Sheryl Lindsell-Roberts

Speaking Your Way
to Success

Houghton Mifflin Harcourt
Boston   New York

Visit our website: www.hmhbooks.com

Library of Congress Cataloging-in-Publication Data

Lindsell-Roberts, Sheryl
    Speaking your way to success / Sheryl Lindsell-Roberts
        p. cm.
    Includes Index
    ISBN-13: 978-0-547-25518-7
    ISBN-10: 0-547-25518-7
1. Business communication. I. Title
    HF5718.L556 2010
    658.4'52--dc22   2009039524

Manufactured in the United States of America
Book design by Joyce C. Weston

1 2 3 4 5 6 7 8 9 10 - EB - 15 14 13 12 11 10

To my parents, Ethel and Max Lorenz

My mother and father were both raised by immigrant parents. My father came to the United States from Hungary when he was a young boy and learned English by being immersed in the culture and the public schools. He knew his success in this country depended on his ability to speak well. And he was successful. My father graduated from New York University and established his own accounting firm in New York City.

My mother's family came from Russia, and she became a stickler for speaking correctly. During my formative years, my mother was like a drill sergeant, teaching me to read, write, speak, and spell. She taught me to spell *antidisestablishmentarianism* and *schizophrenia* when I was quite young, and paraded me around asking me to spell those words for anyone who would listen. As much as I resented it at the time, her insistence on strong English skills shaped my career. My mother did live to revel in my success, although spelling those words hasn't gotten me too far.

Thanks, Mom and Dad, for helping me become the person I am today. You shaped my life in so many wonderful ways—just one of which was instilling in me the need to speak my way to success.

Contents

Acknowledgments

Special thanks to my wonderful husband, Jon Roberts, who sits patiently as my eyes glaze over in the middle of a conversation. It's during these times he knows I'm coming up with a dazzling idea and I'm *writing*. Shortly thereafter I'm at my computer clickety-clacking like a tenacious woodpecker. Jon helps by leaving me alone while I'm writing and by loving me along while I'm writing.

My special thanks to Marge Berube, Senior Vice President, Reference Publisher, for her ongoing confidence in me; to Chris Leonesio, Vice President, Managing Editor, Reference, who jumped in valiantly as my champion after Marge retired; to Catherine Pratt, Editor, who's been an absolute joy to work with through the writing of my last several books; and to Diane Fredrick, who copyedited this book to make sure I dotted my *i*'s and crossed my *t*'s.

I would like to acknowledge the following people (listed in chapter order) who collaborated with me or granted me permission to include their wisdom to enhance this book. You can find many of their websites in their respective sections.

Paul Treuer, Director, Knowledge Management Center, University of Minnesota Duluth
Chapter 4: Tips for College Students

Erica Stritch, General Manager, RainToday.com
Chapter 7: Cold-Calling Scripts That Work: Three Proven Introductions That Break Into and Close New Clients

Stephen Melanson, President, Melanson Consulting
Chapter 8: Verbal Branding

Michael Goldberg, President, Building Blocks Consulting, LLC
Chapter 8: Rules of the Road

Dr. Ivan Misner, Founder and Chairman, Business Network International (BNI)
Chapter 8: Giving and Getting a Hot Referral

Suzanne Bates, President and CEO, Bates Communications
Chapter 11: Manage Conflict

Nancy Settle-Murphy, Principal, Guided Insights
Chapter 11: Multigenerational Considerations
Chapter 13: Survey Results: Multigenerational Differences from the Point of View of the Younger Generations

Roberta Chinsky Matuson, Generational Workforce Expert and President, Human Resource Solutions
Chapter 13: Think Age Diversity Doesn't Affect You?

Dave McKeon, Managing Partner, Game On! LLC
Chapter 13: Common to All Generations

And last, but certainly not least, thanks to my clients, who always inspire me and contribute immensely to my professional growth. I'm so grateful to all of them for their ongoing support and confidence in me.

> Employers list communications skills as one of the two leading job skills employees must have. (The other is attitude.)
>
> — National Center on the Evaluation of
> Quality in the Workplace

Introduction

Speaking is a cornerstone to your success in life. No one will notice you if you're quietly lurking in the shadows. Speak up! Speak well! If you aspire to be a leader, for example, you gain visibility when you conduct a powerful meeting, engage in meaningful conversation, or deliver a dynamic presentation. If you're in sales, you win contracts by demonstrating to potential or current clients how you can solve their problems and have a positive effect on their bottom line.

Statistics show that 75 percent of our time is spent speaking and listening. (The other 25 percent is divided between reading and writing.) Yet, people seem to be losing interest in speaking with each other. Just look around. They send emails, instant messages, and text messages instead of picking up the phone or speaking face to face. They visit restaurants (presumably with people whose company they should be enjoying) and spend time texting and fielding cell phone calls. They spend endless hours in front of the computer or the TV selecting from a glut of channels.

Leave Them Wanting More, Not Running for the Door

Speakers, whether engaging in one-to-one conversation or speaking in front of a large group, should leave people wanting more, not running for the door. Dynamic speakers . . .

- Pay attention to their audience.
- Use interesting language.
- Select words and terms that are relevant and easy to understand.
- Modulate their tone.
- Support their words with body language.
- Introduce visuals when appropriate.
- Interject stories the audience will find interesting.

- Allow for interaction (when appropriate).
- Know when to stop.

Speaking in a Changing Society

Businesses have consistently relied on the influx of new talent to regenerate the workforce. People from different cultures and generations have always had their own ideas, ways of approaching issues, and ways of communicating. These differences are nothing new. What is new is the magnitude of these differences brought about by a global economy and a multigenerational workforce.

As a result of our differences, we bring to the workforce a variety of needs, strengths, motivations, expectations, and communication styles. The companies that thrive (not merely survive) are the ones harnessing the potential of today's rich and diverse cross-cultural and multigenerational workforce. *This makes mastery of communication skills more important than ever.*

You Need This Book If You

- Want to improve the way you come across as a speaker—both in personal conversations and in front of small or large groups.
- Don't have the impact you want to have on your audiences.
- Don't listen as well as you should.
- Want to fine-tune the words you select.
- Need to sharpen your networking skills.
- Wish to hone your interviewing skills.
- Interact with a cross-cultural and/or multigenerational workforce.

Icons in This Book

Scattered throughout this book you'll see the following icons—somewhat like road signs—to help you find pointers, notes, personal stories, and cross-references:

 Hot tip. This may be a time saver, life saver, frustration saver, or just about anything relevant to the information at hand.

 Reminder. This is akin to tying a string around your finger so you won't forget something important, such as packing your umbrella during monsoon season.

 Word from Sheryl. This is an opportunity to share "war stories" from my own experience or my clients' experiences.

Check out a cross-reference. This directs you to a relevant topic within the book.

A Word About Gender

Which word doesn't belong: *aunt, brother, cousin, father, grandfather, grandmother, mother, nephew, niece, sister, uncle*? The answer is *cousin* because it's the only gender-neutral term. I searched for a gender-neutral term for this book to avoid getting into the clumsy *he/she* or *him/her* pronouns but couldn't find one. So I tossed a coin, and here's how it landed: I use the male gender in the even-numbered chapters and the female gender in the odd-numbered chapters. (If this offends you, I apologize.)

Sheryl Lindsell-Roberts, M.A.

PS: Keep this book for easy reference. Don't share it. You may never get it back!

Part One

Getting Down to Basics

I never fail to be amused by those figures of speech that the dictionary labels oxymorons: those combinations of contradictory terms like *jumbo shrimp* and *military intelligence*. But my favorites are *postal service* and *sanitary landfill*.

—Louis E. Boone, American educator and business writer

The tradition of the handshake started as a way of physically validating that a person wasn't carrying any weapons.

—Steve W. Martin, *Heavy Hitter Selling*

Making Introductions

In this chapter

Johnny Carson had Ed McMahon to introduce him; you're probably on your own. Making introductions and mingling with strangers doesn't have to be an angst-provoking experience. After all, what is a stranger? Merely a person you haven't gotten to know yet. Think of an introduction as a way to meet someone new and interesting while expanding your social and professional network. Who knows where these connections may lead? Opportunities often come from the most unexpected sources!

Pleased to Meet You

Many people avoid making introductions because they don't know the right way or can't remember someone's name. Don't be a slave to rules and don't lose your warmth or sense of humor. Just do it! The critical thing is to put people at ease, make them feel comfortable, and get them talking. Following are some general guidelines that can save you embarrassing moments:

- If you're introduced to someone and you didn't hear her name clearly, simply ask her to repeat it.

- If you've previously been introduced to someone, don't assume she'll recall your name. Extend your hand and reintroduce yourself. *Hi, I'm Jenny Smith. We met last year at Sandra's award ceremony.*
- When you're introduced to someone, repeat the person's name back. For example, *I'm glad to meet you, Jane.* This is a gracious gesture and may help you remember Jane's name.
- Rise to the occasion. It's appropriate for both men and women to rise from a seat when they're introduced.
- If you see someone you've met before, this is a great opportunity to engage in conversation. If you don't recall the person's name, don't be shy about asking. Approach the person, extend your hand, and say, *I'm [name]. I don't recall your name, but didn't I meet you at [place] last month?*

Introducing Others

Here's the protocol for introducing people to each other.

Mention the name of the highest-ranking person first.

If you're introducing a four-star general to your colleague, mention the four-star general first: *General Arnold Smith, I'd like you to meet my colleague, Bob Aarons.* It's not likely you'll be introducing many four-star generals, but you can translate that method for use in other situations. For example, if you're introducing the CEO from another company to a manager at your company, the same protocol applies.

Mention a pertinent piece of information.

Mention a bit of information about one or both persons, so you don't leave them in the uncomfortable position of not having anything to say. Think of an accomplishment, hobby, relationship with you, relationship with the host, or something else that's relevant. For example: *In addition to being a top-notch engineer, Jack is a very accomplished pianist.*

Use the right pecking order.

Here's the basic pecking order: Introduce a younger person *to* an older person and a junior person *to* a senior person. Don't get hung up on this stuff, however. The critical thing is to put people at ease, make them feel comfortable, and get them talking.

Younger Person to Older Person: Present a younger person *to* an older person, mentioning the older person's name first.

Mr. Leary, I'd like you to meet my son, Marc, who just graduated from Georgia Tech.

Marc, this is Mr. Leary, my supervisor.

Peers from Different Companies: Present a peer in your own company *to* a peer in another company, mentioning the peer in the other company first.

Ellen, this is Barbara from our communications department.

Barbara, this is Ellen from Ace & Jones.

Nonofficial and Official: Present a nonofficial *to* an official, mentioning the official first.

Congressman Jones, I'd like you to meet my mother, Mrs. Concord.

Mom, I'd like you to meet Congressman Jones, from my district.

Junior and Senior Executives: Present a junior executive *to* a senior executive, mentioning the senior executive first.

Mr. Jones, I'd like you to meet Jim Stanton, who joined our group last week.

Jim, this is Mr. Jones, the vice president of marketing.

Fellow Executive to Client or Customer: Present a fellow executive *to* a client or customer, mentioning the client or customer first.

Stan, I'd like you to meet Grace Petry from our purchasing department.

Grace, this is Stan Gregory, a salesman from ABC Chemical Company.

Men and Women: Present a man *to* a woman, mentioning the woman first. Many feminists feel that the guidelines above should supersede. I guess the jury's still out. Do what's comfortable for you.

Elissa, I'd like you to meet my neighbor, Paul Bates.

Paul, this is my cousin, Elissa Wright.

Make a newcomer feel welcome.

When someone you know joins your company, introduce that person immediately. There's nothing that makes a person feel more left out than standing with a group of strangers. Here are a few suggestions:

- It's appropriate to interrupt a group's conversation to introduce a newcomer: *Excuse me for a moment. I'd like you all to meet [name].*

- Provide some background about the person you're introducing. *Beverly, I'd like to introduce you to some of our guests. This is Jim, who, I believe, also lives in San Francisco. This is Gloria, our HR director. And this is Beverly, my long-time friend and business associate.*

When there's a newcomer in the midst and no one makes an introduction, go over and introduce yourself.

 Avoid using the term *old* friend or *old* business associate; substitute *long-time*. Some people are sensitive about the word *old*.

Use a person's title appropriately.

When you're introducing peers, use a person's title only when you're introducing an older person or someone with status.

Mrs. Peters, I'd like you to meet my friend, Carolyn Kiefer.

Carolyn, this is Mrs. Peters, my supervisor.

Fake memory lapses.

If you want to make an introduction and can't remember the person's name, don't be embarrassed. It happens to everyone. We all get brain cramps at one time or another. Here are a couple of tactful ways to fake it:

- *First I need glasses, now my memory seems to be failing me. I can't recall your name.*
- To a group: *Listen, everyone. This is the wonderful gentleman who just became the president of [company]. I'd like you all to meet him.* (Before long, he'll be going around to the guests, shaking hands and introducing himself.)
- *I can't believe it. I just drew a blank on your name.* Or, *I'm having a brain cramp and I can't remember your name.*

Properly use first and last names.

If you have to think about which name to use, use the last name or full name. Generally, a younger person will call an older person by her last name, unless asked to do otherwise. It's better to err on the side of being too formal. Some people feel that using only a first name is disrespectful.

Use nicknames only when invited to.

Some names hang on from childhood and can be embarrassing in certain business situations. (Your friend may have been called "Pumpkin" as a kid, but that's probably not a name that grew up with her.) Don't use a person's nickname, unless that's what the person is normally called.

Also, don't take it upon yourself to shorten someone's name. If you're introduced to someone named Samuel, don't assume he's called Sam.

Rise to the occasion.

When you're introduced to someone, rise, step forward, smile, and extend your hand for a handshake. Repeat the other person's name. If the group is very large, only those closest to the newcomer need to rise and say hello.

Introducing Yourself

When you don't know anyone at an event, don't just hide out in a safe spot next to the buffet table. You're missing the opportunity to meet new and interesting people. And who knows, there may be someone next to you wishing you'd rescue her from anonymity. You can stimulate conversation by stating your name with a tag line that connects you to the other person.

 Check out chapter 8, "Developing Professional Networks."

Phrases to use

Consider the following phrases when making introductions or introducing yourself.

Opening
- *Hello.*
- *Hi.*
- *Good morning, good afternoon, or good evening.*

Continuing
- *My name is . . .*
- *My friends call me . . .*
- *You can call me . . .*
- *I don't think we've met before.*
- *Haven't we met before?*
- *Nice to see you again.*

Concluding
- *Goodbye or 'bye.*
- *See you.*
- *See you later.*
- *See you soon (or tomorrow, or next week).*
- *Good night.*

Find a commonality.

You were all invited by the host or to the event because of some commonality. What is it? When you keep that commonality in mind, it's easier to introduce yourself.

- *Hi, I'm Barbara. I was invited by James and would like to introduce myself.*
- *Hello, I'm Jim Smith. I'm from the Chicago office.*
- *Hello, I'm Jim Smith. This is my first meeting at the Chamber of Commerce. Are you a member?*

Use the golden opportunity to network.

When you're introduced and someone asks, "What do you do?" it's a great opportunity to market yourself and/or your organization. Here's an example:

Opportunity taken: *I'm the director at [organization], a nonprofit that raises money for [cause] in [region].*
Opportunity missed: *I work at a nonprofit.*

 Check out chapter 8, "Developing Professional Networks," for more about promoting yourself and your organization.

Display your nametag on the upper right portion of your garment.

If you're at an event, wear your nametag on the upper right portion of your garment. When you shake hands, the other person's line of vision will usually travel from your eyes to your right shoulder.

Introducing a Guest Speaker

Take a cue from talk show hosts you may watch. They're the pros. Your purpose in introducing a guest speaker is to increase the audience's interest, attention, and anticipation. Here are some guidelines:

Prepare your mini-talk.

- Ask the speaker in advance if she has a written introduction she'd like you to read. Many experienced speakers have one prepared.
- If the speaker doesn't have a prepared introduction, ask for a fact sheet. Your introduction should be interesting, focusing on the objective, purpose, and desired result. (There's nothing more pointless than

telling the audience the speaker was born in Kalamazoo and won a Michigan elementary school spelling bee.) Make your opening relevant to the audience and the topic.

- If you're introducing someone you know, fold in some things that are personal (your relationship, sports involvements, awards, community projects). This will help the audience to know the speaker better and possibly relate on a different level. (This doesn't contradict the point made above; it personalizes the introduction.)
- If you receive the introduction electronically, consider enlarging the font so you can read it easily.
- Highlight words that begin each thought.
- Make sure you know how to pronounce the speaker's name correctly. Write it out phonetically if you think you may have difficulty.

Deliver with enthusiasm.

- Approach the audience with a smile, pausing for a moment until you have everyone's attention.
- Even though you may be reading, look directly at the audience when you mention the speaker's name.
- Don't steal the speaker's thunder by mentioning too much about the topic.
- After calling the speaker to the appointed place, extend your hand for a firm handshake, and walk away.

 Check out chapter 9, "Speaking in Public," for more tips.

The Golden Handshake

In the United States, the handshake is the classic business greeting. Handshakes create a link between two people. Shake hands when you . . .

- Are introduced to someone.
- Greet a visitor to your office.
- Run into a business associate outside your office.
- Are firming up a deal.
- Say goodbye.

Shake hands properly.

Always extend your right hand for a handshake and look the person directly in the eye. The handshake should be firm (not bone crushing) and should be held for three to four seconds. People tend to think that your handshake matches your character, so don't let it be too strong or too weak.

When you're greeting a business associate in your home or office, you should be the one to extend your hand. On neutral ground, do what's comfortable; it doesn't matter whether you're a man or woman.

Other things to consider:

- If you're holding a drink, you may want to hold it in your left hand so your right hand won't be cold or wet when you need to extend it.
- If you're wearing gloves, remove them. No one can feel the warmth of your hand through fabric. If you're wearing white gloves at a formal celebration, however, don't remove them.

Know when to decline a handshake.

If you're unable to shake someone's hand and the reason is obvious, you don't need to explain. If the reason isn't obvious, offer an explanation. For example, *I'm sorry I can't shake your hand; my carpal tunnel is acting up.* Or, *I'm sorry, I have a slight cold and want to keep my germs to myself.*

I typically carry a small bottle of hand sanitizer and use it regularly. As gross as it sounds, I've seen people cough and sneeze into their hands and then extend the infected hand for a handshake.

2

Become genuinely interested in other people.
—Dale Carnegie

Engaging in Masterful Conversations

In this chapter

- Rating Yourself as a Conversationalist
- Conversation Starters
- Keeping Conversations Going
- Ending Conversations Gracefully
- Gender Differences

When you show genuine interest in others through meaningful conversation (speaking and listening), you make them feel respected and valued. In today's society, people seem to be losing the art of conversation. They go to cocktail lounges that blast loud music; they email, IM, or text; they use headsets; and the list can go on. Just look around. People who are good conversationalists have a big advantage over those who aren't.

Conversation is the social communication that enters into all business and personal interactions—whether we're talking with a supervisor, client, customer, supplier, friend, family member, or John Q. Public. Conversation involves not only the way we speak to each other, but our body language, attentiveness, listening ability, and choice of words.

Rating Yourself as a Conversationalist

People who are good conversationalists are generally well liked and highly successful. Being a good conversationalist requires skills in both *speaking* and *active listening*. Some people are natural-born talkers, but poor listeners. Others are just the opposite. If you want to be considered a good conversationalist, you must do both equally well.

You are a great asset to yourself and your company when you're a great speaker and listener. You can persuade, encourage, praise, charm, motivate, comfort—and in the process, further your career. It's an ability you can acquire. See how many of these skills you already have by checking all that apply to you.

I always or generally . . .

❑ Accept and deliver compliments gracefully.
❑ Can discuss a wide range of safe topics.
❑ Display a sense of humor.
❑ Maintain eye contact.
❑ Make people smile.
❑ Am curious about people.
❑ Question without prying.
❑ Show interest in other people.
❑ Listen with sincere interest.

✓ Check out chapter 4, "Developing Listening Skills."

I never . . .

❑ Break into someone's conversation.
❑ Burst someone's bubble.
❑ Correct someone's grammar or pronunciation.
❑ Exclude anyone present from the conversation.
❑ Interrupt someone who's speaking.
❑ Switch subjects unless it's appropriate.
❑ Pretend to be an expert on a subject unless I am.

Conversation Starters

Be the first to initiate a conversation. People always appreciate it when someone else goes first. Finding conversation starters is a matter of testing the waters. Neutral conversation starters that generally work well include the weather, news, and sports.

Be an interesting person.

Plug into the world by keeping yourself informed of regional and world events and activities, entertainment, politics, and sports. Get involved in activities that interest you and may interest others. Retain a mental list of good conversation starters that have worked in the past—those you've used and those you've heard.

Learn people's names.

People enjoy hearing their names mentioned. As soon as you're introduced to someone, shake hands, make eye contact, and repeat the person's name immediately.

- Unless a person has been introduced by a nickname, don't create one. *Nice to meet you, Jonathan.*
- If the person has a difficult name, ask him to repeat it.

Identify commonalities.

When you and others attend an event, it's because you have something in common. Understand the commonality so you can use it as an opener.

- Are you all in high tech? finance? marketing?
- Are you there to learn new sales techniques? a medical breakthrough?
- Are you all business owners?

 I recently attended a meeting of professional writers and didn't know anyone there. I introduced myself to a gentleman standing behind me as I waited to check my coat. I asked him what kind of writing he does. He told me he was a marketing communications director, and I wound up writing several brochures for his company.

Break the ice with small talk.

When you're introduced to someone, there may be some discomfort as you stand there tongue-tied, not knowing what to say. Some people are naturals when it comes to small talk; others cringe. Once you master this art, you'll have a valuable talent. Small talk is trivial conversation that . . .

- Fills distressing silent moments.
- Puts people at ease when they are getting acquainted.
- Breaks tension.
- Builds relationships.
- Maximizes career opportunities.

Small talk can involve any noncontroversial topic: news events, gardening, books, magazines, movies, TV programs, local performing arts, travel, sports, and much more. Avoid issues that deal with controversial current events, confidential business issues, politics, harmful gossip, your health and personal misfortunes, how much things cost, sex, religion, or anything of questionable taste.

literature, performing arts, and noncontroversial current events. Here are some tips for scanning the newspaper:

- Skim the headlines to get the gist of the news.
- Read the business and sports sections.
- Read the lifestyles section if you're in a city other than your own. It will tell you what's hot in the area so you can talk about it.

Accept compliments.

A compliment should be sincere and make someone smile. When a compliment is paid to you, never downgrade the praise with comments such as, *I don't deserve that,* or *It was really nothing.* Accept it graciously with a *thank you.* We all need praise and should be able to give and receive it gracefully.

Inject humor.

Although you may not be ready for stand-up comedy, you probably have a sense of humor. Nearly everyone does. Laughing at yourself by sharing a funny story, relating ridiculous comparisons, or interjecting a pun can ease a tense situation and add spice to an otherwise dull conversation. Look for opportunities to be spontaneous, but not tedious.

Never use humor if you have any hint that it may be misconstrued— even among friends, humor can be biting. George Bernard Shaw once sent tickets to his latest play to his good friend Winston Churchill. Mr. Shaw included this note: *Here are two tickets to my new play. One for you and one for a friend—if any.* Mr. Churchill returned the tickets with this note: *Sorry, I'm unable to attend opening night. Please send me tickets for another performance—if any.*

Use silence "as golden."

In writing, silence includes white space and punctuation marks to give pauses and breathing room. We also need pauses and breathing room when speaking and listening. Have the confidence to pause for a few seconds between thoughts.

 The consequence of being a good listener is that people like to talk with you, and that may impact your time. Here are a couple of suggestions for helping to remove yourself from lengthy conversations or from long-winded conversationalists:

- *Good morning, Gladys. I have just a few minutes before I have to rush to a meeting. Can you briefly tell me . . .?*

- *I really enjoy hearing about [topic], but I'm up against a tight deadline. Can we revisit this another time?*

Ending Conversations Gracefully

All good (and bad) conversations must come to an end. When a conversation is going nowhere, when you're at an event and there are other people you want to meet, or when it's just time to go, the conversation must end. Body language and key phrases signal it's time to disengage.

Body Language: Here are some signals to give to indicate a conversation is winding down:

- Take a few steps away from the person who's talking.
- Shift your body away from the speaker.
- Start to gather belongings. For example, put things in your briefcase.
- Gaze at something off in the distance.
- Look at a clock or watch.
- Stand up from a sitting position.

Handy Phrases: Saying *I have to rearrange my sock drawer* isn't too polite, but here are some phrases that may be:

- *Goodness, I didn't realize how late it is.*
- *I'd like to continue this conversation, but I have a meeting in a few minutes. Can I give you a call within the next few days?*
- *Thanks for stopping by. We should schedule a time to speak about this in greater detail.*
- *Bob will hunt me down if I don't get this done by [time], so I'd better get going.*
- *I don't want to keep you. I know there are many other people you'd like to meet.*
- *I know this is important, but I can't talk about it. Have you thought of asking Nancy?*
- *I don't want to take up any more of your time. I enjoyed speaking with you.*
- *That's a good point. I'll have to keep it in mind.*
- *It's been a pleasure talking with you, and I look forward to seeing you at the next meeting.*
- *For goodness' sake. The time has passed so quickly I forgot to call my babysitter. Please excuse me.* (Then disappear for a short while.)

Gender Differences

"He/she just doesn't understand me." Have you ever felt that way about your partner, boss, or coworker of the opposite sex? Such feelings are more common than you may think. Perhaps some gender distinctions date back to the ancient hunters (men) and gatherers (women). Men competed against nature to hunt and capture dinner. They competed against each other for tribal status. Winning meant survival. Women were family caretakers and banded together to raise children and perform domestic chores. Avoiding conflict meant survival.

Studies disagree on whether it's nature or nurture, but men and women do have different communication styles. These studies also show that these gender patterns are similar around much of the world. For example, when women disagree, it can affect their relationship. When men disagree, they move to another subject and go out for a drink. Women nod their heads to show they're listening. Men nod their heads to show agreement.

Rate your gender conversation IQ.

Put a check mark to indicate whether you believe men or women fit each situation. Universally accepted answers are on page 20.

Situation	Men	Women
Interrupt speakers more often		
Initiate more interaction		
Talk more at informal public gatherings		
Are less likely to have confidence in ability to persuade		
Take up more physical space when sitting or standing		
Provide fewer reactions when listening		
Speak in clipped sentences and use more jargon		
Ask fewer questions		
Smile and nod when listening		
Are anxious to please		
Are more likely to ask for help and accept it		
Lean backward when listening		
Talk in order to build rapport with others		
Focus on one idea at a time (are single-minded)		

Recognize the differences.

Although there are no absolutes, countless studies have been done, and volumes have been (and continue to be) published on gender differences. Here are some of the differences most commonly referred to:

Men	Women
Vie for leadership.	Work more collaboratively.
Cut to the chase.	Relate stories.
Focus on status.	Share experiences to show commonality.
Dwell on facts.	Discuss feelings.
Are goal oriented.	Are detail oriented.
Think asking for help says *inability*.	Think offering to help says *caring*.
Have no trouble defining themselves as experts.	Appear more modest.
Use definitive language.	Use vague or weak language (such as *Don't you think... Hopefully we can... What do you think?*).
Come to the point quickly.	Use more detail getting to the point.
Make direct statements.	Phrase statements as questions.
End sentences on a low note, taken as more of a command.	End sentences on a high note, taken to mean *Let's talk this over.*
Talk to give information.	Ask questions to gather information.
Think silently and share results.	Think aloud while formulating results
Will say *I'm sorry* when they mean it.	Will say *I'm sorry* to repair a relationship.
Talk about neutral topics such as business and sports.	Talk about people.
Thrive on achieving and competing.	Thrive on harmony.
Resolve conflicts by escalating.	Resolve conflicts by de-escalating.
Need validation, trust, and acceptance.	Need to feel respected, understood, and cared about.

Bridge the gap.

By recognizing and respecting that men and women say and hear things through different filters, you can begin to create a more harmonious environment—at home and in the workplace. Here are a few hints for bridging the gap:

- Before you react in a negative way, understand where a comment is coming from.

Action	Body Language	Message
Shaking hands	Firm grip (but not knuckle-breaking)	You're confident.
	Weak	You're weak and lack confidence.
Listening to the speaker	Maintaining eye contact	You're interested.
	Eyes roaming around room	You're not interested.
Sitting while listening to someone talk	Sitting attentively without slumping	You're paying attention.
	Crossing and uncrossing your legs or fidgeting	You're preoccupied or bored.
As the speaker, making a point	Sitting tall in your chair or standing tall	You're saying something of importance.

Keeping the Fashion Police at Bay

Society as a whole is becoming more casual. Even though today's dress code is often more relaxed than it used to be, there's a big difference between business casual and *oh-my-gosh*. If you want to know what's hot and what's not, check magazines that specialize in fashions for business in your industry. Also, one of my colleagues, Mary Lou Andre, wrote a wonderful book, *Ready to Wear*. Check out her website, www.dressingwell.com, and sign up to have a "Tip of the Month" emailed to you.

All offices have a dress code, no matter how official or unofficial, no matter how conservative or casual. And everyone puts on a uniform to go to work. That uniform may be anything from a three-piece business suit to casual business dress to jeans and a T-shirt.

According to Scott Adams, *The Dilbert Principle,* "When you're at work, take the time to look around and see what other people wear. If you see button-down shirts and blouses, plan to keep your sports jersey in your dresser until the weekend. Contrary to popular belief, it's often your clothing that gets promoted, not you. . . . Always dress better than your peers so your clothes will be the ones selected for promotion. And make sure you're in your clothes when it happens."

Here are some general guidelines for men and women:

- Make sure your clothes fit properly. If you gain weight, either let your clothes out or buy new ones.
- If you wear running shoes or boots (for bad weather), be sure to keep a pair of shoes in your office and put them on as soon as you arrive.
- Never flaunt designer labels.

- Even though a type of clothing may be all the rage, adapt it to your build, your job, your age, and your work environment.

Know what works for men.

Don't get into the habit of wearing the same colors and styles every day. For example, try varied colors and fabrics. Buy pants and sports coats that coordinate with lots of items in your wardrobe so you can mix and match to add variety.

No matter how casual your work environment may be, you must own at least one suit. You'll need it when you eat in a fine restaurant or meet with a client. Your suit must fit properly, whether it's custom-made or off the rack. Here are some guidelines:

- Buy typical suit colors of black, charcoal, brown, dark gray, or navy blue. They may be pinstriped or very muted plaid. In warm climates, you may wear lightweight fabrics, such as seersucker. (Cuffed pants and double-breasted suits fade in and out of fashion, so be careful. Also, double-breasted jackets look best on men who are tall and thin.)
- Wear long-sleeved, conservative shirts. Buy them to match your suits. If you want to add a touch of class, wear a shirt with French cuffs, which require cuff links.
- Make sure your shirttails are long enough to tuck into your pants and your shirt is large enough so the buttons don't strain around the middle.
- Keep ties conservative: solid, printed, or striped. Red ties, and more recently blue ties, are known as "power ties." You may wear one when you want to make a bold statement about yourself, such as when you're the guest speaker at a conference.
- Wear black shoes with black or gray suits and brown shoes with brown suits.
- Select socks that are high enough so that when you sit with your legs crossed you don't show your hairy (or hairless) legs between the tops of your socks and the bottom of your trousers.

Men, you can't expect people to take you seriously if you don't take the time to put yourself together properly.

Know what works for women.

Always wear clothing to complement your body type. If you haven't figured out what looks good on you, consult a salesperson in a high-end department store. You can buy mix-and-match outfits and change their look with scarves and subtle jewelry. Women have gotten away from the "female man's suit," and dress in a more feminine manner. Opt for skirts and blazers, silk dresses, and suits of feminine fabric. You may also wear tailored pants and bright (not loud) colors. Following are a few taboos for office clothes:

- Never wear spike-heeled shoes, no matter how short you are. Instead, wear heels that are medium to low.
- Wear a jacket that covers your seat and your thighs. A jacket of that length is more flattering to most shapes and sizes.
- Save fur coats for the opera. They have no place in the office.
- Save satins, brocades, lamés, and velvets for evening.
- Avoid micro-miniskirts, strapless tops, shorts, or anything see-through, low-cut, or too tight even for streetwalkers.
- Save noisy or outlandish jewelry for parties.
- Wear white shoes and pocketbooks between Memorial Day and Labor Day only.
- Keep an extra pair of pantyhose nearby (in your desk, car, briefcase, or pocketbook) to replace a pair that develops a run.

Women, you too can't expect people to take you seriously if you don't take the time to put yourself together properly.

Understand what business casual means.

The high-tech world has ushered in an entirely new clothing ethos—business casual. For example, in certain industries Gen Xers and Gen Yers might never wear a tie, let alone a suit. The lawyers, accountants, and bankers who interact with the high-tech set often feel a little odd in their three-piece suits, so high-tech is now driving the way the "suits" of the world dress themselves.

Take the example of the prestigious New England law firm Hale and Dorr. The firm has relaxed its dress code, and many lawyers show up for work in sport shirts and corduroys. This is working well for Hale and Dorr's young, sought-after lawyers, whose lives also include child care, working at home, and flextime. However, many older attorneys view the suit as a symbol of their profession, and shun the business-casual look.

 Even though many firms offer *business casual* and *dress-down Fridays,* there's a big difference between business casual and just casual. Business casual generally means something like a sport shirt (no tie) and khakis for men, and pants and a sweater for women. Save your ripped jeans, NY Yankees T-shirt, and flip-flops for the weekend.

Make the most of jackets.

Professionals wear jackets less often than they used to, but there's still a certain etiquette involved when they do:

- *Men who usually work with their jackets off shouldn't wear short-sleeved shirts. If it's warm, it's more appropriate for men to roll long sleeves up to their elbows. However, it is appropriate for women to wear short-sleeved blouses. (If this seems sexist, I don't make the rules.)*
- *Men and women should put their jackets on when meeting with the head honcho of their company, with clients, or with anyone else of importance.*
- *When negotiating, unbuttoning your jacket in front of a prospect will signify an open attitude, saying you're willing to talk, to negotiate. Taking off your jacket is really powerful. And rolling your shirt sleeves up suggests that you're ready to get down to business.*
- *When wearing a double-breasted jacket, keep it buttoned unless you're removing it.*

Know what's appropriate when meeting people from other cultures.

Before you meet people from other cultures (on your turf or theirs), know what's appropriate to wear. Check with a foreign counterpart or someone who's in the know. If you have any doubts about how to dress, err on the side of being formal. Here's a smattering of tips:

- Europeans and Americans have similar dress codes for both formal and casual occasions. Remember, dress codes vary by industry.
- Asians tend to be more formal than Americans.
- In China, white is a symbol of mourning.
- Women traveling to Arab countries shouldn't wear slacks or anything revealing. They should cover up as much of their bodies as possible. In some countries, women must also cover their heads.
- In Israel, people are very informal, so you may dress casually.
- If you visit the Far East or an Arab country, you may be asked to remove your shoes before entering a home. Be sure you don't have holes in your socks or stockings.

Interpreting Gestures

Be aware of the following gestures that suggest negativity:

- Crossing your arms on your chest—suggests defensiveness.
- Dragging your feet—implies lethargy.

- Fidgeting—indicates nervousness.
- Putting your hands in your pocket—implies you're hiding something.
- Tilting your head down and forward—suggests timidity or boredom.
- Drooping your shoulders—implies weakness.
- Extending a weak handshake—says meek and ineffectual.
- Pointing a finger—indicates rudeness.

Make a dynamite first impression.

The first-impression process occurs in every new situation. Within the first few seconds—regardless of the situation—people pass judgment on you. It's much easier to make a great first impression than to correct a negative one. Here are a few examples of how the first-impression process works:

- If you're interviewing, the interviewer is assessing whether you match the corporate culture. This may affect the ultimate decision.
- At business and social events, attendees are assessing whether you're suitable for further interaction.
- If you appear to be of high business status or social rank, you're considered a valuable contact.

Extend your hand for an appropriate handshake.

Handshakes can strengthen or weaken relationships—they may be soft, firm, brief, long, or sometimes painful. The way you shake hands provides clues to your personality. To shake hands, hold the person's hand firmly, shake web-to-web no more than three times, and maintain constant eye contact. Remember:

- Aggressive people often have firm handshakes.
- People with low self-esteem often have limp handshakes.
- Sandwich handshakes (enveloping someone's hand between both of yours) are for people you know very well. Although politicians use them frequently, many people feel they're an invasion of their space.

Men's handshakes are stronger than women's because they have a naturally stronger grip. So, women, get a grip if you want to be noticed.

Respect people's personal space.

Those of you who are (or were) *Seinfeld* fans may remember the episode about Jerry's getting "weirded out" by a close-talking woman. Although there was a lot of humor in that episode, it did deliver a very important message: Don't invade people's personal space. Personal space is the invisible boundary around your body you don't want others to enter unless they're invited. Other than shaking hands when you initially meet people, avoid putting your arm on their shoulder, touching their face, holding their hand, and the like, or you risk making some people uncomfortable. Always remember that personal space is highly variable, depending on culture, social status, family situations, and individual preference.

- Americans, Canadians, and Europeans often like a field of about 18 inches. If you get too close, they'll feel that you're "in their face" and will try to back away.
- People living in densely populated environments tend to require less personal space.
- Affluent people tend to appreciate more personal space.
- People who were raised by affectionate families feel okay with less space.

Be respectful of the personal space of service industry employees such as salespeople, waitstaff, and others. Many complain of touchy-feely customers pulling, tugging, or worse.

Make and maintain eye contact.

Eyes communicate more than any other part of the anatomy. (Gangs have fought and killed over the way people "looked" at them.) Here are some ways to interpret the language of eyes:

- Lively, sparkling eyes say *Talk to me* or *I'm approachable.*
- Polite eye contact shows you're sincere and engaged.
- Looking up shows submission, and looking down shows a lack of interest.
- Staring can create tension and pressure.
- Making and maintaining eye contact when talking and listening shows your confidence, honesty, trustworthiness, and attentiveness. Begin eye contact as soon as the conversation begins and continue until it ends. You don't want to stare, so nod your head and glance away occasionally. Look up or to the side. Don't look down as it will make you appear subservient.
- Shifty eyes with too much blinking suggest deception.
- Lack of eye contact may be construed as showing dishonesty, disinterest, or snobbishness.

Unless you're outdoors on a bright sunny day (or you're a Paris Hilton wannabe), ditch the sunglasses. They prevent people from seeing your eyes.

Smile to show sincerity.

The most famous and most talked about smile of all time is that of the subject of Leonardo da Vinci's masterpiece, the *Mona Lisa*. Many experts question if she was even smiling. (Do you think you could sit in that position posing for a picture for endless hours holding a warm sincere smile? Probably not.)

When you smile sincerely, your body releases endorphins that send a message to your brain, making you feel good. A smile also makes the people you're with feel good. That's why smiles are important facial expressions giving a strong clue as to a person's sincerity and honesty.

- A genuine smile doesn't involve only your mouth. It involves your entire face, including a tightening of muscles around your eyes. It says that you're friendly, interested, empathetic, and engaged.
- A forced smile is evident by a tightening around the mouth. This type of smile can mean you're not telling the truth or you're hiding something.

In addition to expressing yourself by smiling, laugh when something is funny. Don't be the first to laugh at your own jokes, however, or you may seem needy and nervous.

 Smile when you're introduced to someone, but don't keep a smile plastered on your face. It will make you seem insincere.

Don't be a slouch.

Can you recall a teacher saying, *Sit up straight. You don't even look as if you're paying attention*? Perhaps you weren't. You may have been slouched in your seat with your arms crossed and your eyes wandering around the room. Good posture isn't about standing at attention like the guards at Buckingham Palace, it's about carrying your body erect and with confidence.

- Stand in front of a mirror to see yourself as others see you.
- Make sure you suck your stomach in, put your chest out and your shoulders back, and hold your head high.
- Stand straight with your weight balanced on both feet and you'll look secure and relaxed. Then walk around the room.
- Walk back to the mirror and see how much more confident you look.

Use the mirroring technique.

Some experts suggest that when you talk with someone during a critical transaction, you should "mirror" that person's voice, pace, inflections, and gestures. Why? Because people like people who are like themselves. Mirroring indicates maximum communication with the other person.

This means if the other person leans forward, you should lean forward. If the other person speaks at a slow pace, you should speak at a slow pace. If the other person slings his arm across the back of his chair, you sling your arm over the back of your chair. Don't react instantly, or you'll look obvious. And don't mirror every move.

Do you recognize the signs of lying?

A person's words may tell you one thing, but her body language could tell you another. Although this isn't an exact science, the following hints may indicate that someone isn't telling the truth:

- *Avoiding eye contact or staring excessively while speaking.*
- *Touching her face.*
- *Changing arm or leg positions frequently, such as crossing arms over chest or crossing legs.*
- *Turning her body away from you.*
- *Changing the pitch or speed of her voice.*
- *Using lots of* ums *or* ahs.

Interviewers look for these signs of discomfort when asking potential candidates about items on resumes. Lawyers and jurors look for these signs when someone is testifying. (When Bill Clinton lied under oath about his involvement with Monica Lewinsky, he immediately touched his nose. That "scent" a strong signal that he was not telling the truth.)

Being Attuned to Cultural Differences When Gesturing

Very few gestures are universally understood and interpreted. What is acceptable in the United States may be rude, offensive, or obscene in other cultures. In 1992 when George H. W. Bush toured Australia, he gave a V sign to the crowd from the back of his limousine. He intended it to mean "victory." He failed to realize that the correct way to gesture "victory" is with the palm facing outward. To the Australians, President Bush's gesture meant "Up yours, mate."

"When in Rome, do as the Romans do." Don't make assumptions. Before you visit another country, learn all you can about the customs and cultures. Here are a few examples of how gesturing differs:

- **Respecting personal space.** In general, Germans, Chinese, and Japanese appreciate more personal space than Americans, and Americans prefer more personal space than Latin Americans, Italians, French, and Middle Easterners.

- **Shaking hands.** The French like a soft, quick handshake; the Japanese, a handshake with arms fully extended (accompanied by a bow); Middle Easterners, a handshake with the free hand placed on the forearm of the other person. Orthodox Jewish men will not shake the hand of a woman.

- **Giving the thumbs-up.** In the United States and Europe, the thumbs-up means something good. However, it's considered rude in many Asian and Islamic countries and is a sign of displeasure in Spain.

- **Putting your hand up to indicate "stop."** In some Asian countries this means you are requesting permission to speak.

- **Placing hands on hips.** In the United States and Europe, placing hands on hips conveys an open and confident posture; in many Asian countries, it's interpreted as arrogant.

- **Bowing.** Many Asian cultures bow in addition or instead of a handshake. The Japanese bow with their hands at their sides, and the depth of the bow depends on the level of respect shown. The Cambodians bow with their hands in front of their chests. The Thais bow with their palms together.

- **Beckoning with your index finger.** In the United States this gesture means "Come here." In the Middle East, Far East, Portugal, Spain, Latin America, Japan, Indonesia, and Hong Kong, it's insulting, or even obscene.

- **Smiling.** Although this is a universally understood pleasant gesture, in parts of Asia people smile when they're confused, angry, or embarrassed.

- **Forming a circle with your fingers.** In the United States this means "okay." In Japan it means "money"; in France it means "worthless" or "zero"; and in Brazil and Germany, it's obscene.

- **Making the V sign.** It's a sign of victory in the United States. In Europe, if your palm faces away from you, it also means "victory," but when your palm faces toward you, it means "shove it."

- **Having the soles of your shoes showing.** In the United States, it's typical to cross your legs and have the soles of your shoes showing. (Be sure your soles don't have holes.) In Thailand, Japan, France, the Middle East, and Near East, this is a sign of disrespect, because you're exposing the lowest and dirtiest part of your body.

- **Passing an item with one hand.** In the United States, that's the custom. In Japan it's considered rude to pass an item with one hand; two hands are the custom. And in many Middle Eastern and Far Eastern countries, you pass with your right hand only; your left hand is considered unclean.

- **Nodding your head up and down.** In the United States it's a gesture for "yes." In Bulgaria and Greece it means "no."

As a footnote, even within the same culture, gestures are subject to interpretation. Paul Pierce, a popular NBA basketball player, was fined $25,000 for making (what the league deemed to be) a menacing gang gesture. Pierce claimed it was a symbol for blood, sweat, and tears and had nothing to do with gangs.

The Language of "After Hours"

Do business and pleasure mix? They can. Although Americans are less likely than their counterparts in other parts of the world to socialize with coworkers after hours, it is a popular and productive way to schmooze. After-hours socializing can be done in restaurants, clubs, or bars, on the golf course, or at the local watering hole.

Recognize the advantages.

Many people have very demanding jobs and don't have time to get to know each other during normal working hours, even during lunchtime. These people sometimes feel isolated and out of the loop. Socializing outside the office is a good way to see colleagues in a different light and create bonding.

You may be asking yourself, "I work with these people all day. Why do I need to see them outside the office?" Socializing outside the office walls has been credited with creating camaraderie, getting a promotion or larger raise, developing advocates and mentors, building community, and increasing productivity. If you don't do it, you may be missing out. Also, if you're asked and refuse too many times, coworkers may take it personally.

If you . . .
- *have responsibilities caring for elders or young children, try to go occasionally.*
- *don't drink alcoholic beverages for personal or religious reasons, order a soft drink instead. Don't let that stop you from joining the group.*
- *have coworkers who work from home, ask them to join you.*

Be wary of suggestive body language.

Many romances start between people who work together—and I'm talking about the healthy ones between two single people. (Some offices have policies against office romances, so play by the rules.) In any event, know that if you have an office romance and the relationship sours, it can be uncomfortable for one or both persons.

When socializing outside the office (and at the office, for that matter), be wary of the signals you send. Women—you signal interest by flinging long hair, exposing your neck by bending your head back, crossing your legs with toes pointed at a man, subtle touching, fidgeting, and touching part of your face.

Recognize the dangers.

Whether you engage or estrange is up to you. One of the biggest mistakes people make is to let down their guard when outside the walls of the office. Don't!

- Always remember to keep your drinking under control.
- Leave your "loose lips" home and don't talk about coworkers.
- Don't tell risqué jokes or use offensive language.
- Don't stick with your clique. Mingle with everyone.

 "What happens in Vegas stays in Vegas" does not apply here. If you have too much to drink and get up on the stage to do a tacky rendition of Britney Spears, you will regret it later.

4

Nobody ever listened himself out of a job.
—Calvin Coolidge

Developing Listening Skills

In this chapter

- Checking to See If You're a Good Listener
- Developing Active Listening Skills
- Tips for Managers
- Tips for Parents
- Tips for Teachers to Teach Children
- Tips for College Students

Great leaders, winning coaches, successful salespeople, and top-notch facilitators are good listeners. And good listeners are great leaders, winning coaches, successful salespeople, and top-notch facilitators. When you actively listen, you "say" to the speaker *You're important to me; I care about what you think and how you feel.*

Listening is perhaps the most important and the most neglected communication skill. You don't learn anything if you do all the talking. People who don't listen often miss subtleties and signals that could result in their being passed over for a promotion, losing millions of dollars in business, or more. You need good listening skills in order to:

- Better understand the assignments you've been given and what's expected of you.
- Work well as part of a team.
- Answer questions appropriately.
- Resolve problems and issues.
- Build rapport with those around you.

Use the speaking-listening ratio to your advantage.

> "Nature has given to man one tongue, but two ears, that
> we may hear from others twice as much as we speak."
> —Epictetus

The average speaker talks at the rate of about 125 to 150 words per minute (wpm). And that's not a steady pace. Words rush out. The speaker hesitates and pauses. A human being can think at the rate of 500 to 800 wpm. So, while the other person is speaking, you have time to plan and reflect. Use that time to your advantage. Perhaps the suggestions that follow will help you stay tuned and focused:

- Concentrate on each idea.
- Keep track of supporting material to clarify the ideas. You may use the speaker's body language or stories he's sharing.
- Identify your feelings. Understand why the speaker makes you feel comfortable or uncomfortable, happy or angry.
- Analyze the quality of the ideas. Perhaps you wish the speaker would expand on an idea. What are some other ideas he may offer?

Checking to See If You're a Good Listener

Reading, writing, and speaking are taught in schools. Yet listening—the skill that takes about 45 percent of our communication time—isn't. Listening is a skill you must master.

Good manners dictate that you listen to the speaker and treat him with respect. It's a process of internalizing, decoding, and interpreting what you hear. You must mentally do something with the sound, not let it just go in one ear and out the other (as my mother used to say). This is true whether you're involved in an intimate conversation with a small group of people or part of a large audience. How good a listener are you? Check off any boxes that apply to you.

In general, I . . .

- ❑ Listen mainly for the facts.
- ❑ Am critical of the speaker's delivery.
- ❑ Stop listening when a speaker is boring.
- ❑ Interrupt when I don't disagree.
- ❑ Judge the speaker from the opening sentence.
- ❑ Pretend to listen when I'm bored.
- ❑ Avoid listening to difficult material.
- ❑ Finish the speaker's sentences.
- ❑ Let my biases affect my ability to listen.
- ❑ Jump in when I know what the speaker is going to say.
- ❑ Focus on the speaker's mannerisms rather than what he's saying.

In small groups, I . . .

- ❑ Change the subject.
- ❑ Interrupt.
- ❑ Avoid eye contact.
- ❑ Ask for too many details.
- ❑ Rush the speaker.
- ❑ Top the speaker with stories starting with *That reminds me . . .* or *That's nothing, let me tell you about. . . .*
- ❑ Daydream.
- ❑ Fake attention.

In large groups, I . . .

- ❑ Criticize the speaker and his delivery.
- ❑ Get sidetracked.
- ❑ Compose needless rebuttals.
- ❑ Shape what I'm hearing.
- ❑ Ask a question the speaker just answered.
- ❑ Focus on the details and miss the big picture.
- ❑ Create distractions.
- ❑ Look at my watch or out the window.

If you checked any of these boxes, you have some work to do. There are a number of reasons why people aren't good listeners. *They'd rather talk.* When people talk, they're in control and can steer the conversation according to their own agenda. *They're not interested in the speaker or the topic.* No matter how uninterested they may be in the speaker or the topic, they may still learn something. *They're distracted.* They're thinking of other things, such as mentally packing for a trip to Hawaii, rather than paying attention to the speaker.

Listening is more than hearing what the speaker says. It's paying attention to the words he selects and to his tone of voice, expressions, and general body language. Listening is so critical that there's even an International Listening Association. If you think I'm kidding, check out www.listen.org.

Developing Active Listening Skills

The only commonality between listening and hearing is that you use your ears for both. Hearing is the act of perceiving sound; it's biological. Listening is something you consciously choose to do. Listening requires concentration so that your brain processes meaning from words and sentences. Listening leads to learning. Also, people who are great listeners earn more trust than those who are constantly "grabbing the talking stick." The following sections offer some tips for becoming a better listener.

Make time for a conversation.

Before you start a conversation, make sure you have time to complete it. If you don't, perhaps you should wait for a better time. If you're stopped by someone and don't have time to engage in conversation, look at your watch and say, *I'd like to discuss this with you, but I'm late for a meeting. When would be a better time?*

Send the right body language.

Appropriate body language is crucial to letting the speaker know you're actively listening.

- **Remain at the speaker's eye level or lower, if possible.** Have you ever noticed how people squat down when speaking to young children? That's because it's difficult to speak with people when you have to look up. (You want to be looked up to, but not like that.)
- **Face the speaker.** If you're sitting, sit up straight or lean forward slightly to show your attentiveness. If standing, respect the speaker's personal space.
- **Maintain eye contact.** When you're speaking and the other person isn't maintaining eye contact, doesn't that person appear to be aloof and disinterested? Maintain eye contact to the degree that both you and the speaker are comfortable.

Listen with empathy.

You can improve the way that you relate to people by listening with empathy. That means listening with your ears, your eyes, and your heart. That also means listening with the intent of understanding, rather than with the intent of replying. Have you ever needed someone to just listen and had that person jump in with, *I went through something similar. Let me tell you about my experience?*

Listening with empathy takes time and patience, but its returns are abundant. It takes much less time to listen with empathy than it takes to correct misunderstandings. To show you've been listening with empathy, when the person is finished you may say . . .

- *If I understand you correctly, you're concerned about [issue].*
- *I can understand your feelings.*
- *I can understand why you feel that way; however, ...*
- *Other than [issue], is there anything else?*

Show you're listening and understanding the message.

Display a posture of involvement to show you're listening and understanding the speaker's message.

- Face the speaker squarely.
- Adjust your body position in nondistracting ways.
- Nod your head up and down to signal agreement; nod it sideways to signal disagreement.
- Smile to signal agreement; frown to signal disagreement.
- Raise your eyebrows to say *Really?* or *That's interesting.*
- Utter the words *I see, mmmm, right.*

Offer positive encouragement.

Give speakers the space they need with attentive silence. Sit quietly and patiently through pauses or uneasiness. Remember that some people are uncomfortable speaking and some are dealing with difficult personal issues. If the speaker is emotional, accept the emotion without saying *Please don't cry.* Resist the urge to give advice unless asked. Listen with your heart as well as with your ears.

Don't interrupt.

Wait until the speaker completes his thoughts before breaking in with something you want to say. However, it's okay to interrupt if you need clarification. This lets the speaker know you're actively listening, and it also avoids misunderstandings.

Even if the speaker is launching a negative attack against you, wait until he's finished to defend yourself. You'll give the speaker the feeling that he's made his point, so you won't get into an argument. Listen carefully so you can plan your rebuttal.

Ask questions and paraphrase.

Active listening means asking questions to clarify salient points. Pose broad-based questions so you don't get just a yes-or-no answer. This will result in your gaining information you may not have gotten otherwise. Question from a position of goodwill and mutual goals, and recognize the difference between facts and opinions. If you're not sure what the speaker said, ask for clarification: *What I hear you saying is. . . . Is that correct?; So you're saying. . . .; Do you mean . . .?* This verifies the accuracy of what you heard. (This technique is particularly helpful when you're expected to follow instructions.)

Take notes.

When it's important to remember a conversation, take notes. Always make sure the speaker knows you're taking notes. Simply ask: *Would you mind if I take notes?* or *Would you mind if I jot down a few key points?* Then take out a small notebook and pen, and get started. You'll be surprised at how much more accurately you remember a conversation when you write it down.

Mirror body language.

Copy the body language of the person you're speaking with. If he's sitting back with his legs crossed, do the same. If he has his arm over the back of the chair, do the same. When you mirror the body language of the speaker, he will subconsciously understand that you're listening. This works very well during interviews, because people like to hire people who are like themselves.

Be engaged.

Don't shuffle papers, play with your pencil, fondle your hair, doodle, check email, or text. And make sure your cell phone is shut off.

To help master your listening skills, ask yourself these questions after your next conversation:

- Was I facing the speaker and maintaining eye contact?
- What did I learn from the speaker?
- Who did most of the talking?
- Who did most of the listening?

- Did I interrupt?
- What questions should I have asked?
- Did I ask for clarification when I didn't understand something?
- What will I do differently in my next conversation?

 If you find yourself being distracted, apologize: *I'm sorry, I was thinking about [comment] you mentioned earlier.*

Tips for Managers

Whether you sit in the corner office or in a cubicle, to manage effectively you must develop strong communication skills. Too many people are promoted into management positions on the strength of their workplace achievements, while they haven't received any training in basic communication skills—one of which is listening. As a manager, your ability to get your point across clearly often depends on how well you listen. Listen up, listen down, and listen across your organization. This will help you to

- Pick up on problems before they get out of control.
- Understand people's motives.
- Discover options.
- Learn of conditions and trends.
- Build rapport.
- Gather ideas.
- Make better decisions.
- Solve problems.

One of the biggest gripes employees have is that their managers don't listen to them. As a manager: Are you guilty of not listening because your job is full of distractions? Are you flying in a million directions? Are you shifting priorities? Are you trying to put out one fire after another? Do you immediately begin brainstorming and handing out advice? Do you really listen?

Validate your employees.

Stop and listen. When you take the time to truly listen to your employees, it makes them feel validated. Listen to *how* something is said in addition to *what* is said. The emotional and nonverbal messages may be just as important as the spoken ones.

Admit you don't have all the answers.

The command-and-control type of leadership once ruled supreme. Managers "had all the answers," or at least behaved as if they did. Today's managers aren't expected to have all the answers—but they know how to find them and to help others find them. This management style brings out the best in other people and creates a collaboration that drives a winning organization. You can say, *I don't know the answer to that, but I'll look into it and get back to you [when].*

Give your undivided attention.

Listen to your employees and give them your undivided attention.

- Designate hours when you make yourself available.
- Schedule regular meetings to listen to your team, as a group and individually. If you have off-site employees, meet by phone.
- Listen without distractions. Turn off your cell phone, avoid looking at your computer, don't take phone calls, and close the door if necessary.
- Listen with an open and unbiased attitude.
- Ask open-ended questions for clarification.
- Focus on the person's train of thought without trying to formulate your response.
- Don't get defensive.
- Don't rush to fill in gaps in the conversation. Allow for pauses and for the other person to collect his thoughts.
- Take notes on key points you can reference later or can use to sum up the conversation.
- Use *Uh-huh* and *I see* to indicate you're listening.
- Paraphrase what's been said to be sure you understand correctly.
- If the conversation ends without a conclusion, mention what the follow-up will be.

 When listening to your employees, listen for what they're saying, listen for subtleties, listen for what they're asking. They may be asking for a chance to be heard, for respect, or for recognition.

Do you really listen to your employees?

If you ask most high-level businesspeople to name their most valuable company asset, many would say employees. *Do you agree? If so, do you really listen to them?*

- *Do you put what you're doing aside when an employee comes into your office and asks to speak with you?*

- *Do you listen fully without interrupting?*
- *Do you smile and lean forward to let him know you're listening?*
- *Do you ask questions to assure you heard properly?*
- *Do you follow through on anything that comes from the meeting?*

Listening is a gift you give your employees—a gift that will pay back big time!

Tips for Parents

Parents always complain that their children don't listen. Part of the reason is that kids are just being kids. But some of the reason may be that parents don't listen—really listen—to their kids, and they don't teach the kids how to listen either. Some suggestions for leading by example follow.

Set aside time to listen.

Set aside time when you and your children can listen to each other. The 10-minute drive to school or to after-school activities isn't necessarily the time for quality conversation. If you eat dinner together, take turns sharing how everyone's day went. Ask: *What was your favorite part of the day? What frustrated you? What made you happy?* If you don't eat dinner together, schedule periodic family talks. Get creative. Have talks at a family picnic or during some other quiet activity everyone enjoys.

Show real interest with open-ended questions.

Ask about your child's ideas regularly. When he knows you're interested in what he thinks, he'll be comfortable expressing his feelings and thoughts to you. Ask the types of questions that will promote conversation, not reach a dead end: *Tell me about your day at school. How did the teacher . . .? Tell me about your favorite part of the day. It sounds as if you're angry with [name]—can you tell me what happened?*

 Watch for signs that your child wants to end the conversation. They include staring into space, giving silly answers, and the like.

Play listening games.

"Simple Simon" is a popular game that makes children listen carefully. If you say, *Simon says, raise your left hand,* the child should raise his left hand. However, if you say, *Raise your left hand,* the child shouldn't raise his left hand, because you didn't say, *Simon says.*

Read a story.

Most young children love to have an adult read to them. Read a story and ask the child to retell the story. Ask questions about the story.

- *Why do you think [character] did . . .?*
- *If you were [character], what would you have done?*
- Read partway and ask, *How do you think this will end?*

Reading to children helps them not only to listen, but to comprehend and develop reading skills.

Get down to size.

When you speak to a young child, crouch down, sit down, or lift the child up so you're at eye level. It's important to look directly at your child when you speak. You can find many messages in your child's face and body language that can help you understand his feelings. Is he sad? happy? angry? Also, when you look at your child, he knows he has your undivided attention.

Stop what you're doing when your child has something important to say.

When your child wants to talk to you about something important to him, don't "listen" as you continue reading, watching television, vacuuming, emailing, or busying yourself with whatever you're doing. Give that child your undivided attention. All the "stuff" you're currently working on can wait, but you can never recapture that precious time with your child.

When you want to speak to your child about something important to you, you can then expect the same measure of his full attention.

Listen without interrupting.

Give your child the same respect you'd give an adult. If he hesitates, you can prompt with a leading question or a comment such as *Tell me more.* Identify your child's emotions and let him know it's okay to have and express that emotion. Your child needs to express emotions and feel assured that you'll listen.

- Speak in a quiet tone of voice, even a whisper, so your child has to work a little to listen.
- Respect your child and use a courteous tone of voice. If you speak to your child as respectfully as you would with a friend, he may be more likely to seek you out as a confidant.

Offer praise when your child earns it.

When your child is helpful, courteous, does chores, completes homework, or does other things worthy of praise, lavish it on. This will build your child's confidence and open the door to better communication. Parents are often too quick to offer criticism when something is wrong. Be sure to flip the coin.

 If you really feel that your young child isn't listening, perhaps that child isn't hearing. When one of my sons was young, I used to get frustrated because he didn't listen to me. I soon came to suspect that he had a hearing problem. That was verified by an audiologist, and fortunately it was just a minor hearing loss. I learned to speak a little louder, and that made all the difference. Of course, he still had "selective hearing," as all children do.

Tips for Teachers to Teach Children

Good listening skills will enhance children's communications, improve the classroom climate, build reading skills, and prepare children for life. Here are a few suggestions for teachers for promoting listening skills in children:

- Make sure they're comfortable.
- Suggest that they close their eyes and listen.
- Encourage them to listen for pleasure, not just to follow instructions.
- Ask them to sit quietly and listen to their own breathing.
- Play a listening game. Ask them to sit quietly for a short period and think of the noises they hear. Then ask them to describe the noises.
- Give them specific directions about how to draw something. Then compare how they drew it with what they were told.

Tips for College Students

Studies show that the average college student spends about 14 hours a week attending lectures. The University of Minnesota Duluth compiled these tips for college students to improve listening skills:

- **Maintain eye contact with the instructor.** Of course, you will need to look at your notebook to write your notes, but eye contact keeps you focused on the job at hand and keeps you involved in the lecture.

- **Focus on content, not delivery.** Have you ever counted the number of times a teacher cleared his throat in a 15-minute period? If so, you weren't focusing on content.

- **Avoid emotional involvement.** When you are too emotionally involved in listening, you tend to hear what you want to hear, not what is actually being said. Try to remain objective and open-minded.

- **Avoid distractions.** Don't let your mind wander or be distracted by the person shuffling papers near you. If the classroom is too hot or too cold, try to remedy the situation if you can. The solution may require that you dress more appropriately for the temperature of the room.

- **Treat listening as a challenging mental task.** Listening to an academic lecture is not a passive act—at least it shouldn't be. You need to concentrate on what is being said so that you can process the information into your notes.

- **Stay active by asking mental questions.** Active listening keeps you on your toes. Here are some questions you can ask yourself as you listen: What key point is the professor making? How does this fit with what I know from previous lectures? How is this lecture organized?

- **Use the gap between the rate of speech and your rate of thought.** You can think faster than the lecturer can talk. That's one reason your mind may tend to wander. All the above suggestions will help you keep your mind occupied and focused on what is being said. You might begin to anticipate what the professor is going to say as a way of keeping your mind from straying. Your mind has the capacity to listen, think, write, and ponder at the same time, but achieving this takes practice.

5

The difference between the almost right word and the right word is really a large matter—'tis the difference between the lightning bug and the lightning.
—Mark Twain

Making Proper Word Choices

Language abounds with words that are rich, colorful, and precise. These words are not just functional, they can be used to engage or disengage, sadden or gladden, strengthen or weaken, persuade or dissuade—whether your audience is one person or a room full of people.

Words for Impact

Keep it short and simple (KISS).

Every word that doesn't add to the effectiveness of your message wastes the audience's time and reduces interest. In the left column you see short, straightforward words. Why use the "overkill" expressions in the right column?

Simple	Overkill	Simple	Overkill
Agree	Come to an agreement	Although	Regardless of the fact that
Always	In all cases	Apply	Make an application
Because	Due to the fact that	Before	Prior to
Conclude	Arrive at a conclusion	Consider	Give consideration to
During	During the course of	Examine	Make an examination of
Experiment	Conduct experiments	Find out	Ascertain
If	In the event that	Investigate	Conduct an investigation of

45

Simple	Overkill	Simple	Overkill
Invite	Extend an invitation to	Meet	Hold a conference
Read	Peruse	Refer to	Make reference to
Return	Arrange to return	Save	Realize a savings of
Show	Give an indication of	Then	At that point in time
Use	Utilize		

Be clear, concise, and to the point.

In November 1863 a large crowd gathered to listen to Edward Everett, a leading orator of the time, dedicate Gettysburg's National Cemetery to the Civil War's fallen heroes. He spoke for two hours. After his speech, Abraham Lincoln got up and delivered the 278-word Gettysburg Address in fewer than three minutes. Lincoln's address is one of the most memorable of all times. *Eighty-one percent of its words are one syllable.* Everett's speech is all but forgotten.

Contrast Lincoln's address during the Civil War to this mandate issued by the government during World War II: "Such preparations shall be made as will completely obscure all federal buildings and non-federal buildings occupied by the government during an air raid for any period of time from visibility by reason of internal or external illumination." (It's amazing the United States won the war with gobbledygook like that.) President Franklin D. Roosevelt revised the message. "Tell them," he said, "that in buildings where they have to keep the work going, to put something across the windows."

Keep your language clear, concise, and to the point so your audience will understand your message. Eliminate all words that don't add value to your topic. (Imagine that every word you use will cost you $100.)

> **Clear:** We should send all major projects to outside shops so ours aren't tied up should an emergency come in. (19 words)
>
> **Unclear:** Because we have a small shop with limited personnel whose primary purpose (in my opinion) is to support the reactor operations and experiments, I recommend we send all major projects to outside shops who have better machines and capabilities so as not to tie up our machinists for extended periods of time, which can be a problem if an emergency job is required and they are interrupted. (67 words)

Draw upon positive words, phrases, and experiences.

Presenting yourself as an optimist is a winning strategy. (The glass is half full, rather than half empty.) Words such as *benefit, bonus, congratulations, generous, of course, please, pleasure, proven, satisfactory,* and *thank you* are positive; whereas words such as *broken, careless, complaint, disappoint, inconvenient, problem,* and *unable* are negative.

- Be mindful of "un-" words. For example, "the toy was determined to be safe" sounds more positive than "the toy was not determined to be unsafe." Although two negatives equal a positive, you want the listener to hear the word *safe*, rather than the word *unsafe*.
- Sounding positive can be a matter of saying what you can and will do, rather than what you can't and won't do.

Positive: I'm glad to tell you that your shipment will arrive on April 5.
Negative: Unfortunately, your shipment won't arrive until April 5.

Positive: Once you pay the past due balance, we'll be delighted to ship your order.
Negative: We can't ship your order until you pay the past due balance.

 My client invented an electrical appliance and asked me to write a brief handbook. He asked me to put on the cover, "This is no more harmful than a hair dryer." The word *harmful* would have stood out like a wart on the end of his nose. Therefore, I wrote, "This is as safe as a hair dryer."

Avoid tentative language so you sound confident.

Many speakers fear sounding too confident, so they use tentative language. This includes expressions such as *I guess, I think, practically, it may be that, in effect, more or less, to some extent, for all intents and purposes, suggests that, it may be argued that,* and more. To appear confident, use language that projects confidence, as in the following examples:

Self-assured: One of the main reasons businesses fail is because of. . . .
Tentative: One of the main reasons businesses fail might be because of. . . .

Use the right tone.

Keep the talk short and simple. Use language that's clear, concise, and conversational. Use positive words and the active voice. Be sensitive to word associations, sarcasm, and sexist language. There are three specific ways to achieve the right tone and stress your message:

1. Phrase your sentences so they're strong and have impact.

Strong: Financial planners believe that the market will continue to rise.
Weak: There's a belief among financial planners that the market will continue to rise.

2. Use a highlighter or a bold font for text you want to emphasize. When speaking, use your voice to stress words or phrases.

The goldfish is in the sink. (Nothing is stressed.)
The **goldfish** is in the sink. (As opposed to the shark.)
The goldfish **is** in the sink. (In case you doubted it the first time.)
The goldfish is **in** the sink. (As opposed to near the sink.)
The goldfish is in the **sink**. (As opposed to in the bathtub.)

3. Indicate pauses in your notes. The word *PAUSE* or double slashes (//) may do the trick.

Include alliteration or rhyme.

Alliteration and rhyme can be memorable parts of your talk.

Alliteration: Really rigid requirements!
Rhyme: You may remember the famous rhyme that came out of the O. J. Simpson trial: *If the glove don't fit, you must acquit.*

Think internationally.

It's a small world and shrinking quickly. International travel is commonplace. If you have occasion to speak before a foreign audience (even foreigners visiting or living in your own country), display international savvy. Consider the following suggestions when speaking to people from foreign countries or cultures.

Dos

Here are a few audience enticers:

- Start your talk by expressing your sincere honor at being able to address the group.
- Be aware of current events within the country or culture, and be sensitive to those issues.
- Quote a well-known person from your audience's country or culture. Make sure that person is someone your audience can admire.
- Speak to the need for international communication. Use statistics, anecdotes, or stories.
- Deliver a powerful line or phrase in the audience's native language and be aware of how things translate.

Taboos

Here are ways to avoid shooting yourself in both feet:

- Do not insult your audience with cute remarks that could be interpreted as social blunders. For example, if you're from the United States and are speaking to people from Greece, do not announce that in the United States all the diners are owned by Greeks.
- Do not tell off-color jokes or use profanity. This holds true no matter who's in the audience.

 Check out chapter 12, "Communicating Cross-Culturally."

Don't get lost in the translation

When Secretary of State Hillary Clinton first met with her Russian counterpart, she presented him with a mock "reset button" to symbolize a break from the snarling relationship between the two powers during the Bush administration. The Americans had printed on the button the word *peregruzka*, which was intended to mean "reset." Instead, it meant "overcharge."

Think of analogies to foster understanding.

The American Heritage® Dictionary defines an analogy as an inference "based on the assumption that if two things are known to be alike in some respects, then they are probably alike in other respects." I was listening to a radio talk show on finance. The caller mentioned that he has investments in stocks and real estate. He said that when the stock market starts to fall, he sells, and when the market starts to climb, he buys. The talk show host was having trouble convincing the caller that this is poor strategy. Finally the host offered an analogy in the form of a question: When the real estate market falls, do you sell your real estate investments and purchase them back when the real estate market rises? Aha! A light bulb went on. Analogies can do that.

Use contractions.

Years ago contractions belonged only in the labor room. Today, however, contractions in speech are preferable because they're conversational. *Hasn't* rather than *has not, can't* instead of *cannot, won't* instead of *will not,* and others.

Think plural.

Masculine pronouns were once pervasive, and people typically used *he* or *him* to denote doctors, lawyers, politicians, and the like. That's all changed. Instead of getting into clunky *he/she* or *his/her* situations, use plurals when you can.

Plural: Doctors are trained to heal their patients.
Singular: A doctor is trained to heal his/her patients.

Plural: All candidates for the human resources position must submit their applications before [date]. They must include their educational backgrounds.
Singular: Every candidate for the human resources position must submit his/her application before [date]. He/she should include his/her educational background.

 Notice how I solve that problem in this book. As mentioned in the introduction, I use female pronouns in the odd-numbered chapters and male pronouns in the even-numbered chapters.

Use repetition for emphasis.

Consider using repetition to create a strong effect or to emphasize an intense feeling or point. Immediately following 9/11, New York City Mayor Rudy Giuliani delivered a powerful speech that inspired our nation. (Notice how he strategically repeated the word *stronger* three times to intensify the message.)

> "The people in New York City will be whole again. We are going to come out of this emotionally *stronger*, politically *stronger*, much closer together as a city, and we're going to come out of this economically *stronger* too."

Here's another example of repetition used to strengthen a point:

Strong: Why should we adopt this policy? We should adopt it because it will give us the competitive edge. And we should adopt it because it will give us a 50 percent profit.
Weak: Why should we adopt this policy? Because it will give us the competitive edge and a 50 percent profit.

If you're not trying to emphasize a point, avoid wordy, repetitive, repeated, and repetitious redundancies, such as the ones that follow:

Simple	Overkill	Simple	Overkill
As soon as	At the earliest possible date	Breakthrough	New breakthrough
Consensus	General consensus	Developments	New developments
Essential	Absolutely essential	Fact	True fact
Factor	Contributing factor	First	First and foremost
Fundamentals	Basic fundamentals	Group	Group together
Loan	Temporary loan	Opposite	Complete opposite
Outcome	Final outcome	Result	End result
Status	Current status	Truth	Honest truth

Speak in the active voice unless there's a reason to speak in the passive voice.

Imagine this scenario: You're vacationing in the tropics with your loved one. The fiery crimson sun is sinking slowly into the distant horizon and the waves are crashing on the craggy shore. You and your companion interlock arms and you sip vintage wine from each other's glasses. That special someone then whispers in your ear . . . *I love you.* Doesn't that make you feel affectionate? Now imagine that same scenario, and that special someone whispers in your ear . . . *You are loved by me.* Doesn't that make you want to check the classifieds? Well, that's the difference between the active and passive voices.

Active Voice

The active voice makes your words come alive. When you speak in the active voice, you start the sentence with the doer—the person, place, or thing performing the action. Here are a few examples of the active voice:

- Jon will prepare the agenda on Monday. (Jon is the doer.)
- The people in Wisconsin experienced a warmer-than-usual winter. (The people in Wisconsin are the doers.)
- Check Parts A and B for accuracy. (The doer is implied; it's the listener.)

Passive Voice

When you speak in the passive voice, you make the subject the receiver of the action. In these examples, the passive voice is effective:

- The manager was recognized for his outstanding performance. (You want to focus on the manager, not the person who cited him.)
- The quota for Q2 wasn't met. (You want to be diplomatic and hide something or protect someone.)

When you use the passive voice, you'll always use a form of the verb *to be* (*is, are, was, were, will be, should be, should have been, must be, must have been, could be, could have been,* and the like).

- The course *will be* taught by Gene Rodden.
- The contract *should be* checked for accuracy.
- The office *is* shared by Jim and John.

Pepper your sentences with adjectives.

In addition to using the active voice, use adjectives to add pizzazz to a message. (Here's a mini-English lesson.) An adjective is a word, phrase, or clause that modifies, describes, or limits the noun or pronoun it's describing. Following are a few examples of interesting and boring sentences.

Interesting: The darkly charred steak sizzled atop the smoky grill, its surface beaded with hot, red juices.
Boring: The steak was cooking on the grill.

Interesting: Three hundred CIOs, impressive in black tie and tails, joined the conference in the warmth of the Miami sun.
Boring: Three hundred CIOs attended the conference in Miami.

Put the focus on your audience, rather than on yourself.

Have you ever been to an event and been cornered by a bore who talked incessantly about herself? It's pretty annoying. The next time you see that bore, would you be anxious to spend more time with her? Of course not. You'd probably hide behind the tallest plant you could find. Engage your audience with inclusive words such as *we, our, you,* and *your.*

Use euphemisms.

Euphemisms are substitutes for words or phrases that may be blunt, offensive, negative, or distasteful. Here are a few:

Euphemism	Less appealing
Casualties	Deaths, injuries
Deposit, initial investment	Down payment
Direct report	Subordinate
Downsize	Terminate, fire
Economical	Cheap
Fatal injury	Death
Opportunity	Problem
Passed away	Died
Previously owned	Used
Supervisor, manager	Boss
Unsophisticated	Ignorant

Know when to use jargon, acronyms, and initialisms.

Jargon is specialized "shop talk" that's unique to people who have common interests or are in the same profession or industry. When you speak to people with whom you share a common language, it makes no sense to water down your words. When you speak with outsiders or a mixed group, however, avoid jargon, because it may alienate or exclude certain listeners.

When using acronyms or initialisms, be certain your audience will understand what they stand for. For example, do you know what ABA stands for? It's the American Bar Association, the American Banking Association, the American Booksellers Association, the American Basketball Association, and the American anything-with-a-B Association. So if an attorney is speaking with a banker about an ABA meeting, they'll have different frames of reference. Make sure those listening to you will understand your references. If in doubt, mention the reference in full the first time you say it: *I went to the March meeting of the American Booksellers Association (ABA) recently and. . . . At the ABA meeting, I met. . . .*

Avoid clichés like the plague.

A cliché is a group of words that is overused. When new, these words paint a picture or convey an idea. When overused, they become boring. Popular clichés include "That's the way the cookie crumbles," "When in Rome, do as the Romans do," "As happy as a clam," "What happens in Vegas stays in Vegas," "What goes around comes around." People use clichés when they speak because they haven't developed new and interesting descriptions, so they resort to what they know and what they've heard. The cliché police won't cite you for using one on occasion, but using too many will weaken your message and cause your audience to tune out.

Remain clear and consistent.

Following are some hints for remaining clear and consistent.

- **Be consistent with wording.** If you make reference to a "user manual," don't later call it a "reference manual" or "user guide." Your audience may think you're referring to separate documents.

- **Avoid ambiguity.** Using the words *should* or *may* can make your message ambiguous. "Don't smoke when operating this equipment" is definite. "You shouldn't smoke when operating this equipment" carries a hint of maybe.

- **Be precise about locations.** Locations are relative and are determined by where you are and which way you face. Use clear terms like "As you face the front of the computer" or "Rotate the dial 45 degrees clockwise."

Think seriously about being funny.

Humor—when used properly—can be a wonderful way to lighten a heavy topic or create a bond between you and your audience. Your humor should, however, relate to your topic. But remember that there's often a fine line between being humorous and being offensive. This is especially true when you're communicating with people of different cultures. Many points have been missed and international contacts lost due to the misunderstanding of humor.

 I attended a workshop where the facilitator made a religious comment he thought was funny. When a few people openly took offense, the facilitator tried to explain that he's a member of that religious group, so he wasn't being offensive. But the people who were offended didn't want to hear any explanations; several walked out of the workshop.

Pronounce words correctly.

Unless someone corrects you, you may not even realize that you're mispronouncing a word. Rather than finding out in an embarrassing manner, look at the following list to see if you misspeak any of these words. If you mispronounce these or any other words, practice, practice, practice!

Correct	Incorrect	Correct	Incorrect
Accessory	Assessory	Across	Acrossed
Affidavit	Affidavid	All	Alls
All right	Awright	Any	Iny
Ask	Aks	Asked	Axed
Asterisk	Aksterik	Athlete	Athelete
Candidate	Cannidate	Center	Cenner
Cinnamon	Cimmanon	Could have	Coulda
Didn't	Dint	Dilate	Dialate
Escape	Excape	Espresso	Expresso
Etcetera	Excetera	Federal	Fedral
Figure	Figger	Film	Fillum
Give me	Gimme	Going to	Gonna
Hierarchy	Hiarchy	Interesting	Inneresting
Jewelry	Jewlrey	Masonry	Masonary
Nuclear	Nucular	Oriented	Orientated
Particular	Paticular	Perhaps	Praps
Picture	Pitcher	Plenty	Plenny
Pollute	Plute	Prescription	Perscription
Probably	Probly	Regardless	Irregardless
Relevant	Relvant	Specific	Pacific
Supposedly	Suppossably	Triathlon	Triathalon
Verbiage	Verbage	Want to	Wanna
Would have	Woulda	You	Yous

For more on pronunciation controversies, check out *100 Words Almost Everyone Mispronounces,* from the Editors of the American Heritage® Dictionaries. You can hear many of these words pronounced on a podcast at http://www. hmhbooks.com/ahd/100words.shtml.

With all due respect, getting rid of overused expressions isn't rocket science.

Now that the United States is so interwoven with the rest of the world, some of the expressions we use have little or no meaning in other parts of the world. And sometimes they're downright confusing. For example, if you told an American to *look out*, that person would probably duck. If you told someone in a European country to *look out*, that person would probably take you literally and look out the window. Here are just a few tired old expressions that have been used so often, they've lost most of their meaning and all of their originality. If you use any of them, try something more meaningful.

24/7	At the end of the day
By the close of business	Can't hold a candle to
Defining moment	Enclosed please find
Fallen on hard times	Get down to brass tacks
Give me a break	Having said that
Heart-to-heart talk	I personally think
It's a nightmare	It's in the bag
Leave no stone unturned	Leaves much to be desired
Lion's share	Middle of the road
Now you're cooking with gas	Nuts and bolts
Off the charts	Play by the rules
Please do not hesitate	Put your nose to the grindstone
Run of the mill	Take a hike
The food chain	This isn't rocket science
Value added	We are pleased
With all due respect	

Punctuation

You may have looked at the heading "punctuation" and wondered what it has to do with speaking. It has everything to do with speaking. Punctuation was created in days of yore for actors, chanters, and other readers to indicate verbal pauses and stresses. For example, a period is to a stop sign what a comma is to a yield sign. Look at the following sentences and notice how the punctuation marks create a different "voice."

Use em dashes for high emphasis. The ABC Company—winner of the Service Award—just introduced its new product line. *The em dashes create a raised voice when saying, "winner of the Service Award."*

Use parentheses for low emphasis. The ABC Company (winner of the Service Award) just introduced its new product line. *The parentheses create a lowered voice when saying, "winner of the Service Award."*

Use commas for neutral emphasis. The ABC Company, winner of the Service Award, just introduced its new product line. *The commas create a neutral voice when saying, "winner of the Service Award."*

The Power of Punctuation

To experience the power of punctuation (and what text may look like without it), read the following to see if it makes sense:

Dear Tom I want a man who knows what love is all about you are generous kind thoughtful people who are not like you admit to being useless and inferior you have ruined me for other men I yearn for you I have no feelings whatsoever when we're apart I can be happy forever will you let me be yours Sheila

Did you have a problem? If so, here's how punctuation dramatically changes the meaning of the text.

Warm message
The placement of periods, commas, and a question mark create a warm and loving message.

Dear Tom,
I want a man who knows what love is all about. You are generous, kind, thoughtful. People who are not like you admit to being useless and inferior. You have ruined me for other men. I yearn for you. I have no feelings whatsoever when we're apart. I can be happy forever. Will you let me be yours? Sheila

Cold message
The placement of periods, commas, and a question mark create a cold and calculating message.

Dear Tom,
I want a man who knows what love is. All about you are generous, kind, thoughtful people who are not like you. Admit to being useless and inferior. You have ruined me. For other men I yearn. For you I have no feelings whatsoever. When we're apart, I can be happy forever. Will you let me be?
Yours, Sheila

Common Grammatical Faux Pas

When you were a kid, do you remember asking your mother, *Mom, can Pat and me go to the movies?* Perhaps your mother replied, *That's Pat and I,* and she didn't give you the money until you corrected your grammar. Although you didn't think so then, your mother was doing you a favor. Poor grammar didn't get you far with your mother, and it doesn't get you far in the world.

We all know the importance of dressing properly in order to be successful. No matter how well you're dressed, if you use incorrect grammar, you'll appear to be a wolf in sheep's clothing—fashionable on the outside, but sloppy on the inside.

Swat pesky pronouns.

Simply stated, pronouns are small words that replace nouns. Pronouns keep you from being repetitious. When you have two pronouns together in a sentence, use them in two sentences to see how they sound separately and you'll always know whether they've been used correctly.

> The odds were against *you and me.*
> The odds were against *you.* The odds were against *me.*

Always be certain your pronoun relates to someone or something specific. In the first sentence that follows, it's unclear whether the pronoun *he* refers to George or to Steve.

> Steve first met George when *he* was a trainee.
> Steve first met George when George was a trainee.

Compare for clarity.

Use *-er, more,* or *less* to compare two things. Use *-est, most,* or *least* to compare three or more.

> Marc is my *older* son. (Tells you I have two sons.)
> Marc is my *oldest* son. (Tells you I have three or more sons.)

Don't dangle your participles.

Dangling participles or misplaced phrases are constructions that are too far away from what they modify. If your phrases are misplaced or your participles dangle, don't worry. The condition is curable.

> **Dangling:** At the age of five, my mother bought me a cat. (Your mother wasn't five when she bought you a cat.)
> **Not dangling:** When I was five, my mother bought me a cat.

Make subjects and verbs agree.

Use a singular verb with a singular subject and a plural verb with a plural subject. Some grammatical constructions present complications.

Singular: The file folder listing the companies is sitting on my desk. (The singular "file" is sitting, regardless of what's in it.)

Plural: Here come two of my favorite candidates. (They come . . .)

 Use a singular verb for collective nouns that emphasize the group—such as *panel, audience, class, jury, company, bank, association, committee,* and the like.

Singular: The committee is being asked to . . . (The singular group)

Plural: The committee members are being asked to . . . (Multiple members)

Don't use double negatives.

If you have ever said, "I don't want no liver," you have said you do want liver. Two negatives equal a positive. Never use two negatives to express one positive idea.

Correct: I don't want any.
Wrong: I don't want none.

What about split infinitives?

Was Gene Roddenberry wrong in saying *To boldly go . . .*? For years it was thought so, but now many English experts are saying it's okay to split infinitives. You split an infinitive when you put another word between *to* and the verb.

He tried *to understand* the meaning thoroughly. (Not split)
He tried *to thoroughly understand* the meaning. (Split)

End a sentence with a preposition when changing it would make the sentence clumsy.

I know you were probably taught in school that it's a no-no to end a sentence with a preposition. It's okay to do so if changing the sentence will make it sound clunky. Following is a quote from Winston Churchill that is a comment against clumsy avoidance of a preposition at the end of a sentence: "This is the sort of English up with which I will not put." Although that sentence is grammatically correct, you'd sound like a pompous "you-know-what" if you spoke like that.

Know thyself.

Don't use words such as *myself, yourself, himself, herself, itself, ourselves, yourselves,* or *themselves* when you should correctly be using *I, me, you,* and so on. Use *-self* only when the subject acts upon itself.

Correct: I asked *myself* that same question.

Correct: He hates *himself* for what he did.

Incorrect: Bob and *myself* ate lunch at Barlow's yesterday. (Should be "Bob and I...")

Pair off.

Little words can make a big difference. Some change the meaning of the message entirely; others are just incorrect. Can you imagine the nursery rhyme as "Mary had a little lamb, its fleas were white as snow"? The good thing about speech is that listeners may not hear a difference between "fleece" and "fleas." Following are examples where they will notice a faux pas, however.

Access/Excess

He gained *access* to the locked room. (Admittance)

The truck carried a load in *excess* of the allowed limit. (Extra)

Adapt/Adopt/Adept

You must *adapt* to changing situations. (Adjust)

The company will *adopt* a stringent policy on absenteeism. (Choose)

He is *adept* at cycling. (Proficient)

Adverse/Averse

Many patients had *adverse* reactions to the drug. (Unfavorable)

Are you *averse* to being interviewed? (Opposed)

And/But

Jack was new to consulting *and* outperformed expectations. (Infers this was expected)

Jack was new to consulting *but* outperformed expectations. (Infers this had been doubtful)

Between/Among

He couldn't decide *between* stocks or bonds as an investment. (Two entities)

He chose ABS from *among* all the options. (Three or more entities)

Biannual/Biennial

The board meets *biannually*. (Same as semiannually—twice during the year)

The graduates have a reunion *biennially*. (Every other year)

Can/May

I *can* give you an answer tomorrow. (Being physically or mentally able)

May I stop by your office to discuss the issue? (Asking for permission)

Continual/Continuous

Speaking well requires *continual* practice. (Happening repeatedly)

The *continuous* humming of the machine is annoying. (Without interruption)

Different from/Different than

This message is *different from* the one we received yesterday. (Comparison is between two things)

She found the town *different than* she remembered it. (Comparison is expressed by a full clause)

Disinterested/Uninterested

Let's ask a *disinterested* person. (Impartial)

James was *uninterested* in the lecture. (Didn't care)

Either-or/Neither-nor

Either a letter *or* a phone call would be appropriate at this time. (One of two options will be chosen/exercised.)

Neither a letter *nor* a phone call would be appropriate at this time. (Neither of two options will be chosen/exercised.)

Eminent/Imminent

Dr. Marshall is *eminent* in his field of medicine. (Well known)

The storm is *imminent*. (About to happen)

Ensure, Assure, Insure

I want to *ensure* that nothing will go wrong. (Make certain)

I want to *assure* you that nothing is wrong. (Give confidence)

I want to *insure* this diamond for $7,500. (Protect against loss)

Farther/Further

This is *farther* than I've walked in a long time. (Notice the word *far*, meaning distance)

That couldn't be *further* from the truth. (To a greater degree)

First/Firstly

First we'll eat, then we'll talk. (First, second, third)

Firstly we'll eat; secondly we'll talk. (Firstly, secondly, thirdly)

Good/Well

This is a *good* proposal. (An adjective that describes a noun)

She ran *well* in the race. (An adverb that describes a verb)

She has not been *well* for a long time. (An adjective that describes health or condition)

Irrelevant/Irreverent

That evidence is *irrelevant* to the case. (Inappropriate or unrelated)

It's *irreverent* to eat in church. (Disrespectful)

Its/Their
The company will celebrate *its* tenth anniversary. (Singular)
Both companies will celebrate *their* tenth anniversaries. (Plural)

Moral/Morale
He is a man with strong *moral* values. (Good and honorable)
After the loss of the final game, *morale* was low. (Spirit)

Number/Amount
There are a *number* of issues we need to discuss. (Countable quantity)
The *amount* of energy that machine uses is staggering. (Sum total)

Precede/Proceed
Creating a good storyboard *precedes* writing a good speech. (Comes
   before)
Jim *proceeded* to the rear exit. (Moved)

Regard/Regards
That information is *in regard to* what we discussed yesterday.
   (In relation to)
Give my *regards* to Geraldine. (Best wishes)

That/Which
Jack's horse *that* has one white leg won best in show. (Jack has more than
   one horse, and you identify the one that won best in show by mentioning the horse's unique leg.)
Jack's horse, *which* has one white leg, won best in show. (Jack has only
   one horse, so it doesn't matter what color its legs are. Notice that when
   it's written, you set the clause off with commas.)

Titled/Entitled
What is that book *titled*? (Named)
He's *entitled* to a rebate. (Having a right or claim)

Wait on/Wait for
We need more staff to *wait on* customers. (Serve; used in the hospitality
   industry only)
We're *waiting for* Joan to arrive. (Pass time till an expected event
   happens)

Who/Whom
Here's a sure-fire rule for remembering this distinction for the rest of
your life: When you can substitute *he/she/they,* use *who.* When you can
substitute *her/him/them,* use *whom.* Simply notice the *m* endings, and
you'll never confuse them again. The same holds true for *whoever* and
whomever.

Whom will Jack send to Hong Kong? (Jack will send him.)
Steve is the person *who* needs the least amount of supervision.
　　(He needs the least . . .)
Always be courteous to *whoever* calls. (He calls.)
Who should I say is calling? (She is calling.)

If in doubt, substitute.

If you're ever in doubt as to which of two similar words to use, see if you can change the word or the sentence. For example, in the first sentence that follows, say you don't know whether to use beside *or* besides. *Rather than frustrate yourself, substitute something else.*

　The file cabinet is beside *the window.*
　The file cabinet is next to *the window.*
　The file cabinet is near *the window.*
　The file cabinet is by *the window.*

6

Being politically correct means always having to say you're sorry.

—Charles Osgood, CBS News anchor

Using Politically Neutral Terms

In this chapter

- Using Neutral Terms
- In the Workplace
- Communicating with People with Disabilities
- Dispelling Fears of Potential Employers

I searched one of the online booksellers to see what was out there on political correctness. I found everything from politically correct (PC) scrapbooks, bedtime stories, and holiday stories to wars, hunters, and guns. In its truest sense, being PC means using neutral language that doesn't reinforce stereotypes, offend, exclude, devalue, or diminish.

Using Neutral Terms

Without getting into the ridiculous, such as merging Christmas, Hanukkah, and Kwanzaa to get a holiday called *Christmahanukwanzakah* (which I've seen, by the way), let's get a grip. Following are some neutral terms that should never offend anyone.

Instead of . . .	Use . . .
Acting like wild Indians	Out of control
Bitchy or PMS-ing	Assertive
Blind person	Person who is visually impaired
Broken home	Dysfunctional family
Bum	Homeless or displaced person
China (dinnerware)	Porcelain
Deaf person	Person who is hearing impaired

Instead of . . .	Use . . .
Flip chart	Easel (*Flip* is a negative term for Filipinos.)
Guys (denoting a mixed group)	Friends, folks, group
Gifted children	Advanced learners
Girls (denoting coworkers)	Women
Half-breed	Multiethnic
Handicapped person	Person with special needs, person who is physically/mentally challenged, person with disabilities (Focus on *person*)
Indian	Native American
Manning a project	Staffing a project
Middleman	Intermediary
Midget	Person of short stature
Old folks	Seniors
Oriental	Asian (or the specific nationality)
Physically disabled	Functionally disabled
Race	Ethnicity, nationality
Retarded	Developmentally challenged
The wife	My (his) wife
Uneducated	Lacking formal education
Wheelchair-bound, paraplegic, quadriplegic, crippled person	Person in a chair, person in a wheelchair

Respect people's choices.

Honor people's rights to choose the language and words that best describe their own race, class, gender, sexual orientation, or physical ability. Don't get defensive if someone rejects language that disempowers, marginalizes, or diminishes his or her own group of people.

Explain terms that may appear exclusionary.

This gets down to knowing your audience, which is likely to include people of different backgrounds and generations. To be taken seriously, use language that includes all of them and doesn't offend any subgroup.

- If you're talking to a group of technical people who understand your lingo, by all means use the lingo. If some don't, explain a few terms.

- In a mixed group, if you mention a holiday everyone may not understand, explain the term. (For example, Yom Kippur is a Jewish holy day and Mawlid al-Nabi is a celebration of the birthday of the Prophet Muhammad.)

Use gender-neutral terms.

An early awareness of political correctness emerged with the onset of the women's movement. Women protested the use of terms such as "male dominated" (instead of *patriarchal*), "chairman" (instead of *chair*), "man-made" (instead of *synthetic*), and the like. Some even went so far as to suggest "personhole" (instead of *manhole*). Following is a list of gender-neutral terms that have become commonplace.

Instead of . . .	Use . . .
Anchorman	Newscaster
Cameraman	Cinematographer
Chairman	Chairperson, chair, moderator
Clergyman	Member of the clergy
Delivery boy	Delivery person, messenger
Fireman	Firefighter
Forefather	Ancestor
Insurance man	Insurance agent
Layman	Nonprofessional
Man-made	Synthetic
Mankind	Humanity, human race
Newsman	Reporter, journalist
Policeman	Policewoman, police officer
Postman	Letter carrier
Repairman	Repairwoman, service technician
Salesman	Salesperson, sales representative
Spokesman	Spokesperson
Steward, stewardess	Flight attendant
Waiter, waitress	Server
Weatherman	Meteorologist
Workman	Worker

 When talking about female adults, refer to them as *women*. They're not *girls, gals, chicks, dames, broads,* or *babes*.

Use politically neutral colors.

Staff at a coffee shop in Glasgow, Scotland, refused to serve a customer who had ordered a black coffee, believing the term to be racist. The patron wasn't served until he changed his order to *coffee without milk*.

Instead of . . .	Use . . .
Black sheep	Outcast
Blacklisted	Banned
Blackboard	Chalkboard
White lie	Fib

Neutral Terms in Children's Literature

There's even a movement afoot to "cleanse" children's literature.

- Snow White and the Seven Dwarfs *is alternatively* Snow White and Her Seven Vertically Challenged Companions.
- Baa, baa, black sheep, have you any wool? *is alternatively* Baa, baa, transparent sheep, have you any wool?

When the prince in storyland appears as the savior, is that chauvinistic? Is the ugly stepmother an unfair depiction? (I certainly hope my daughter-in-law thinks it's unfair.)

In the Workplace

We are instinctively drawn to people who are like ourselves—those who share the same backgrounds, interests, and physical features. Just look around the cafeteria where you work and notice how people who are alike tend to cluster.

Step out of your comfort zone.

It's easy to misunderstand someone from a different ethnicity, religion, or country, so step out of your comfort zone. Reach out with sincerity to those who are unlike you. Ask respectful questions to learn about differing norms and values. You will bridge many gaps, find many commonalities, and make your life richer. Political correctness is more than watching what you say. It's learning about others and respecting the differences that make us all unique.

Be wary of humor.

It's been well documented that humor reduces stress, boosts morale, brings people closer, and wards off burnout. Although laughter is the best medicine (as the saying goes), it all depends on who's laughing. Our interpretation of what we hear is colored by our backgrounds and experiences. What one person finds humorous, another may find offensive.

Your place of employment should be safe and productive for every employee. Jokes about minorities, women, gays, weight, disabilities, seniors, and the like have no place there. If you use undesirable language in the workplace, you can damage your reputation, lose your job, or be judged unworthy of a leadership position. Here are some questions to think about in regard to workplace humor:

- Are you using humor to say something negative that you wouldn't dare say seriously?
- If you're teasing someone, do you know him well enough to understand his inner reaction?
- Is there someone in the group who may find the humor painful for reasons you don't know?

As for jokes: If you're not sure how a joke will be received, don't tell it. Most of us are not comedians who can tell jokes about the quirks of society and make us laugh at ourselves.

Communicate respectfully.

There is some language that is always offensive; other times it's merely a matter of people's sensitivities.

- Don't call people by nicknames you invented. (I worked with a man who often referred to a sexually promiscuous female coworker as "Mini the Mattress." When a high-level manager overheard that comment [and Mini was his administrative assistant], the offender was severely reprimanded.)
- Avoid talking about sexual issues, even in the restrooms. You never know who may be in the stall next to you.
- Engage in easy-to-understand conversation so you don't intimidate people with more limited vocabularies.
- Think before you speak!

Be correct for the circumstances.

Your actions, as well as your words, should send the right message. In 2008, when the CEOs of the "Big Three" automakers appeared in Washington to plead for billions of dollars to save their ailing companies from the jaws of bankruptcy, they arrived in their own luxurious, private jets. They were denied funding. Reprimanded for the brazenness of their extravagant entrance, the next time they drove from Detroit in fuel-efficient cars. So, if you're visiting a client who's starting a business and struggling to make a go of it, you may want to leave your jet in the hangar and your Bentley in the garage.

Take control of an uncomfortable situation.

Here are a few tips to try if you find yourself in an uncomfortable conversation:

- Excuse yourself and walk away. *I have some things back at my desk that I must get done.*
- Change the topic. *Do you remember when . . .?*
- Express your discomfort. *I really don't think we should be saying things like that behind [name's] back. Would you say that to his face?*
- Agree to disagree. *I disagree with your politics but respect your opinion. Perhaps we should move on.*
- Refer to office policy. *Please remember that it's against office policy to be discussing [topic].*

If you need to voice your opinion, do so in a way that suggests you're open to the opinions of others. *I appreciate what you're saying, Jim, and wonder if you thought about. . . .*

Remember the golden rule.

The simplest way to ensure politically neutral or tolerant behavior in the workplace is to treat others the way you would want to be treated. If you treat others with respect and caring, your overall professional experience will be much more positive.

Communicating with People with Disabilities

William Arthur Ward, American author, said, "A true friend knows your weaknesses but shows you your strengths; feels your fears but fortifies your faith; sees your anxieties but frees your spirit; recognizes your disabilities but emphasizes your possibilities."

People without disabilities are often uncertain of how to act when they're around people with disabilities. The simple answer is: Treat them as you'd like to be treated. It's estimated that five out of every six people with disabilities weren't born that way. They acquired the disability later in life through natural causes or accidents. Therefore, each one of us is merely an incident away from joining the ranks. Remember, *Do unto others. . . .*

Use appropriate terms.

People may have a variety of disabling conditions: mobility impairments, blindness and visual impairments, deafness and hearing impairments, speech and language impairments, mental and learning disabilities, and the like. Regardless of a person's disability, always put the word *person* first. For example, a person is not an *epileptic*, but rather a *person who has epilepsy*. This stresses that people with disabilities are people first and foremost, and that their disabilities are incidental.

Keep in mind that even people with disabilities don't always agree on what's correct when it comes to certain terms. What everyone agrees on, however, is the importance of being respectful. Here are a few guidelines:

Unacceptable	Acceptable
Cripple/Disabled/Handicapped or handicapped person/Defective	Person with a disability
Cerebral palsied/Vegetable	Person with cerebral palsy
Blind/Blind as a bat	Person who's visually impaired
Gimpy/Peg leg	Person with paralysis or loss of a limb
Lisper/Mute/Mumbler	Person who's speech impaired
Retard/Moron/Imbecile/Idiot	Person with developmental disability
Wheelchair user/Uses a wheelchair/Confined to a wheelchair/Wheelchair-bound	Person in a chair, person in a wheelchair

Always remember: People sometimes say things they don't mean or say things that simply come out wrong. If someone has no past history of insensitivity, give him a break. To err is human.

Ask before you offer assistance.

In general, before you offer assistance to a person with a disability . . .

- Ask first.
- Understand what assistance the person needs.
- Acknowledge that people have "help" preferences.

If you want to learn more about disability issues, here are two of many websites to check out: www.eeoc.gov/types/ada.html and www.nod.org.

Work comfortably alongside coworkers with disabilities.

People with disabilities feel that some of the biggest obstacles they face in the workplace are the attitudes of people without disabilities. Those of us who have disabled family members, friends, or coworkers are undoubtedly sensitive to their needs. But people who haven't had a lot of contact with people with disabilities are often uncertain how to behave when faced with the prospect of a coworker with disabilities.

There are many assumptions made about the quality of the lives of people with disabilities or their ability to function as contributing members of society. A person with disabilities is trying to live as normal a life as possible. We must do everything we can to honor and encourage that person's independence.

Dos

- If you notice that a person with disabilities is in any immediate danger, by all means intervene.
- Always encourage a person to participate in business functions. He might tend to be withdrawn, and a little extra urging may make all the difference. Be sensitive to the person's reactions, and don't be too pushy.
- If a third party (server, salesperson, or other) responds to your companion with disabilities by speaking to you instead, don't answer. Also, avoid eye contact. That will encourage the third person to speak directly to your companion. And you'll teach the third party a valuable lesson.

Taboos

- Assuming a person has multiple disabilities. For example, don't speak loudly to a person who's blind—he can hear you.
- Staring. It's rude to remind someone that he's different in any way.
- Asking a person about his disability, especially someone you've just met. Those who wish to share their experiences will volunteer to do so.

 I learned a few years ago that what's intended to help one group with disabilities may harm another. I was chatting with a business associate at a busy intersection in downtown Atlanta, Georgia. All of a sudden I heard horns honking and brakes squealing. I turned around and noticed a person who was visually impaired in the middle of the intersection. He was in a panic. I ran toward him, took his arm, and brought him back to the sidewalk. He explained that the down ramps intended for wheelchairs can be a nightmare to the visually impaired. Their canes don't always let them know they're walking off the curb. What a frightening experience it was for this man, and what an enlightening one for me.

People Who Are Visually Impaired

People who are visually impaired are just like the rest of us in most ways. They can use a phone, use computers, and perform a full range of activities. They learn to do much by touch, sound, and special equipment.

Dos

- Talk in a normal voice.
- Introduce yourself and those with you. For example: *Hi, Ginger. It's Sheryl Lindsell-Roberts. With me to your left is Jon Allan. Shall we shake hands?*
- It's okay to use the word *see*, such as in *I'll see you later.* A person who's visually impaired may use it.
- If you're giving directions, be as specific as possible. Use the terms *right* and *left* relative to the direction in which the person is facing. For example: *Walk about 100 feet to your left and make a right at the corner.*
- If you go to a restaurant, read the menu and the prices. You can verbally locate the salt and pepper shakers and any other items on the table. When the meal is served, tell the person where the items are on his plate, using the clock. For example: *The potatoes are at three o'clock, the fish is at six o'clock.*
- If the person visits your home or office, lead him to a chair and then gently place your hand on his arm or back. If he's staying with you for any length of time, be certain to describe the floor plan and identify where the furniture is.
- When taking a person who's visually impaired to a strange place, tell him where everything is and who's there.
- When there's a visually impaired person in a room you've entered, go over and identify yourself. When you're ready to leave, make sure that person knows you're leaving.
- Many elevators have Braille buttons identifying the floor numbers and a bell that rings at each floor. If an elevator is crowded, it's polite to say, *Which floor would you like?* And if the elevator is noisy and he can't hear the ring, it's polite to say, *We're at the [third] floor.*
- Allow the person to take your arm at or above the elbow. This will enable you to guide rather than propel or lead the person.
- When offering seating, place the person's hand on the back or arm of the seat.

Taboos

- Grabbing the person's arm in offering assistance. Ask, *May I help you across the street?* If the person wants assistance, let him reach for your arm.
- Playing with or feeding a guide dog. The dog is there to be the eyes of the person and shouldn't be distracted.
- Leaving doors partially ajar. (That can also be very dangerous for sighted people who aren't paying attention to where they're walking.)

People Who Are Hearing Impaired

There are all degrees of hearing impairments, from a partial hearing loss to no hearing at all. If someone suffers from a partial hearing loss, you may need to speak a little louder or repeat a remark he may have missed. To attract the attention of someone who has moderate hearing loss, call the person by name. To attract the attention of someone who has little or no hearing, tap the person gently on the arm or shoulder. If someone suffers from a severe hearing loss, look at him when you speak. Many people who are hearing impaired read lips.

Dos

- If you know American Sign Language (ASL), by all means use it.
- To get the attention of a person who's hearing impaired, tap the person on the shoulder or wave your hand.
- Look directly at the person and speak naturally, but not too quickly.
- Look directly at the person and don't walk around while you converse. Your expressions and lip movements will help him hear you.
- Be patient and willing to repeat something the person may not have understood.
- If the hearing loss is in one ear, sit on the side of the person's good ear during times you can't face him.
- Speak expressively, because the person will rely on your facial expressions, gestures, and eye contact.
- If you need to, write a note. (But don't talk while you write.)

Taboos

- Yelling. A person with a total hearing loss won't be able to hear you, and a person with a hearing aid may hear as well or better than you do. Also, yelling distorts sounds accepted through hearing aids and inhibits lip reading.
- Exaggerating lip movements. Distorted lip movements can make speech reading difficult or impossible.

People Who Are Speech Impaired

You may come across people whose speech is impaired for a wide range of reasons. Here are some ways to help:

Dos

- Give the speaker your full attention.
- Speak in a normal tone of voice. These folks don't have a problem hearing.
- Keep questions simple so the person you're speaking to can reply with short answers or a nod.
- Be patient. If you have difficulty understanding the person, repeat what you understand.
- Ask short questions that require short answers or a nod of the head: *Tell me about your experience in Ireland* rather than *I understand you were in Ireland last year. I bet you had a lot of interesting experiences. Tell me about some of them.*

Taboos

- Not allowing the speaker to finish his thoughts without interruption.
- Pretending you understand something you don't. Casually repeat what you thought you heard. If you phrase your uncertainty with a question in your voice, the person can nod or merely say yes or no. For example: *You'll be arriving at five and will be ready by six?*

People with Paralysis or Loss of a Limb

A person who has lost a limb or suffers from paralysis may lead a close to normal life. Some embarrassing situations may arise if you don't realize a person has a problem. People with these types of disabilities have been criticized for not helping to carry packages or not helping in other ways. If you're the person with the disability, there is nothing wrong with saying, *I'm sorry I can't help you. I have a bad arm.*

If a person has an artificial limb, he may need help in certain situations. Remember to ask, *May I help?* When talking with a person in a wheelchair for more than a quick conversation, grab a chair and sit down. That puts you at his eye level.

When approaching someone who has lost his right hand or arm, you may feel some uncertainty during an introduction. If you know the person has lost his right hand or arm, let him take the lead when you're being introduced. If the person . . .

- Smiles and says *Hello* without extending a hand, respond by smiling and saying *Hello.*

- Extends his left hand, shake his left hand.
- Extends an artificial limb, shake hands as you normally would.

People in Wheelchairs
Please consider the following:
- To greet someone who cannot shake hands, touch the person on the shoulder or arm to welcome him and acknowledge his presence.
- Never patronize people using wheelchairs by patting them on the head or shoulder.
- When addressing the person, never lean on the wheelchair. The chair is part of that person's personal space.

People with AIDS
If you're one of the growing number of people who know someone infected with the AIDS virus, you need to have a special sensitivity to the problems this group faces. Unlike other disabilities, this one carries with it a stigma and a fear. Feel free to offer help to a person with AIDS without fear of becoming infected. You cannot get the AIDS virus through everyday contact. The AIDS virus is transmitted through unprotected sex or by sharing injection drug needles. It may also be passed from infected mothers to their babies during pregnancy or birth. Most people with AIDS can lead active lives for long periods, and the prognosis is getting better and better. Each person with AIDS is different and is affected by the disease in a different way.

Dos
- Above all, keep an upbeat attitude.
- Feel free to talk about the disease and gently encourage the person with AIDS to do the same. Often, people—especially those who have the illness—need to talk about the disease in order to come to terms with it.
- If the person has difficulty getting around, get him water from the cooler or lunch from the cafeteria.

Taboos
- Ignoring your own emotions. Share your feelings and get support if you need it.
- Ignoring the caregiver. If you know the person with AIDS well, offer to help the caregiver so that he does not feel isolated. He may need a break from time to time, a free afternoon, or someone to talk to.

Dispelling Fears of Potential Employers

People with disabilities are often more conscientious, punctual, and reliable than their counterparts without disabilities. So, if you're looking to hire a great employee, go for a person with a disability! The following will help dispel some of the reservations an employer may have:

Question	Answer
If I hire this person, will my insurance premium increase?	No. Experts don't know of a single case where this has happened. Rates are based on the relative hazards of the workplace and the company's accident experience.
If I have to lay this person off, am I opening myself up to a lawsuit?	No more so than with anyone else. Persons with disabilities are no more likely to be laid off than those without disabilities.
Will the person get along with coworkers?	There's no reason to suspect otherwise. A person with a disability can defuse this thought at the beginning of an interview by saying, *I generally develop great rapport with my coworkers. We're all rooting for each other.*
How will the person get to work?	If the person is applying for the position, he's already figured out how to get there.
Will there be safety issues?	No, he'll figure out what he needs to do.

 Set the person up with a buddy in case there's a fire or other emergency.

Conduct interviews with ease.

Conduct interviews as you would with anyone else. People with disabilities don't expect special treatment—just equal treatment.

Dos
- Shake hands.
- Speak directly to the candidate.
- Conduct interviews in a manner that emphasizes abilities, achievements, and individual qualities, just as you would with any other candidate.

- Be clear and candid in your questioning.
- Ask for clarification of terms or issues when necessary.
- Ask only job-related questions that address the functions of the specific job.
- If you offer to help, wait until the offer is accepted. (Don't insist, and don't be offended if your offer isn't accepted.)
- If you question the candidate's ability to perform certain tasks, ask appropriately. People with disabilities often develop innovative solutions.
  Appropriate: *This position requires [task]. Do you foresee any difficulty in doing that?*
  Inappropriate: *I notice you're in a wheelchair, I wonder how you would perform [task].*

Taboos
- Expressing sympathy.
- Commenting on the candidate's disability.
- Asking personal questions about the candidate's disability.
- Avoiding eye contact.
- Expressing admiration for the candidate's courage.

 If you know in advance that a candidate has special needs, ask ahead of time how to accommodate those needs. Also check out how to best interview candidates with specific needs earlier in this section.

Prepare to be interviewed.

If you have a disability, prepare for an interview well in advance. Know how long it will take you to arrive at your appointment, and learn of any obstacles you may encounter. Although buildings today require accessibility to all, it pays to ask the following questions:

- Are there accessible parking spaces nearby?
- Where is the nearest train or bus stop?
- Is there a ramp or step-free entrance?
- Where are the accessible restrooms?
- If the interview is not on the first floor, does the building have an elevator?
- Are there water fountains and telephones at the proper height for a person in a wheelchair?

Part Two

Getting Down to Specifics

I didn't say that I didn't say it. I said that I didn't say that I said it. I want to make that very clear.

—George Romney, American industrialist and former governor

7

This [telephone] has too many shortcomings to be
seriously considered as a means of communication.
The device is inherently of no value to us.
—Western Union internal memo (1876)

Using the Telephone Effectively

In this chapter

- Inbound Calls
- Outbound Calls
- Managing Telephone Time Efficiently
- Telemarketers
- Voice Mail
- Cold Calling
- Cell Phone Etiquette
- Call Centers/Customer Service

Upon hearing that his obituary had been published in the *New York Journal*, Mark Twain said, "The reports of my death are greatly exaggerated." Despite all the new communications technology, the telephone is (other than face-to-face communication) the best way to make personal connections and set the record straight. I've heard people say they'd rather send an email because they don't want to bother people by phoning. You're not bothering people when you have a legitimate reason to call. Remember that emailing, which is one-way communication, is very impersonal. Calling, which is two-way communication, is highly personal. Phone someone the next time you want to . . .

- set up a business meeting
- get together for lunch or coffee
- build or rekindle a relationship
- learn if someone has any questions
- follow up on a confusing or misunderstood email.

Inbound Calls

Despite how far communications technology has come, the phone is still the primary means of contact for businesses. The way you answer the phone will often form someone's first impression of you and your business. The following tips will help callers know they're dealing with a person and/or a business that cares.

Answer the call by the third ring.

When possible, answer the call by the third ring with a voice that's warm and enthusiastic. (If you can't answer by the third ring, have your answering machine pick up on the fourth ring.) Here are some ways to say hello and win the caller's favor:

When you answer your own phone

Appropriate:	*Jim Logan speaking.*
	Hello, this is Jim Logan.
Casual:	*Jim speaking.* (Okay in some offices)
Abrupt:	*Logan speaking.*
	Logan here.

When you answer the phone for someone else

Appropriate:	*Good morning. This is ABC Technologies. How may I help you?* (Rather than *May I help you?*, which calls for a yes or no answer.)
Long, but okay:	*Good morning. This is the Marketing Department, Mr. Logan's office.*
	Good afternoon. ABC Technologies. This is Susan in the Marketing Department.
	Good morning. This is Mr. Logan's office. Kathy speaking.
Inappropriate:	*Hi, this is Kathy.*

Other things to consider:

- Take telephone messages accurately and completely. If there's a part of the message you don't understand, ask *Would you repeat that, please?* If you can't spell someone's name easily, ask *Would you please spell that for me?*
- If you're a manager and suspect that incoming calls aren't handled appropriately, here's a (devious) tactic you may try: Call your company incognito (or ask someone else to do it) to see what impression you get of the company from the person who answers the phone. You may pose as a job candidate or prospective client.

Be mindful of your voice and expressions.

When you hear someone's voice on the phone, you make a generalization about that person—about her education, background, ability, and personality. Although that's akin to judging a book by its cover, it's done. What impression is your voice making? Here are a few things to remember:

- Be certain to enunciate clearly and speak slowly.
- If you typically inject *um, like,* and other such expressions into your conversations, be careful to avoid using them.
- Instead of saying *I don't know,* say, *Let me find that out for you.*

Smile even if the caller is grumpy.

We've all had to deal with grumpy or irate callers. People who are upset tend to take their frustrations out on the person who answers the phone, even though that person had nothing to do with causing the problem. Following are a few ways to soothe a savage beast:

- **Don't yell back or be rude.** It's difficult to continue being angry when the person at the other end is polite. Let that polite person be you.
- **Suggest that the caller talk to someone who is in a more appropriate position than you to deal with the situation.** Offer to transfer the call, or give the caller the name and number she needs.
- **Ask if you may put the caller on hold briefly.** Then take a few moments to explain the situation to the person to whom you're forwarding the call.
- **Mention the person's name.** Using a person's name personalizes the conversation and may help to defuse anger.
- **Politely ask the caller to slowly repeat her complaint so that you can write it down.** This may also help to defuse anger.

And finally, don't ever be an irate caller. Remember, the person you speak to isn't necessarily the person who caused your problem—it's the person you hope will help solve your problem.

Don't leave a caller in "hold limbo."

Never put a caller on hold for any length of time without the caller's permission. Always ask, *Would you mind if I put you on hold for a moment?* If the person agrees, make sure it's only for a moment. If the caller is waiting for another party to pick up, get back every 30–45 seconds and ask if she'd like to continue holding. If not, take a message.

While your caller is in holding mode, it's perfectly acceptable to use the listening time to your business advantage. Offer tips of the trade, talk about a special promotion, or give driving directions. Make sure you change your recording regularly so callers don't feel they're listening to the same-old, same-old. I recently called my financial planner's office and was put on hold for a short time. Instead of music, her message was an announcement about an investment seminar she was offering. The message gave a preview of some of the tips she would share. I got some wonderful information just from listening to her message, and it whetted my appetite. I reserved a seat at the seminar.

If you're piping music into someone's ear, make sure it's easy to listen to. Remember, however, music isn't a license to keep someone on hold indefinitely. The caller didn't dial in to listen to Beethoven's Fifth Piano Concerto in its entirety.

Get rid of a chatty caller politely.

Some people are chatty and are hard to get off the phone. Here are a couple of tactful ways to get rid of such a caller:

- Explain that someone just handed you a note for an urgent call or for a meeting you should be at.
- Politely say, *Jack, before I hang up . . . or, I know we have a lot to talk about, why don't we plan to. . . .*

Once I was desperate to get rid of a chatty caller. I started saying, *Hello, hello, hello,* as if we had lost the connection. I'm not suggesting you do that, but desperate times call for desperate measures.

Screen calls without the caller realizing it.

Busy executives often ask their administrative assistants or others to screen calls. You must exercise great tact to hide the fact that you're doing that. Otherwise the caller will feel "unloved."

Appropriate:	*Ms. Smith is out of the office this morning. May I ask who's calling?*
Inappropriate:	*May I ask who's calling?* (If you then say the person isn't available, it will make the caller feel shunned.)

Never ignore a caller.

If the caller is someone you don't want to speak with, have someone relay an appropriate message. For example, if there is someone who's been trying to reach you about a job you listed and you don't want to speak to her, have your administrative assistant tell the caller that you'll be in touch with all candidates who qualify by a certain date.

More to think about:
- Check your messages several times a day. If you're away from the office, dial in from a remote phone. There may be a new client or an existing client who's facing a dilemma.
- Return your calls in a timely manner so you're not thought of as rude or uncaring.

Use good judgment when dealing with emergencies.

Understand what constitutes an emergency. You may have to interrupt an important meeting if you think it's critical—"If in doubt, pull her out." Use good judgment. When you must interrupt a meeting, knock on the door and ask either to speak to the person you need, or that she be handed a note.

Outbound calls

Before you place an important call, stand up and stretch. This puts animation and enthusiasm into your body that will be reflected in your voice. (You don't want the person you phone to think you need a defibrillator.) And, unless the caller knows you intimately, it's egotistical and rude to expect someone to recognize your dulcet tones. Unless someone has caller ID and says, "Hello, [your name]," identify yourself immediately. You can say something as simple as *Hello, this is Mary Jones from [company]*.

Prepare for the call.

Always know why you're calling, what information you want to get or convey, and what to say if you get the person's voice mail. Following are some tips to prepare you for your phone call:

- Make a list of the items you want to talk about in order of priority.
- Have all the files and papers you need close at hand.
- If your call is a difficult one, write out what you want to say beforehand.

Leave a clear, detailed message.

When you reach someone's voice mail, leave a brief, detailed message that states your name, reason for the call, your phone number, and the best time to reach you. Think about this in advance so you're not caught off-guard.

Also, say your name and number at the beginning and the end so the person can write it down correctly.

Call during prime time.

Research shows that hard-to-reach people are often in their offices before 9:00 and after 5:00. Also, during that time they're more apt to answer the phone themselves.

Don't just hang up if you misdial.

If you misdial, it's rude to just hang up. Following is an example of a pleasant conversation:

Caller: *May I please speak to John Doe.*
Callee: *I think you have the wrong number.*
Caller: *I'm sorry to have bothered you.*
Callee: *No bother. Have a nice day.*

If the caller rings you again:

Caller: *May I please speak to John Doe.*
Callee: *This is the same number you just called. I think you're calling the wrong number.*
Caller: *What number is this?*
Callee: *I'd rather not give out my number. What number are you trying to reach?*
Caller: *[number]*
Callee: *This isn't the number you're trying to reach. Please recheck it.* (In this era of unsolicited and unwanted phone calls, it's often better not to give out your phone number.)
Caller: *I'll do that. I'm very sorry to have bothered you.*
Callee: *No bother. Have a nice day.*

Getting through to a human

Are you tired of calling companies and pressing dozens of numbers before you get through to a human? (That's somewhat of a rhetorical question, because we all are.) The May 2008 issue of Reader's Digest *listed a few things to try.*

- *Push zero several times.*
- *Keep saying* operator *or* agent.
- *Call headquarters, sales, investor relations, or some other specific department.*
- *Select the Spanish option. You can get a bilingual operator/agent.*

- *Call from a friend's phone instead of the one you're registered with. The rationale is that potential customers leapfrog to the front.*
- *Check out www.gethuman.com for phone shortcuts to reaching a human at 1,000 major companies.*

Managing Telephone Time Efficiently

The telephone is meant to be a valuable business tool, not an intrusive oppressor that governs your working day. When you follow a few basic strategies, you'll be in control.

Be in control of outgoing calls.

Keeping Contact Information Updated

In addition to making sure you have the right phone number for each person, make a note of what days the person may have off (some people work three-day weeks), what time she typically starts and ends work, what time zone the person is in, and so forth.

Scheduling Phone Calls

If you initiate a call and anticipate that the subject will involve a lengthy conversation, here's how you may handle the call: *Hello, this is [name]. I'm calling [reason] and would like to set a convenient time to discuss this. What would be a good time for you?* This not only saves time, but avoids putting the callee on the spot.

Be in control of incoming calls.

When you answer the phone with *Good morning, this is ABC Technologies. How may I help you?*, this immediately lets callers know they have reached the right number and puts the responsibility on them to answer the question without a lot of chitchat. Always keep a pad and pen or pencil (that writes) near the phone so you can take messages.

Determining When to Handle a Call

Many calls are simple inquiries that can be handled quickly—such as calls asking about your hours of business, your email address, and the like. Other calls may come at an inopportune time, may involve tracking someone down or locating information, or may require you to engage in time-consuming dialogue. If the latter is the case, always ask when it would be convenient to call back.

Fielding Frequently Asked Questions

If your incoming calls involve answering the same questions repeatedly, keep a list of those questions and their answers in plain sight so you don't have to search for them each time.

Summarizing the Conversation

Get in the habit of ending phone calls with a summary of whatever action you and the other person have agreed to. This will take only a moment and can help avoid miscommunications. You may say,

- *What I hear you saying is . . .*
- *I look forward to meeting you and Joe at your office tomorrow at 9:00 so we can review the Smith contract.*

Practicing Good Cell Phone Etiquette

In today's on-the-go society, cell phones help keep us in constant touch with the world. They're at once one of the biggest blessings and one of the biggest curses in communications today. If you've ever been in a theater or nice restaurant and overheard people speaking loudly on cell phones, you know how poorly people observe good cell phone etiquette.

Telemarketers

You can always identify calls from telemarketers. There's a momentary pause before they start talking. Then the caller asks for you by name and poses the give-away question: "How are you today?" Once the caller inquires about your health, you know there's a "sell" coming for storm windows, insurance, widgets, or something else you probably don't want.

Get off the calling lists.

If you're plagued by unsolicited phone calls (Sorry, telemarketers!), you can get off these lists by placing your number on the National Do Not Call Registry at www.donotcall.gov. Alternatively, you can write to the following address. Include your name, address, and phone number. They don't take phone calls!

Telephone Preference Service
Direct Marketing Association
P.O. Box 9014
Farmingdale, NY 11735-9014

In the meantime, don't just hang up on these pesky people or put them on hold for all eternity. Instead, tell them you want your name taken off their calling lists. They're obliged by law to remove your name. If they continue to plague you, notify your phone company; you may be entitled to monetary remuneration.

Stay off the calling lists.

Whenever you order something by phone, be sure to tell the person taking the order that you don't want your name sold for telemarketing purposes. There's a special box to check off. If you don't make that clear, you'll be back on everyone's calling list.

Know the exemptions.

There are exemptions from this Do Not Call list that include calls made . . .

- by charitable organizations.
- with your prior express invitation or permission.
- on behalf of any person or entity with whom you have an established business relationship.
- within 30 days after you contact a business to inquire about the potential purchase of goods or services.
- urging support for or against a political candidate or ballot issue.
- to conduct political polls or to solicit opinions, ideas, or votes.

Voice Mail

Many people are intimidated by answering machines and feel foolish talking into a mechanical device. However, the answering machine is a fact of life, and you must use it appropriately.

Make your outbound message brief.

Following are tips for recording a brief, professional message that won't make the caller feel like hanging up:

- **Keep your outbound message brief.** No one wants to listen to your commercial.

- **Before you record the message, practice what you want to say.** After you record it, play it back. If it isn't something you'd want to listen to, try again.

  Example: *Hello, this is [name]. I'm not able to take your call, but I do want to speak with you. Please say your name and number twice so I can be sure to record it correctly, and I'll call you back just as soon as I can. Thanks for calling, and have a wonderful day.*

- **Don't make your caller wait too long.** Don't let too much time elapse between the time the machine picks up and the time the caller can start leaving a message.

- **Always keep your message updated.** If you're going to be away even for a day or two, mention that in the message so people won't expect you to return the call immediately. (If it's appropriate, leave your cell phone number or the name of someone the caller may contact in your absence.)

To stand out from the crowd, leave a clear inbound message.

Be certain the message is clear. Include your name, phone number, and a brief message. Plan in advance what you'll say, because you may very well get an answering machine. Here are a few hints for leaving a clear message:

- *If your name isn't straightforward, spell it out. For example, I have a friend named Dave Farrison. If he doesn't spell his last name, people think it's Dave Harrison.*
- *Be brief. Remember, you're not auditioning for a part in a Shakespearean play. Say what you have to clearly and briefly.*
- *Make sure that your phone number and other numbers that may be part of your message are clear. For example, say, "Sixteen. That's one, six." Otherwise, the number 16 may sound like 60.*
- *At the end of the conversation, repeat your name and phone number.*
- *Don't hang up without saying goodbye.*

Telephone etiquette in review

As a wrap-up, here are a few things to remember:

Generalities	• Identify yourself when placing and answering calls. • Return calls within 24 hours.
Placing someone on hold	• Ask the person if she can hold, don't just put her on hold. • Never leave a person on hold for more than 30–45 seconds without checking back. • When you return, thank the person for holding.
Interoffice	• Don't hover over coworkers while they're on the phone. Leave and come back later. • Never comment on something you might have overheard.

Outgoing voice message	• Include your name, company, and perhaps a tag line or something about your company. For example, I end my message with *Have a wonderful day, and always remember, [pause] You make more dollars when you make more sense,* which is my tag line. I get wonderful comments. • If applicable, let the caller know how to reach you in an emergency. • Keep your message current. For example, when you return from vacation, replace the vacation message.
Call waiting	• Unless you're expecting a critical call, don't interrupt a conversation. • If you're waiting for a critical call, mention that at the outset of the call you are already on: *Normally I don't respond to call waiting, but I'm expecting a critical call, so I may have to ask you to excuse me briefly. I hope that will be okay.*
Speakerphone	• Use this feature sparingly, because your voice may not be as clear as when you hold the phone to your ear/mouth. • When you are on speakerphone and others in the room can hear, let the person at the other end know who's in earshot.
Cell phones	• Turn off your phone in public places. • Leave a public area when talking on the phone.

Cold Calling

Sourcing new sales leads and recruiting new customers is crucial to all businesses. Love it or hate it, cold calling is a direct-marketing method that can be a very cost-effective way to generate new business. Although many people will think of any excuse to put off making a cold call (such as rearranging their sock drawers), this effective sales tactic works. When done properly—and that includes making sure you're reaching your target audience—cold calling can open the doors to new business. Conventional wisdom recommends calling early in the morning when prospects are typically more energized. The following tactics can help you take the chill out of cold calling.

Leave enticing voice messages when prospecting/cold calling.

If you're frustrated because people don't call you back when you prospect (or cold call), take a good look at the messages you're leaving. Here's a booooring message, much like the ones most people leave. Would you be inclined to return this call?

Booooring

Hello, this is [name] calling. I'm an account rep with [company]. We provide [exhaustive listing of services]. Our services are praised by our customers, and I'd like to get together with you to learn more about your business and how I can help you. Please call me at [number] to set up a time we can speak.

The callee would probably delete this message after the first few words. Remember that this isn't about you; it's about the potential customer. When you research a company and can talk about the value proposition—*from the potential customer's point of view*—your message is enticing. Notice how the following message differs from the booooring one.

Enticing

When I reviewed your company's literature, it became clear to me that you're facing [critical issue or industry need]. After working with companies such as yours for more than [number of years], we've helped them to increase sales by as much as 25 percent within the first year. I have a few ideas I'd like to share with you. Of course, I can't promise you identical results, but I think a brief conversation may be worth a few minutes of your time. Please call me at [number] to see if there may be a fit. My name is [name]. Again, my name is [name], and my number is [number]. I look forward to speaking with you.

 Another method cold callers use is to say *Hello, this is [first name]. Please call me at [phone number].* This may pique the callee's interest.

Send something in advance.

Consider sending a promotional item, magazine or newspaper article, or a letter that tells the prospect you'll be calling on a certain day. This gives you a reason to follow up and helps break the ice.

Understand your company's unique selling points.

My colleague Steve Melanson, principal of Melanson Consulting, helps companies develop their uniqueness. He suggests that "95 percent of the companies in all industries do about 95 percent of the exact same things as their competitors. So, you have to look at the remaining 5 percent of what you do to develop a differentiated positioning message." Understand what differentiates you from your competitors. There must be something, because your customers have chosen you. If you're not sure of the differentiator, ask a few customers.

Find a quiet place and set time aside.

Find a quiet place where you can make your calls without interruption. Consider using a hands-free set so you can take notes easily without twisting your neck. Also, set time aside to make your calls, rather than trying to fit them into your free time.

Stand tall and smile.

If you anticipate rejection and you're hunching over your desk filled with dread over making the call, your prospect will immediately pick up on it. Then rejection will become a self-fulfilling prophecy. Instead, stand tall, and you'll sound more energetic. Smile, and the prospect will "hear" the smile in your voice. This isn't as corny as it may sound—it affects your neurophysiologic state. You feel better and will come across better.

Treat gatekeepers as allies, not roadblocks.

One of your best allies can be the "guardian of the gate." Always be pleasant, and develop strategies, such as *Good morning, this is Carol Grayson. I'm hoping you can help me.* The gatekeeper can lead you to the right contact, get you a phone number, or find specific information.

Keep detailed records.

Your records should include anything you sent, promises you or the prospect made, details of the call, and any follow-ups that are necessary. There are many contact management software programs that can make this process easier.

Follow up.

The call doesn't end after the initial contact. If the call went well, design ways to keep in touch. Be on the lookout for relevant articles you can send. Include the prospect (with permission, of course) on your mailing list. Send the prospect a newsletter or e-zine you publish. Call periodically just to stay on the prospect's radar screen.

Don't give up.

Studies show that more than 75 percent of new sales are made after you've touched the prospect five to seven times, yet most people give up after the second time. The "touches" don't all have to be phone calls. You can mix in an email, postal mailing, or anything else that's appropriate.

Don't take it personally.

Remember that sales is a game of numbers, and you won't wow everyone you speak with. If the prospect . . .

- Isn't interested and tells you that immediately, that's okay. It's far better to hear that at the outset than to waste time wooing a dead-end prospect.
- Hangs up or ends the call abruptly, you haven't failed. That person may be having a bad-hair day.
- Is one of many with whom you don't get to first base, then you need to consider restructuring your message or the times at which you're calling.

 You can turn a cold call into a warm call by name-dropping. Mention a mutual contact such as a friend, relative, client, or someone you met at a function. That's one of the best icebreakers of all.

Cold-Calling Scripts That Work: Three Proven Introductions That Break Into and Close New Clients

The following article is being used with permission from Erica Stritch, general manager of a wonderful newsletter, "RainToday." She shares what you should do and say for cold-calling success. Here are three proven cold-calling scripts that have helped service businesses break into new clients:

Script #1
My name is John Smith, and I am with Smith, Smith & Smith, we're a <insert type of firm>.

We've been scheduling brief phone calls to introduce ourselves and share best practice information. We'd like to tell you how other <industry> companies are . . .

- Protecting their global shipping operations and ensuring continuous cash flow
- Achieving the best possible efficiencies by connecting all <blank> disciplines
- Using <our client's special expertise> to create competitive differentiation and capture market share.

The information will give you a framework for assessing your situation at <company name>. I'm wondering if you'd like to talk with me and one of the partners here at Smith, Smith, & Smith on <date>.

Script #2
My name is Jane Smith, and I am with Smith, Smith, & Smith—we're a <insert type of firm>. As a part of that work, we have just completed a

benchmark study where <industry> firms rate over 350 major suppliers in those areas critical in deciding who they will do business with.

What we've been doing as a way of introducing ourselves is to share with some select suppliers survey details specific to you:

- How (company name) rates on six critical success factors
- Where your competition stands in relation to you
- What areas you can focus on that will have the greatest impact on increasing your share of wallet

That's it. Even if you decide not to pursue this any further than this first meeting, at least you'll have valuable intelligence as a result.

What does your calendar look like next Wednesday or Thursday?

Script #3

My name is Jane Smith, and I'm calling from Smith, Smith & Smith. We are a <insert type of firm>.

The reason I am calling is to schedule a brief telephone meeting to review the findings of the work we have been doing on what makes the biggest difference in <topic area> for leaders who are looking to <do something specific that benefits the company>. It is fascinating stuff, especially since in the next ten years there will be <an important industry dynamic that you need to attend to>.

If you're interested, we'll even make some recommendations as to what areas to focus on that will make the biggest difference in your particular situation.

It's fascinating intelligence, and I was hoping you might have some time on the morning of <date> or anytime in the afternoon during the week of <date>. What would work for you?

The Essentials of Effective Scripts and Cold Calls

What's similar in these three examples?

1. *The business developer introduces themselves and provides a brief overview of their firm (one sentence, not a 20-second elevator pitch).*

2. *They immediately move to the WIIFM ("What's in it for me?") and pitch a value-based offer. This is not "an introductory meeting" where you go in and pitch a sales presentation on your clients, services, and successes. It is a presentation where you are sharing your expertise and insights and applying it to the prospect's situation.*

3. *There is a simple, non-threatening call to action. You are not going to sell your services on the first call, but you might schedule a 10-, 20-, or 30-minute teleconference in which you share your valuable insights. This will also help position you as an expert and thought leader in your field.*

4. *The business developer closes with asking the prospect to look at a spe-*

cific time on their calendar. This turns the question from being one of yes/no to being one of when.

5. In the introductory meeting the service company actually delivers the best practices, the benchmark research, the findings that they promise in the cold call. The pitch is not a sales presentation in disguise, but a conversation where actual challenges and advice are shared.

It is important to note that these scripts are never read word-for-word—prospects can smell this kind of rookie mistake from a mile away. The script is a starting point and the best business developers internalize these scripts and make them their own.

Before making the call you must be ready to have a peer-to-peer conversation around business issues facing your prospect. These conversations appear as though they'll end in two minutes with a yes or a no, but often times they can go for thirty minutes or more. If you can't be conversational without a script in front of you, you shouldn't be making the calls.

An extraordinary script and value proposition with a mediocre business developer will get you nowhere. An extraordinary business developer, adjusting their value-based pitch along the way from direct prospect feedback, will get you introductions with top prospects—without having to resort to deceptive tactics.

© Wellesley Hills Group
Permission from Erica Stritch, General Manager
(www.RainToday.com)

Cell Phone Etiquette

With the advent of cell phones, it's becoming increasingly possible to reach people anytime, anywhere. As convenient as cell phones have become, their usage is out of control, and no public or private venue is immune. Remember the following to put some sanity back into cell phone usage.

Turn your phone off in public places.

Unless you're in a profession where people's lives are hanging in the balance if people can't reach you immediately, turn off your phone in public venues such as theaters, restaurants, places of worship, funeral homes, museums, courthouses, libraries, elevators, concert halls, or any other place where a quiet atmosphere is appreciated and expected.

Here are a few things to consider:

- If you're expecting a very important phone call, let people know that in advance. Simply say, *I'm expecting an important phone call. I have the phone on vibrate, so please excuse me if I have to run out for a few minutes.*
- If you have a multimedia phone, consider using options such as email, instant messages, or text messages, which minimize disruptions.
- Switch to a silent ringer and check your messages during a break.

Don't have La Cucaracha as your ringtone.

Although you may think the Oscar Mayer jingle is a cute ring, will others? It may be cute when you're with your kids, but it's not cute in a professional setting. Some cell phones offer environment settings. If yours does, set one ringtone before you head into a meeting and another when you pick your kids up from school.

Be mindful of your voice level.

Not everyone within a mile of where you are needs to know the details of your conversation. For some reason, perhaps because of poor connections, people yell when they're talking on the cell phone. If you have a poor connection, yelling won't make the connection any better. Either tell the person you'll call back or move to another location.

I was at an airport recently and the man behind me in line was yelling into the phone, *Can you hear me now?* (just like in the commercials). I turned around and said, *The entire airport can hear you.* He looked insulted, but he toned it down.

Be sensitive when using your phone in business.

Always keep your voice down to a reasonable level, especially in a cubicle or open-office environment. Never discuss confidential or sensitive information in an area where you may be overheard. Turn your phone off during meetings, workshops, seminars, or presentations.

Observe road safety.

The Insurance Information Institute reports a dramatic rise in the number of accidents caused by drivers talking on cell phones. Therefore, several states have passed legislation banning hand-held cell phone use while driving. Even hands-free sets can be distracting. If you must talk, pull over, let voice mail pick up, or allow a passenger to answer the call.

Here are some options for those of you who can't refrain from keeping your phone turned on:

- Place your phone in a cradle so you can talk with your hands free.
- If your cell phone rings while you're on the road, let your voice mail pick up the message.
- Pull the car over to a convenient spot if you must talk en route to your destination.
- Let a passenger in your vehicle answer the call.
- Don't text while driving. You can't pay attention to the road when you're looking at the keys.

Teach your children proper etiquette.

Many children have their own cell phones; teach them to use the phones safely and properly. Here are a few suggestions that may be helpful:

- Insist that children don't talk on the phone during class, while at the library, during a concert, or in other public places.
- Advise them to speak in a moderate voice and to be considerate of those around them.
- Keep the ringtone volume low.

Consider a calling plan with minimal minutes to limit phone use to brief chats rather than lengthy conversations. The same advice applies to texting.

Family Phones

There comes a time in every child's life when she falls in love with the telephone. Here are some hints for consideration and safety:

- *Teach children to dial 9-1-1 in case of emergency. Many young children have been credited with saving the lives of family members by doing this.*
- *Don't inflict your children on others, unless it's Grandma. Friends don't really want to speak to your children on the phone.*
- *Teach children to answer the phone properly by saying, "Good morning, [last name] residence."*
- *Practice techniques for having children answer the phone when they're old enough. They must learn never to give a hint that they're alone in the house. If a stranger calls and asks whether the child's mother is home, the child should answer, "Sorry, but my mother can't come to the phone right now. Let me take your phone number, and I'll have her call you when she's free."*

Call Centers/Customer Service

We've all called a call center/customer service representative only to hear an "attitude" on the other end. It's quite obvious that that person doesn't like her job. These representatives are most likely the first point of contact with your company for new and potential customers. Because 80 percent of the calls are complaints, it can be discouraging for people to listen to customers venting all day. Therefore, you must hire the right people and train them well. They must be professional and upbeat at all times. Given knowledge about your products and services, they will be well equipped to cross-sell as well as resolve problems.

Make the most of the phone call.

Have you ever called for customer service and had to press what seems to be hundreds of buttons before you're put on hold for an endless period of time? Intermittently a pleasant voice interrupts the obnoxious music to say, "Thank you for your patience. Your call is very important to us, and someone will be with you just as soon as our customer service reps have finished servicing all of Asia."

Here are a few tips for providing superior telephone service.

Dos
- Have a human answer the phone—with a smile—by the third ring.
- If you must use an automated answering machine, limit the options and make customer service the first button mentioned. Make sure someone returns that call as soon as possible, not the next day.
- Allow angry customers to vent by listening carefully. Don't take their anger personally. They're not angry at you.
- Listen actively to the customer and ask probing questions such as *When did you place the order? Describe exactly what was wrong,* and so forth.
- Use problem-solving skills to resolve issues before they escalate.
- Document everything that transpires during the call, including the date, time, description of the issue, action taken, and follow-up required. Keep all this information in the database.
- Project a we-can-work-it-out attitude.
- If you can't solve the problem during the call, take the customer's phone number and ask when it would be convenient to return the call.
- After an issue is resolved, follow up with the customer to make sure the resolution was to her satisfaction.

Taboos

- Putting a caller on hold without first asking permission.
- Putting a caller on hold for a long period of time. It is better to return a call than to keep someone on hold too long.
- Interrupting the caller.
- Badmouthing your organization.
- Being the first to hang up.

Guard your customers with your life.

Are your customers satisfied only because you're no worse than your competition and they're used to mediocrity? Or are they raving about you because you constantly raise the bar on service?

Even when your sales team is landing lucrative accounts, if your call center/customer service department isn't constantly raising the bar, you're losing business. According to customer loyalty expert Frederick Reichheld of the management consulting firm Bain & Company, "a 5 percent increase in customer retention can increase an organization's profitability by 25 to 100 percent. On the other hand, an organization that sees its customer retention rate slip by 5 percent may see its bottom line drop by as much as half." Therefore, the success of your company may be in the hands of these frontline agents.

Too many companies have as their motto "superior customer service," "outstanding customer service," or "our service is number one," and provide fair service at best. You must provide more than words; you must provide the service.

Technical call centers are also using IM to "chat" with customers. The IM chat can be saved so there's a permanent record of the "conversation" that can be used by others in the company to serve customers better. Prior to the advent of this technology, calls were recorded and call center employees had to type the conversation into a database.

 Many customer service centers are starting to use instant messaging (IM) to provide immediate responses to customers. They rely on IM's "presence awareness," which means they can check who's active in the company's IM service. A typical scenario may be the following: A customer calls about the status of a purchase. The customer service representative sends an IM to someone in the appropriate department who's logged on, and the representative can give the customer an immediate answer. This eliminates having to track down the right person and get back to the customer. The customer gets satisfaction on the spot.

8

Networking is like banking—you have to make deposits before you can make withdrawals.

— Alice Ostrower, Executive Director, BNI Connecticut

Developing Professional Networks

In this chapter

- Elevator Pitch
- Tag Line
- Verbal Branding
- Business Cards
- Name Badge
- Work a Room
- Referrals
- Trade Shows and Conventions
- Social Networking

Networking is *not* about selling your product or service to the people you meet. It's about developing relationships and building those relationships. You can "work the world" and expand your network wherever you go. There's a popular networking expression, "It's not what you know, but whom you know." New relationships and new business opportunities come from the people you meet and the people they know.

So how can you build new relationships when you don't have time to squeeze networking into your already overtaxed life? The answer is you don't have to. Instead of trying to make extra time, concentrate on meeting more people in doing the things you already do. Networking takes place at conferences, conventions, trade shows, chambers of commerce, professional associations, community service groups, and more. Networking also takes place in (and at) gyms, airplanes, banks, sporting events, golf courses, supermarkets, dog parks, doctors' offices, restaurants, sushi bars, cocktail parties, nightclubs, or just about anywhere.

One of my colleagues was attending his aunt's funeral. At the funeral he met a cousin he hadn't seen in a long time. He asked her what she had been doing, and she mentioned she had been working in corporate training. He said, "I have someone you should meet." He introduced me to his cousin. I'm now training her to facilitate some of my workshops, and we've become personal friends. She's also introducing me to her clients.

When I was flying back to Boston from California, I met a fantastic woman who was seated next to me. She's the CEO of a biotech firm in New Zealand and was heading to Boston for a conference. We exchanged business cards. Long story short . . . I invited her to my home for dinner while she was in Boston. When my husband and I visited New Zealand a year later, we stayed with my friend and her husband (now also our friend). She worked to set up a business-writing workshop for me to facilitate while I was in New Zealand. That shows how you can form new friendships and business relationships in the most unusual places!

Elevator Pitch

Imagine you're in an elevator with someone you've been anxious to meet. Now's your chance! You're probably not riding to the top of the Sears Tower, so you may have about 30–60 seconds for that person to want to learn more about you. Your elevator pitch can mean the difference between the person asking you to step out of the elevator to continue the discussion or thanking you and making a beeline for the elevator door.

In essence, an elevator pitch (or elevator speech) is a short statement about who you are and what your business does and why it's unique. It speaks to what excites you about your business. It has integrity. What is it about your business that really motivates you? If you're genuine about who you are and what you do, it will show. The opposite is also true.

Avoid the cheesy, cookie-cutter templates you find on the Internet that say, "Insert your company name here." You want your pitch to be about *your* unique business, not everyone else's.

Keep it targeted.

This isn't the time to tell your life story or detail how you got started in the business. You don't even know this person, so he doesn't care where you were born, how many kids you have, or what you did during your summer vacation. He wants to know what you can do for him. Touch briefly on your products or services, the market(s) you serve, successes you've experienced, and your competitive advantage.

Identify your niche.

Think big and serve small. You can't be all things to all people, so don't try to be. If you position yourself as a specialist, not as a generalist, you make a larger impact.

Articulate what makes you different.

Your elevator pitch is about results, not processes. What do you do that's better or different than what your competitors do? Are you rolling out a new product or service? Did you just win a major contract? Do you have a market niche?

When you're asked what you do, do you answer, *I'm an accountant; I'm a writer; I'm an engineer; I'm a realtor,* or whatever? Most people answer this question literally and don't differentiate themselves from others in the profession. Those answers are very ho-hum, and they're not memorable.

Prepare a robust answer that states a benefit and a catchy line. A realtor may say, *I help first-time home buyers to purchase their dream homes. So if you know of a first-time buyer, tell them to call me and start packing.* Think about what makes you different. Why do your customers/clients keep coming back? If you don't know, ask them.

Keep your pitch fresh.

Once you establish your pitch, don't let it get stale. Business vocabularies change and cultures change. You want to make sure that your pitch is always timely and relevant, so revisit it regularly.

Know your audience's pain.

One thing all businesses have in common is that they want to surpass the competition and make a profit. Your pitch must show that you understand a potential client's unique concerns, frustrations, and pain. Stress that you have a unique solution to alleviating the pain.

Keep it simple.

Keep it simple and relevant by thinking in sound bites, not paragraphs.

- Avoid acronyms and jargon.
- Focus on problems your clients have encountered and how you helped to solve them.
- Think of numbers in terms of growth, innovation, quotas, dollars saved, percentages increased/decreased, and the like.

Write it down.

Use the guidelines in this section and give it a try. Realize that you may not get it right the first time. An elevator pitch is always a work in progress. You see what works and what doesn't work.

 Here's the evolution of an elevator pitch I use for my business-writing workshops that differentiates me from every other business-writing facilitator in the galaxy:

First iteration: I conduct business-writing workshops.

Second iteration: I conduct business-writing workshops **that help companies to cut writing time by as much as 30 to 50 percent and get the results they want.**

Third iteration: I conduct business-writing workshops that help companies to cut writing time by as much as 30 to 50 percent and get the results they want. **One client recently used the process to write a proposal that closed a $70 million contract.**

Practice, practice, practice!

Practice your pitch until it sounds natural and authentic. Convey passion, confidence, and enthusiasm.

- **Practice in front of a mirror and tape your words.** Rehearse, but don't overrehearse; you want to sound natural.
- **Pitch to trusted colleagues.** Ask for honest feedback. Did you differentiate yourself? Would they engage your services if needed? If not, what else would you need to say?
- **Go live.** The first few times you go live with your elevator pitch may be a bit uncomfortable, but it gets easier. Stand tall, smile, sound proud, and stay professional. After a while, your pitch will become second nature. When it does, you will be glad you honed this invaluable skill.

Use your pitch at meetings.

When you're wearing your name badge and are face to face with one or two people, you don't have to say your name after you've been introduced. (Learn how to make memorable name badges later in this chapter.)

However, when you're at a meeting where people take turns introducing themselves, start and end with your name and company name. The following picks up on the third iteration of my elevator pitch earlier in this chapter:

I'm Sheryl Lindsell-Roberts, Principal of Sheryl Lindsell-Roberts & Associates. I conduct business-writing workshops that help companies to cut writing time by as much as 30 to 50 percent and get the results they want. One client recently used the process to write a proposal that closed a $70 million contract. [Slight pause] Sheryl Lindsell-Roberts, Principal of Sheryl Lindsell-Roberts & Associates.

Tag Line

Unlike an elevator pitch, a tag line (also known as a motto, or memory hook) is a short, clever sentence that makes your business more memorable. It positions your company in the marketplace and becomes the basis for your marketing, advertising, and public relations campaigns. Place your tag line on your business card, stationery, website, brochure, emails, and other places where your name appears. Here's a tag line I use that gets wonderful kudos.

You make more dollars when you make more sense!

Seven Second Marketing, a book by Ivan R. Misner, PhD, discusses using a memory hook "that engages the other party's interest positively and creates an unbreakable connection between you and your product or service."

Verbal Branding

Branding has been a buzzword for many years. Most people are familiar with *visual* branding, where you create a mental image with your logo and other visual images. This distinguishing visual brand should appear on your website, business cards, stationery, envelopes, and anything else your company shows to the world. Although you may not be in the same arena with the powerhouse companies such as IBM, Google, Starbucks, and others, when people see your visual brand, they know who you are.

Verbal branding, on the other hand, is where everyone in the company is "speaking the brand," so those outside the company hear the same clear and consistent message, whether it's from a CEO, salesperson, customer service representative, the media, or anyone else. Verbal branding isn't merely a catchy tag line or elevator pitch; it's an entire verbal strategy to distinguish your company.

Verbal branding differs from an elevator pitch or tag line in that it will take the conversation in the direction you want it to go. A tag line doesn't have a clear foundation in how an organization positions itself in its market space, and an elevator pitch doesn't account for the remainder of the interaction.

To help me write this section, I interviewed Stephen Melanson, president of Melanson Consulting and a positioning and verbal branding expert. Steve defines verbal branding as "managing conversations so brand positioning is what impacts people and is what they most easily remember."

Be the 5 percent in your market space that stands out.

According to Steve: "Ninety-five percent of your competitors do 95 percent of what you do. You must identify the 5 percent that makes you different." So, the time you spend verbally wading through the 95 percent common to you all is doing the opposite of branding. It's making you seem more and more like the competition, rather than positioning you as different and better. If your clients or customers don't remember your best brand positioning a day, or even a week, after a conversation someone from your organization had with them, you missed the branding opportunity.

The general idea behind branding is to own an idea in the mind of your customers or clients. For example, the Target store chain is known as the "hip discounter" and is clearly branded as an alternative to its conventional mass-market competitors. Its red bullseye is one of the most commonly recognized logos, nudging out Apple's apple and the Nike swoosh.

Create your brand.

From a brand positioning perspective, the trick is to figure out what makes you different and better than the competition. Think of some of the popular brands. When people think of Apple computer, they immediately think of "cool technology." When they think of Walmart, they think of "inexpensive." You must associate these terms *with the company,* because "cool" and "inexpensive" alone aren't necessarily good. Who would be attracted to cool cement or a cheap hospital?

The following guidelines will help you to begin developing your unique brand positioning.

Answer these questions

- What assumptions already exist in the market about the kind of business you're in?
- What do you do to re-create the market space you're in? (Think of how Netflix re-created the way people rent movies, or how Saturn re-created the no-haggle pricing structure.)
- What's the unique impact you're offering? (No one cares what you do; they care about what you can do for them.)
- What gaps do you fill in your market space?

- What's the next generation of product or service within your market space? (Describe how you'll get there first.)
- Who's No. 1 in your market space? Position yourself against that company. (Avis masterfully positioned itself against Hertz by launching a brilliant branding campaign, "We try harder." This tripled Avis's market share within one year.)
- What do you do better than anyone else in your market space?

Cull to find differentiation

- Review your answers, searching only for *concepts* that represent how you're different. To differentiate his company, Steve says, "I'm the only one who teaches verbal branding in a classroom setting, having translated brand positioning development into a verbal platform for direct communications."
  The core meaning of this sentence, and the part that truly represents differentiation, is in the words *teaches verbal branding.* (When Steve meets someone, he tells him his name and follows with "I teach verbal branding.")
- Pull out ideas and concepts. Do this for every answer you've detailed. In all likelihood, you'll end up with about 6 to 12 ideas.

Cull again to shorten the list

- Whittle your list down again, with the goal of choosing the top three differentiators. Do this by asking yourself if others in your market space make the same claim. If yes, cross that item off your list. You may have words such as *strategic* and *consultative* on your list. Which one represents you more accurately?
- Put these three differentiators in order of importance, from most to least. Also, decide if any of these concepts can logically be associated with the others. For example, in Steve's case, if his concepts were (1) teach verbal branding, (2) develop rapid positioning, and (3) produce higher sales, he'd be able to eliminate the last two, because the first is the key differentiator, with the other two extending from it.

Test the marketplace

Congratulations! You've pared your differentiated positioning concepts down to one or two of your best ideas.
- Test this every time you can. Introduce yourself by telling people your name, your title, what organization you represent, and your differentiator—your verbal branding statement.
- Monitor the results. Note if your message creates curiosity and moves the conversation in the direction you want it to go. If not...
- Be prepared to repeat the process. The entire process may take weeks or months, but it's well worth the effort. Once you develop a solid verbal branding statement, it will impact your bottom line in a very positive way.

Direct the conversation.

Using the strategy just outlined, you can direct conversations so people remember what differentiates you from the competition. Here's how a typical conversation may go:

Speaker 1: Hello, I'm [name] and I work at [name] law firm. Our firm is different because we *become part of the profit strategy* for our clients!

 After you've introduced yourself this way, allow for a pause and don't say another word until Speaker 2 responds. The person should be curious and want to know more.

Speaker 2: What do you mean, *part of the profit strategy*?

Speaker 1: We work mainly with emerging companies to help them get venture funding and be profitable more quickly. All our services—from offering strategic planning and connecting them to our network to providing lower-cost legal services—are geared toward making this happen.

Speaker 2: Hmm . . . interesting. So you must practice corporate law. Is that right?

Speaker 1: Yes, we do, but lots of firms do that. The important thing about us is that we're better than other firms in how we work with clients to attain higher and quicker profitability.

To learn more about verbal branding, you can purchase Stephen's book *Jaw Branding*™ by visiting www.melansonconsult.com.

Business Cards

Your business card is one of your most important marketing tools. Give it to prospects and customers, tuck it inside of presentation folders, drop it in letters, and use it in a myriad other ways to remind people of who you are and what you do.

Although swapping business cards is the most basic form of networking, don't distribute yours like candy. If it's not valuable to the recipient, he may throw it away. Give your cards only to people with whom you have shared a meaningful conversation. If someone doesn't have a card, take out one of your own and ask the person to write down his contact information. Some business card tips follow.

Create your business card.

Every business card should include your name, title, address, website, email, and phone. Optional inclusions are cell phone, fax, or IM/ICQ Internet chat address. If you have a tag line, include that as well. Here are other things to think about:

- Make sure your card's design reflects your business. An investment banker would have a more conservative card than a graphic designer.
- Use a legible font; avoid those that are too small or otherwise hard to read.
- Limit the size to 3.5" by 2" or it won't fit in a standard card holder. (Business cards in Europe tend to be larger.)
- If you do business internationally, have the information from the front of your card translated on the back into the language of the country you visit.
- Proofread the card a million times before going to print. Then have others do the same. It's quite embarrassing to have a typo on your card. (I was trying to reach a colleague who had recently joined a company, and each time I dialed I got another person in the company. The last two digits of my colleague's phone number were transposed, and this was the first time that it came to his attention.)
- If your business isn't obvious from its name, consider including pertinent information on the front and contact information on the back. (See how I do it on mine.)

 Unless you have very strong graphic design skills, don't design your own card. If your card looks homegrown, you lose credibility. Use a graphic designer or one of the many online services that are very reasonably priced. A popular one is VistaPrint, www.vistaprint.com. Beware of the free cards, however, because VistaPrint puts its name on the back, and the cards shout that you had them done on the cheap.

Distribute your cards.

I can't believe how many people show up at networking events without business cards. Or they rifle through their briefcases and pockets trying to find them. Keep your cards handy so you can give them out gracefully. Here are some tips to remember:

- Keep your cards current. If you change your phone number, address, email, or anything else, have new cards printed. Scratching out the old information is tacky and unprofessional.
- When someone hands you a card, take a moment to read it. It's rude to just put it away.
- Take every card you're offered; it's rude to refuse. If you're not interested in continuing the relationship, it's not necessary to give your card in return. Just smile and say thank you.
- If you want to give your card to someone who hasn't asked for it, request his first.
- Buy an attractive case in which to keep your cards.

- As you meet new people, jot down notes on their cards to jog your memory later. You may want to remind yourself to invite someone for coffee or to send someone an article.
- At networking events, try to wear a garment that has two side pockets. In one pocket you can put business cards from people you want to continue a relationship with, and in the other you can put the cards to discard.
- Make sure your hands are clean when you distribute (and accept) cards. No one wants to take a card from a hand that's covered with guacamole.

Name Badge

When name badges are prepared properly, they let people know at a glance who you are and what you do.

- Don't use your business card as your name badge. It's probably printed in a font size that the average person would need a magnifying glass to read.
- Be sure the lettering on your name badge is large enough for anyone to read at arm's length.
- Wear the badge on your right side, so when people shake your hand they're looking at your badge and can see your name easily.
- Come up with something intriguing. (I met a financial planner who had the word MONEY under his name. He said that many people approached him to find out what he does. This humorous tactic paid off.)

Here's a sample of a badge I use. You can see my first name is large, and I include my company's tag line. No one will look at my badge to get my contact information; that's what business cards are for.

Sheryl
Lindsell-Roberts & Associates

*You make more dollars
when you make more sense!*™

 Always bring your own name badge to a networking event. Many organizations have preprinted name badges with your name and their organization. That may be good for the organization, but it's not good for you.

Networking isn't selling.

Recently I joined a networking group. At the first meeting an insurance agent asked me to meet him afterwards for a cup of coffee. Immediately he pulled out an application asking for personal information. I asked him what he was doing. He answered that if I filled out the form it would help him get to know me better. Sure! There was no way I was going to put any personal information in his pushy hands. He was asking me to fill out the form so he could try to sell me insurance. I'm an old hand at networking and was wise to him immediately.

Apparently he tried to "sell" other people in the group, and was asked to leave. That's not networking, that's selling.

Work a Room

"Working the room" is an old political phrase that used to invoke the image of obese, cigar-smoking politicians cutting deals in back rooms. Today, however, it means attending a gathering of people and mingling. Even if you were the high school wallflower, you can learn to meet people and emerge as the prom king or queen. Don't squander the chance to make valuable professional and social contacts. If working a room seems daunting, remember, you're not working an entire room, just one or two people at a time.

Before an event, remember to bring a pen (to jot down information on someone's business card) and breath mints (depending on what you ate for your previous meal).

Before you attend a business function, understand how you may benefit, both professionally and personally. Here are just a few benefits:

Professional	Personal
• Establish new contacts	• Gain confidence
• Enhance your career opportunities	• Feel good about yourself
• Gain new information	• Have fun
• Increase your income	• Meet new people
• (Add your own)	• (Add your own)

Before the event

Preparing for the event is as important as showing up.

Keep your sales materials handy.

Keep an ample supply of business cards, brochures, and other handouts in your car at all times. Take a few into the event; you can run out to your car if you need more.

Set goals.

Some events may list attendees in advance; others may give out rosters when you arrive. If you have access to the guest list, decide in advance whom you want to meet. Do you want to meet people from certain companies, people in your field, educators, or CEOs? Limit the time you spend with each person to just a few minutes. If you anticipate a budding relationship, mention that you'll call for a follow-up. Make a note of that on the person's business card.

If you don't know anyone, get the name of a contact person. It may be the person hosting the event or the person to call for further information. In this way, you will have forged a relationship and have someone to look for when you arrive.

Arrive early.

Get there before the other guests, and play host. This is quite easy. When you arrive early and stand not too far from the entrance, you'll notice others with white knuckles who seem uncomfortable at not knowing anyone else. Go over to one of these people, look at the name tag, and introduce yourself: *Hello [name], I'm [name].* Then drum up a brief conversation.

People will be glad you took the initiative. (I've gotten business by doing this.)

 Eat before you arrive at the event. It's not easy to juggle food, beverages, business cards, and handshakes.

During the event

Try the buddy system.

If the thought of entering a room alone makes you fear you'll create a fire hazard by standing in the doorway for the duration of the gathering, bring a buddy. Your buddy may know people you don't, and vice versa. You can introduce each other, but don't be joined at the hip. You and your buddy should split as soon as you have met new people, otherwise you defeat the purpose of going to the event.

Find one kindred spirit at a time.

Stand in high traffic areas (such as near the bar or the food) and look for positive body language. Perhaps someone looks your way or someone smiles at you. That's an opportunity to say hello and initiate some small talk. Also look for people who are by themselves and have that won't-someone-please-talk-to-me look. They'll be delighted.

When you see a group of three people, stand nearby without interrupting. Observe the body language. If they're shoulder to shoulder, they're all engaged in conversation. However, two of them will typically be chatting with each other. The "odd man out" may start talking with you, and before you know it you're part of the conversation.

 Check out chapter 2, "Engaging in Masterful Conversations," for good conversation starters.

Focus your conversation on that kindred spirit.

If you introduce yourself and then jump into a litany of your accomplishments, you'll be brushed away quickly. Instead, get the other person to talk about himself. Engage in small talk, asking open-ended questions.

How did you find out about this event?
What's your line of work?
Are from this area?

When I'm approached and someone asks about my line of work, I typically answer, *Have you ever sat in front of your computer waiting for pearls of wisdom to appear on the screen? I specialize in helping people to get started quickly and be more profitable and productive through the written word.*

Remember names.

Some people have a knack for remembering names, but most of us don't. Here are a couple of tried-and-tested techniques that may help:

- Repeat the other person's name as you're introduced: *It's nice to meet you, Janice.*
- Form a mental association: Long-haired Larry, freckle-faced Fran, tall Tom, smiley Sally, and so forth.

Meet the big shots.

Be sure to introduce yourself to the host or people from the host company. Learn all you can beforehand so you can ask leading questions. If members of the media are present, seek them out as well. Don't be intimidated. (We can all recall the story of the lonely, beautiful prom queen. Guys were too intimidated to approach her, so she sat home on Saturday nights. The same holds true for the media; don't be shy.)

Connect with someone you've met before.

If you see someone you've met before, this is a great opportunity to engage in conversation. If you don't recall the person's name, don't be shy about asking. Approach the person, extend your hand and say, *I don't recall your name, but didn't I meet you at Warren Bergstein's office last month?* Introduce that person to someone else in the room.

Hold drinks in your left hand so you can shake with your right hand. No one wants to shake a cold, clammy hand.

Don't pass up opportunities.

Talk to people in the parking lot, in the registration line, at the coat check, or in the restroom. You can ask basic questions such as *Are you going to the [name] meeting?* or *Did you have a hard time finding this place?*

Sit with people you don't know.

Don't sit down too early in the event. This is about networking, not sit-working. When it's appropriate to sit and seats aren't assigned, find a table where few people are seated and sit with people you don't know. You can greet each person who sits down and drum up a conversation.

Exit with class.

Networking isn't about spending lots of time with one person; it's about meeting many people. Here are a few tips for ending a conversation with class:

- *I know we're both here to meet new people, so I don't want to take up any more of your time. (If the person is interesting . . .) Why don't I give you a call tomorrow and we can schedule a time to meet for coffee.*
- *I enjoyed hearing about your trip to Africa, but I don't want to monopolize your time. I enjoyed meeting you.*
- *[Name], it was nice talking with you. Now, will you please excuse me, there are a few people over there I'd like to say hello to.*

Once you extricate yourself, visibly move to another part of the room.

 If someone doesn't respond to your introduction in the way you'd hoped, it's not the end of the world. Don't take it personally, and move on.

After the event

All your networking will be beneficial only if you follow up with key people.

Follow up with a note.

When you meet someone at an event and you want to grow the relationship, follow up right away with a note. This is where the notes you made on the back of business cards will be valuable. Don't write "Dear [name]: I enjoyed meeting you at the [event] [when] and hope we can meet again soon." It's b-o-r-i-n-g. Get a little more creative.

- Mention something you discussed that you had in common.
- State something relevant to that person.
- Send something that may be of interest (an article, perhaps).
- Suggest the next step, such as meeting for coffee. (You take the initiative.)

Remember the small things.

The name of the game is all about keeping in touch.

- Follow through on a promise you made (to call or send something).
- When you see an article you think will be of interest, send it along.

- Invite acquaintances to another networking event you think would be of interest.
- Introduce that person to other colleagues of yours.

 Before you give out the name of any contact, first get the okay from that person.

Rules of the road

In his book More Prospects! More Referrals! More Business!, *networking guru Michael Goldberg, president of Building Blocks Consulting, LLC, lists the following rules of the road for networking:*

- *Have your tools of the trade.*
- *Look the part.*
- *Realize that selling and networking aren't the same.*
- *Be professional, positive, and respectful.*
- *Talk less and listen more.*
- *Remember that it's NEVER about you.*
- *Don't give your business card out—unless asked.*
- *Eat and drink strategically.*
- *Initiate conversations by introducing yourself.*
- *Terminate conversations by excusing yourself politely.*
- *Introduce others with passion.*
- *Don't talk to any one person for longer than 6–8 minutes (if possible).*
- *Keep your eyes focused on the person you're speaking with.*
- *Have a goal and a plan.*
- *Have an array of questions to ask.*
- *Have a target market or niche.*
- *Plan to take the initiative to follow up.*
- *Have fun!*

For more information on Building Blocks Consulting, LLC, check out www. buildingblocksconsulting.com.

Referrals

When you need a financial planner, doctor, accountant, or any other professional, do you look in the phone book? Of course not. You probably ask a friend or colleague to refer you to a professional who has a stellar reputation. In essence, referrals are about connecting good people with other good people.

Make referrals part of your marketing strategy.

Building your business on referrals is powerful. There's nothing stronger than a personal endorsement from someone who knows you and trusts you. Your referral base can be an endless network of contacts. Why? We all like to do business with people we know, like, and trust. Therefore, it's not only the people you know, but the people they know that makes networking so powerful and far reaching.

When you provide prompt, reliable, and high-quality service, people—your friends, relatives, customers, and clients—will be happy to spread the word. Let them know you welcome referrals. People who know you personally and/or enjoy working with you will be anxious to tell others, but it may not occur to them. Putting that idea into their heads isn't pushy; it's good business. Simply say, *Do you know of any other HR professionals I can help in the same way I've helped you? If yes, I'd appreciate it if you would call them and tell them how I've added value to your company.*

When do you ask for a referral to be given? Conventional sales wisdom may say the best time is immediately after your client experiences success as a result of your efforts. This may be a little aggressive. Give your clients time to experience your service or product before asking for a referral.

Giving and getting a hot referral.

If you've watched David Letterman, you know about his Top Ten lists. He presents topical theme-based lists, delivered countdown style, with No. 1 being the "hottest." Here's the same principle applied to types of referrals, going from the least effective to the most effective.*

12. Giving a key contact name.
11. Giving a key contact name along with contact information.
10. Having literature, bios, and company information sent on your behalf.
9. Being authorized to use someone's name.
8. Having a written testimonial and/or letter of recommendation sent on your behalf.
7. Having a letter, handwritten note, or email of introduction sent on your behalf.
6. Having an introduction call made on your behalf.
5. Having an introduction call and promotion made on your behalf.
4. Having a meeting arranged.
3. Receiving a face to face introduction.

*Source: *Business by Referral* by Ivan R. Misner, PhD, and Robert Davis.

2. Having someone else assess needs and interest on your behalf.

1. Having someone endorse you while describing your products and services.

Get testimonials.

When a customer or client compliments you on your work, ask him to put it in writing. He may write it on your behalf or ask you to draft something. Always get the person's written permission to use his name.

Join one or more networking groups.

There are many networking groups that can help you to grow your business. Some are industry specific or peer specific. Also, consider one of the international networking groups such as Business Network International, known as BNI (www.bni.com), or LeTip International (www.letip.com). Each group allows one person from a profession in each local chapter, giving each member an exclusive spot. For example, a local chapter may have a chiropractor, writer, travel agent, realtor, financial planner, accountant, architect, and so on. (One of my sons is a chiropractor. He belongs to a LeTip group in Columbia, MD, and says that 25 percent of his business comes from referrals from his LeTip group.) There are also local independent groups that function in much the same way.

Other things to consider:

- Check out several groups to make sure the one you join is a good fit. Look for people in your sphere—those who can be natural referral sources. For example, one of the first groups I joined had a graphic designer and a marketing strategist. With my business-writing skills, the three of us referred lots of business back and forth and worked together on many projects.

- Be sure you get to know people in your group very well before referring them. You want to refer only people you know and trust. Although these groups try to bring in people with high ethical standards who offer quality goods and services, there can be a few rotten apples.

Get paid.

Some referral partners work on a percentage basis, giving a percentage of an assignment to the person who made the referral. That's a good incentive for someone to recommend you.

When someone gives you a referral, keep that person in the loop (whether or not there's a financial arrangement). You may send a quick email saying, *Thanks for referring me to [name]. I called him, and we'll be meeting next Wednesday. I'll let you know how it goes.*

Send a thank you—always, always.

People always appreciate your taking the time to thank them for a referral—and I don't mean an email or phone call. In most cases a handwritten note is adequate. However, if the person went to great lengths to get you the referral, you may want to give him a bottle of fine wine, a fruit basket, gift certificate, or anything else you think would be appropriate.

Trade Shows and Conventions

Trade shows and conventions are great events for rekindling old business friendships, creating new friendships, increasing your base of contacts, buying and selling products, and having fun. Keep in mind that this is a business event.

 Don't give verbal or nonverbal messages that could be used as ammunition against you once you're back at the office. Watch your drinking at after-hour events, and be aware of the clothing you wear (such as around the pool).

Plan for the experience.

Don't wait till your plane touches down to start planning, regardless of whether you're an exhibitor or "floor walker." Plan ahead.

- Plan as well as you can for your office to run smoothly while you're gone. This will give you peace of mind and let you maximize your benefits.
- Arrange your travel so you have time to relax and recover from jet lag before you have to "hit the floor running."
- Carry a small notebook to jot down ideas and information.
- Decide in advance which booths, meetings, hospitality suites, and parties to attend. Most trade shows and conventions distribute (or display online) a detailed floor plan and description of the events.
- Carry a tote so you can bring goodies back for the kids.

Work the booth.

As an exhibitor, have giveaways such as calendars, pens, pads, magnets, candy, mugs, and anything that has your company name and/or logo. Also, have an ample supply of business cards, brochures, flyers, announcements of specials, and such in clear view. Although some people attend trade shows for the freebies, you need to reel in the serious attendees.

I attended a trade show where a company was offering complimentary coffee in the back of the booth. The booth was packed. People were hanging around while holding a hot cup of coffee, which made the booth look busy and attracted even more people.

If you have an attractive booth, friendly people, an interactive display (quiz or game), regularly scheduled demonstrations, prizes and drawings, and the like, you'll be swarming with visitors. When a person approaches your booth, don't say, *May I help you?* because you'll give the attendee the chance to say, *No, thanks. I'm just looking.* That may cost you a contact or hot sale. Be creative.

- Smile, extend your hand, and make an upbeat introduction.
- Take a peek at the attendee's name tag and say, *Good morning, [name]. Isn't your company the one that just . . . ?*
- Discuss an on-the-spot promotion scheme: *If you sign up now, you get . . .*
- Have someone at the booth at all times. If you're alone and must step away, leave a note indicating when you'll return.

Quickly end a conversation with an unqualified lead.

If someone who isn't a potential prospect tries to monopolize your time, it takes you away from serious attendees. Accompany the following phrases with a smile and handshake:

- *I've taken up enough of your time. Thanks for stopping by.*
- *Based on the information you shared today, I don't think [product/ service] can help you.*
- *I'm glad we had a chance to talk and am sorry we can't help solve your problem.*

Follow up immediately.

Studies show that nearly 60 percent of all trade show attendees plan to buy one or more of the products or services exhibited at a trade show or convention. If you have a booth, success relies on immediate follow-up by mail, email, personal meeting, and/or phone call. Why let a hot prospect become a cold lead by not making contact within one week of the show? When making a phone call or sending a letter or email, refer to the conversation you and the prospect had. Any way you can personalize the message will yield greater impact and encourage the prospect to take action.

Social Networking

Now that you have mastered the art of face-to-face networking—handing out business cards, wearing your badge on your right side, and more, along comes another way of networking—social networking. There are social networks for businesspeople, teens and tweens, dating, many different personal interests, and more.

Increasing your presence on the Internet is paramount for any business. Social networking sites have much higher traffic than other websites, and you get exposure to hundreds of thousands of people (or more). However, don't jump at every offer to join a social network.

Here's how it works:

- You join a site. Popular sites include www.linkedin.com, www.facebook.com, www.plaxo.com, www.twitter.com, and others.
- A friend or colleague invites you to join the network.
- You create a profile describing yourself and your interests.
- You connect to your friend's or colleague's network and then expand your own network via message boards and blogs, connecting to members with similar interests.
- You can join online conversations and groups.

Fine-tune your profile.

Social networking sites may have places to post photos, audio recordings, and videos. Don't put anything on your site that may embarrass you. If a potential employer finds a picture of you drunk with a lampshade on your head, do you think he'll hire you?

Prepare for face-to-face contact.

Just because you have met someone online doesn't mean the relationship can't go live. Social networking sites often connect people through meetings and events. (Unless you know someone who knows the person, though, be wary of whom you meet online.)

Personalize your site.

Some people use blogs to post advice, get advice, share information, and so on. I've seen people post "I'm on the train to New York right now"—to which you may ask, "Who cares?" However, a colleague who is also on his way to New York, or who lives in New York, may read that notation and want to set up a time to meet. If not for the posting, he wouldn't have known you were in the neighborhood. If you don't know how to get started, ask a friend or colleague. There's no excuse for not putting yourself out there.

9

The most important parts of any talk are the opening and closing. And they should be as close together as possible.
—George Burns

Speaking in Public

In this chapter

- Planning Your Talk
- Developing Your Text
- Delivering Your Talk
- Resources

Do you remember show-and-tell when you were in grade school? You'd bring in something to *show*, and you'd *tell* your classmates about it. It was exciting and it was fun. No one felt intimidated. That was an early introduction to public speaking. Somewhere along the way, however, most of us have lost that spark.

According to *The Book of Lists* by David Wallechinsky and Amy Wallace, public speaking is the No. 1 human fear. Would you believe that death is actually No. 7? "So," asks Jerry Seinfeld, "at a funeral, you would rather be lying in the casket than delivering the eulogy?" Glossophobia, otherwise known as fear of public speaking, doesn't have to be one of life's terrors. While it's true that some people are innately talented public speakers, anyone can deliver a successful speech.

 Watch the masters. Notice what makes them successful; check out their styles. Although you want to be yourself and not copy anyone else, there are certain characteristics you may want to incorporate.

Planning Your Talk

When you're asked to give a talk (or have your arm twisted to do so), what you deliver should be the *pièce de résistance*. Invest the time to prepare properly, and you'll be a hit.

Use the Start Up Sheet.

Use this Start Up Sheet to walk you through elements for strategic planning. Following the sheet is a detailed explanation of how to fill it in.

START UP SHEET

Audience

1. Who is my primary audience? _____

2. What does my audience *need to know* about the topic?

    _____

3. What's in it for my audience?

    _____

4. Does my talk need a special angle or point of view?

    _____

5. What is my audience's attitude toward the topic?

    _____

    _____

Purpose

6. My purpose is to _____, so my audience will

    _____.

Key Issue

7. What's the one key point I want my audience to remember?

    _____

Audience

1. Who is my primary audience?

If you want to hit your target, you must know exactly where to aim. Identify your audience and your relationship with them (if any).

- Is the audience comprised of managers, peers, subordinates, clients, customers, potential customers, others?
- Are they internal to your organization or external?
- Are they technical or nontechnical?
- What are the demographics?

2. **What does my audience *need to know* about the topic?**
The focus is on *needs to know*. Too often we tell audiences everything we know about a topic. Think of what they *need to know*. You don't want to give too much or too little information. Consider these questions:
- What's the audience's level of knowledge about the topic?
- Do they have any preconceived notions?
- Are there barriers to their understanding your message?
- What acronyms, jargon, or abbreviations should you use or will you need to explain?

 People with academic, scientific, or technical backgrounds tend to be process oriented and benefit from step-by-step explanations. Those with backgrounds in business or law are answer oriented and respond to quick answers. Creative people are usually visually oriented and benefit from charts, tables, and other visual representations.

3. **What's in it for my audience?**
When you hear a message, you mentally ask yourself these questions: *What's in it for me? Why is this worth my time?* Your audience will ask those same questions. Maybe what's in it for them is an opportunity to earn more money . . . make their jobs easier . . . look good to their superiors . . . be more knowledgeable . . . propel their careers . . . jump on a wonderful opportunity. Understand what's in it for them.

4. **Does my talk need a special angle or point of view?**
You determine the point of view by understanding the needs of your audience. Managers, for example, are big-picture people. They need the key issue. Technical people need the details. Salespeople need benefits.

5. **What is my audience's attitude toward the topic?**
You may not always tell people in your audience what they want to hear, but you must tell them what they need to know. Will they be responsive (glad to hear your message)? Will they be neutral? Will they be unresponsive or disappointed?
- Are you disputing existing data?

- Will they lose face by accepting your recommendation?
- Are you creating more work for them?
- Will they get pressure from managers because of your message?

Purpose

6. My purpose is to _____, so my audience will _____.

My purpose is to . . . Whether you think your purpose is to communicate, inform, sell, teach, or whatever, chances are you're trying to *persuade* someone to do something or think in a certain way.

So my audience will . . . When your audience knows exactly what they will learn or what action you want them to take, they can digest your message more intelligently.

Key Issue

7. What's the one key point I want my audience to remember?

Billboard advertisers, ad people, and designers know that people read on the fly. Put on your advertising hat. Pretend you have to write a 15-second commercial. If your audience forgets everything else, what's the one point you want remembered? Condense this key point into one sentence.

Don't bury the lead.

My friend and colleague Suzanne Bates talks about this in her latest book, Motivate Like a CEO. *Suzanne is president and CEO of Bates Communications (www.bates-communications.com) and a former newscaster. "Don't bury the lead" is a common expression in the news business that refers to putting the most important facts—the* what *and* why—*first.*

Here's a case in point: I was coaching a client who works at a large company. She was preparing a presentation for a group of high-level people within the company. She showed me the draft of her PowerPoint presentation titled "How We Can Become No. 1." It consisted of a dozen slides of identical-looking charts. (If I were in the audience, my eyes would have glazed over when she put up the second slide, if not the first.) I asked her about the one key point she wanted the audience to remember. She explained that the company is No. 2 in its market space and is looking to move into the No. 1 spot. "So what?" I kept asking, "What does this mean for the bottom line?" After much probing, she revealed that moving into the No. 1 slot would mean an estimated $250 million added to the bottom line the following year. Nowhere in her presentation did she mention that extraordinary number. She expected her audience to read between the lines. Okay, we had some work to do.

The end product

She titled her new presentation "Adding $250 Million to Our Bottom Line by Becoming No. 1." She pared her dozen slides down to three: (1) depicting where the company currently excels, (2) showing where the company is mediocre, and (3) explaining where the company needs to improve. When I asked her how many people actually needed the level of detail her original slides showed, she said very few. She agreed to provide them with a link to the original slides.

The result

*She called me after the presentation to let me know how well it went. The presentation turned into a brainstorming session that stimulated some very strong action plans to move the company to No. 1. **Don't bury the lead!***

Ask yourself the basic questions.

Prepare a chart with two columns. At the left list the six basic questions— Who? What? When? Where? Why? How? In the first column list the specific questions in each category that you anticipate from your audience. In the second column, list the questions you need to ask yourself. You may not need to answer all of the questions, and you may have several answers for some of them.

Your audience will want to know	You need to ask yourself
Who...	
• is responsible? • will be impacted by the change? • will benefit? • will be adversely affected? • are the stakeholders?	• is the audience? • will be supportive and make supportive comments? • will be adversarial and make combative comments? • is my contact person for logistical and other issues? • will introduce me? • is on the program before/after me?
What...	
• are the advantages/disadvantages? • are the alternatives? • is the next step?	• are the major concerns of my audience? • materials do I have to help them address those concerns? • props/visuals should I show? • stories can help them to remember the key points? • do they know about the topic?

Your audience will want to know	You need to ask yourself
	• is my relationship with the audience?
	• is the occasion?
	• is my purpose?
	• objections may I expect?
	• obstacles may I encounter?
	• discussion points should I encourage?
	• questions will I be asked?
	• are the logistics?

When...

• does this take effect?	• is the best time to deliver this presentation?
• do you need a decision?	• should I distribute handouts?— before? after? at all?
• can we start?	

Where...

• will the funding come from?	• is the talk taking place?
• can I get more information?	• can the audience get more information?
• can I get more resources?	

Why...

• are you recommending that?	• is the audience attending your presentation?
• can't we . . . ?	• was I chosen?

How...

• will we measure success?	• will I open the presentation?
• can I apply this information?	• will I stay calm before the presentation?
	• will I close the presentation?
	• will this talk benefit me?
	• many people are expected?

Note: When speaking to large audiences, consider having someone interpret using sign language.

How to Feed a Martian

This is an exercise I use when I facilitate my presentation workshops. At first, participants think I'm crazy (and you may too), but it does prove an essential point.

Scenario

It's the year 2050, and you're conducting business intergalactically. You have a group of 25 Martians coming to attend your presentation on mak-

ing a peanut butter and jelly sandwich. The Martians speak English, and you've already purchased the ingredients.

Your assignment
Prepare a presentation to teach the Martians how to make a peanut butter and jelly sandwich. I hope you'll PAUSE HERE and try this exercise, because there's a method to this madness.

Then . . . assess what you did
If you're like most people, you may have thought this exercise was quite easy. Perhaps you even jotted down information for some basic slides with directions much like these:

> *1. Open the jar of peanut butter.*
> *2. Open the jar of jelly.*
> *3. Smear the peanut butter and jelly on the bread.*

Learning from this exercise
Check out some questions you should have thought about in order to have made a clear and informative presentation that would have accomplished your goal.

- *What level of understanding did the Martians have? Would they necessarily understand your terminology? Would they know a jar of peanut butter from a jar of jelly? Even though they speak English, they only understand the terminology they've been exposed to—just as earthlings do. (Would you be able to distinguish montmorillonite from another mineral next to it? Do you even know what the word means? Just because you speak English doesn't mean you understand everything. You understand only what you've been exposed to.)*

- *Did you give the Martians all the information (and steps) they needed? Would they understand how to remove the lid from the jar? Would they hit the jar with a hammer to get inside? If you told the Martians to unscrew the lid, would they know in which direction to turn it?*

- *Is your peanut butter like that from a health store, where the oil separates? If so, did you tell the Martians to mix the oil with the gooey stuff?*

Aha!
Then comes the realization that slides may not be the best way to communicate this information. Perhaps an audio, video, audience participation, or live presentation would work better.

Lesson learned
Just as important as knowing how to prepare a slide presentation is knowing whether one is appropriate.

It's interesting to note that during my entire four-hour presentation workshop, I don't use a single slide. The entire workshop is interactive, and participants prepare part of a presentation they need to deliver. I give them handouts and worksheets, but those are the only visuals.

Developing Your Text

Have you ever sat in front of your computer, staring at a blank screen, trying to develop text, hoping the right words will magically appear? Even prolific writers such as Mark Twain had trouble getting started. At the end of each writing session he'd leave a sentence unfinished, so that when he sat down for his next session, there would be an easy starting point. Preparing a talk doesn't have to be wishing for magic.

Create a storyboard.

Take your first step by creating a storyboard. A storyboard is a visual display broken into segments of talking points and visuals/other. The storyboard lets you see the continuity of your message, identify any gaps, and discover if you told too much or too little. Here's how to set up a storyboard:

1. Create two columns.
2. Populate the left column (talking points) with highlights of the information you want to deliver verbally. Not your full text, just key words and thoughts.
3. Populate the right column (visuals/other) with the information you want to present. This doesn't necessarily mean PowerPoint slides. You may include slides, audio recordings, presentations from others, questions, handouts, individual or group activities, and anything else that may be appropriate.

Keep in mind that you don't have to start at the beginning of your talk in creating your storyboard. Start at the point that's easiest for you to develop. Following is a portion of a storyboard—actually, Step 4—that I generated when I was first preparing my business-writing workshop.

TALKING POINTS	VISUALS/OTHER
WHITE SPACE • Use 1 to 1½" margins on the top, bottom, and sides of printed pages. • Leave one line space between each paragraph. • Leave one line space above and below bulleted and numbered lists.	
PARAGRAPH AND SENTENCE LENGTH • Limit paragraphs to 8 lines of text. • Limit sentences to a maximum of 25 words.	
BULLETS AND NUMBERS • Discuss the difference between numbered and bulleted lists. • Use bullets when everything on the list is of equal value. • Use numbers when • there's a sense of priority • there's a sequence of events • you need to refer to items on a long list • you've already mentioned the number of items on the list.	
CHARTS AND TABLES Etc.	

Next, fill in the Visuals/Other section. On page 131 you see how I did that for Step 4 of my business/technical writing presentation:

TALKING POINTS	VISUALS/OTHER
WHITE SPACE • Use 1 to 1½" margins on the top, bottom, and sides of printed pages. • Leave one line space between each paragraph. • Leave one line space above and below bulleted and numbered lists.	Show examples. Show examples. Show examples.
PARAGRAPH AND SENTENCE LENGTH • Limit paragraphs to 8 lines of text. • Limit sentences to a maximum of 25 words.	Show examples.

BULLETS AND NUMBERS
 	
• Discuss the difference between numbered and bulleted lists.
 	
• Use bullets when everything on the list is of equal value.
 	
• Use numbers when
  • there's a sense of priority
  • there's a sequence of events
  • you need to refer to items on a long list
  • you've already mentioned the number of items on the list.
	Slide: Bullets vs. Numbers
	Simple sentence
	Xxxxxxxxxxx.
	
	Bulleted list
	• xxxxxxxxxxxxxx
	• xxxxxxxxxxxxxx
	
	Numbered list
	1. xxxxxxxxxxxxxx
	2. xxxxxxxxxxxxxx

CHARTS AND TABLES Etc.	

And there's more.
- Get a clicker that will allow you to black out the screen when there's nothing to display.
- Don't display slides that read "Discussion" or "Questions." They serve no purpose and take the focus off of you and your audience.

Always keep in mind that your audience attends your presentation to listen to you. *Your visuals—if you need any at all—are your aids, not your focus.* They're not meant to be your teleprompter.

Creating appealing and informative PowerPoint presentations

How many PowerPoint presentations have you sat through (or slept through) where the presenter bored you with an endless avalanche of slides? Don't use PowerPoints as a teleprompter; they're not a crutch. Some of the best speakers don't use any PowerPoints.

As a presenter, your brilliance doesn't matter if you can't communicate effectively. Use PowerPoint presentations and other visuals only to clarify ideas, emphasize key points, show relationships, and provide supporting information. Present the big picture.

Prepare a master slide so all the slides have the same fonts, colors, and banner. Include your logo on all slides. If you make a presentation to a client or potential client, include the client's logo on each slide as well.

Present the big picture.
Audiences remember concepts, trends, and impressions, not raw data or minutiae. Each visual should address one of these questions:
- *What is it?*
- *What are the benefits?*
- *Where is it?*
- *How much is there?*
- *How does it work?*
- *What are the parameters?*

Craft text strategically.
Use text to clarify ideas, emphasize key points, show relationships, and provide supporting information.
- *Craft headlines that make the visual aid readable, even from the worst seat in the room.*
- *Use active, high-impact words that benefit your audience.*
- *Prominently display the words* you *and* yours, *when possible.*
- *Use upper- and lowercase, even for headlines.*
- *Limit visuals to 5–7 lines of text.*
- *Include bulleted or numbered lists.*
- *Use a 24-point font for the headlines and an 18-point font for the text.*

Use graphics to enhance the message.
Remember that a picture is worth a thousand words.
- *Show pictures, diagrams, and charts to make your visuals memorable.*
- *Use lines, shapes, and colors to clarify your message.*
- *When preparing charts, label axes and data lines.*
- *Create a legend to explain a graphic.*
- *Use a graphic to add value to your text or to jazz up an otherwise dull slide, as in the one that follows:*

Example

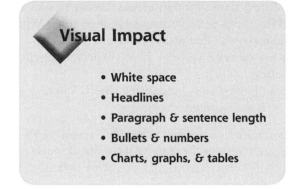

Notes:
- *Bring an electronic copy of your presentation. (I typically carry mine on a memory stick that I wear around my neck so I can't lose it.)*
- *Show up early to check the equipment. Never assume your presentation will work on someone else's laptop.*
- *Don't leave your laptop in Standby mode.*
- *Don't leave your screensaver on; black out the screen when you're not projecting.*
- *Avoid the need for frequent mouse or keyboard interaction; it's very distracting.*

 One size does not fit all when it comes to learning. Pat may learn easily by reading instructions. Leslie may see something done once and be able to repeat the process. Jim may need to be shown step-by-step. Deliver your materials in a variety of formats to accommodate various learning styles.

Create a memorable opening.

People typically remember what you say in the first 30 seconds (because they're assessing you). They also remember what you say in the final minutes. Don't waste either of these opportunities. Limit your opening remarks to one or two minutes. The comedian George Jessel once said, "If you haven't struck oil in your first two or three minutes, stop boring." Here are a few things to consider:

Opening Dos
- **Think of an interesting opening.** Relate a story. Ask a thought-provoking question. Use a quotation. Cite a statistic. Tell a joke. Show something.
- **Make a brief statement about your qualifications.** This is to establish credibility, not to dazzle your audience.

- **Make a strong statement that speaks directly to your audience's needs.** Why is this presentation worth their time? What can they expect to leave with that will be of value?
- **Address any concerns up front.** If you expect negativity, build rapport at the outset.
- **If you aren't introduced, introduce yourself.** You may say something as simple as, *Good morning, I'm [name].*

 I often hear speakers start with, *For those of you who don't know me, my name is [name].* Isn't the name the same for those who do know you?

Opening Taboos
- **Weak statements.** These include: *Today I'll attempt to . . ., I'll be speaking on . . .,* or *Today you'll be listening to. . . .*
- **Forecasts of doom and gloom.** They're instant turnoffs. If you must present doom and gloom, fold it into something positive, but certainly not at the outset.
- **Personal experiences that aren't related to the topic.**
- **Overworked quotations or trite phrases.**
- **Dictionary definitions.** They're condescending and boring.

After your catchy opening, share personal information so you establish your credibility. This helps the audience to relate to you.

Bill Clinton vs. Bob Dole
Your choice of words is critical. Read the following opening statements made by Bill Clinton and Bob Dole at the first 1996 presidential candidates' debate. Notice the difference in tone and content. Do you think speeches such as this one helped Bill Clinton to get elected?

President Bill Clinton's Opening Statement
Thank you, Jim. And thank you to the people of Hartford, our hosts. I want to begin by saying again how much I respect Senator Dole and his record of public service and how hard I will try to make this campaign and this debate one of ideas, not insults.

Four years ago I ran for president at a time of high unemployment and rising frustration. I wanted to turn this country around with a program of opportunity for all, responsibility from all, and an American community where everybody has a role to play. I wanted a government that was smaller and less bureaucratic to help people have the tools to make the most of their lives. Four years ago you took me on faith. Now there's a record: Ten and a half million more jobs, rising incomes, falling crime rates and welfare rolls, a strong America at peace.

We are better off than we were four years ago. Let's keep it going. We cut the deficit by 60 percent. Now let's balance the budget and protect Medicare, Medicaid, education and the environment. We cut taxes for 15 million working Americans. Now let's pass the tax cuts for education and child-rearing, help with medical emergencies and buying a home.

We passed Family and Medical Leave. Now let's expand it so more people can succeed as parents and in the workforce. We passed the 100,000 police, the assault weapons ban, the Brady Bill. Now let's keep going by finishing the work of putting the police on the street and tackling juvenile gangs.

We passed welfare reform. Now let's move a million people from welfare to work. And most important, let's make education our highest priority so that every 8-year-old will be able to read, every 12-year-old can log onto the Internet, every 18-year-old can go to college. We can build that bridge to the 21st century, and I look forward to discussing exactly how we're going to do it.

Senator Bob Dole's Opening Statement

Thank you. Thank you, Mr. President, for those kind words. Thank the people of Hartford, the Commission, and all those out here who may be listening or watching.

It's a great honor for me to be here, standing here as the Republican nominee. I'm very proud to be the Republican nominee, reaching out to Democrats and Independents.

I have three very special people with me tonight: My wife Elizabeth; my daughter Robin, who has never let me down, and a fellow named Frank Carafa from New York, along with Ollie Manninen who helped me out in the mountains of Italy a few years back.

I've learned from them that people do have tough times. And sometimes you can't go it alone. And that's what America is all about.

I remember getting my future back from doctors and nurses, and a doctor in Chicago named Dr. Kelikian. And ever since that time, I've tried to give something back to my country, to the people who are watching us tonight.

America is the greatest place on the face of the earth. Now I know millions of you still have anxieties. You work harder and harder to make ends meet and put food on the table. You worry about the quality and the safety of your children—the quality of education. But even more importantly, you worry about the future, and will they have the same opportunities that you and I have had.

And Jack Kemp and I want to share with you some ideas tonight. Jack Kemp is my running mate, doing an outstanding job. Now, I'm a plain-speaking man, and I learned long ago that your word was your bond. And I promise you tonight that I'll try to address your concerns and not try to exploit them. It's a tall order, but I've been running against the odds for a long time. And again, I'm honored to be here this evening.

Omit trite or inappropriate expressions.

Following are inappropriate expressions that people often use. In parentheses, see the audience's possible reactions.

- *I'm really not prepared.* (Then why should we waste time listening to you?)
- *I don't know why I was asked to speak here today.* (Are we being victimized by someone's poor judgment?)
- *As unaccustomed as I am to . . .* (Thanks for sharing that. I should have stayed away.)
- *I won't take up too much of your time.* (This is going to be a sleeper.)
- *I don't want to offend anyone, but . . .* (Oh, here comes an insult.)
- *Have you heard the one about . . .* (Oh, we have a comedian here.)
- *Please give me a few more minutes.* (It's already been too long.)

 Always keep the storyboards, visuals, and notes from speeches you deliver. If you're presenting to an entirely new audience the next time, you can use all or part of your original speech. Of course, *make sure everything is current.* For example, when I deliver my email workshop, I typically show current headlines from newspapers to point out how each subject line should be as informational as a newspaper headline.

Prepare the middle.

Many people struggle with how to start or how to end. Why not start in the middle, which is the nuts and bolts of your presentation? The middle may be the easiest place to start your storyboard, because once you're on a roll, your opening and closing will evolve. Here are some suggestions for developing the middle:

- **Brainstorm.** Generate a series of points you want to raise.
- **Organize those points into strategic order.** If you're delivering a message your audience will view as good or neutral, open with the main point. If you're delivering a message they'll view as negative or contrary to popular belief, build up to that point.
- **Never try to overwhelm the audience with too much information.** It's better to make a few powerful points rather than too many weak ones.
- **Think about the visuals that will enhance your talk.** Prepare the visuals after you prepare your talk. Remember that people are there to listen to you, not to see your props.

End with a bang.

Take one or two minutes to wrap up. A good talk ends with a bang and must include some of your strongest material. Don't end by saying *That's it* or *That's all there is.* (You'll sound like Porky Pig announcing, *That's all, folks.*)

- Thank your audience for coming.
- Recap your major theme or major points.
- End with an appeal.
- Use a quote.
- Relate a story.
- Leave the audience with a thought-provoking question or food for thought.
- Revisit something you opened with.
- Ask for any questions.
- Use gestures or your voice to let the audience know you're finished.

 Offer your audience a reason to stay in touch with you. Do you have online courses that may interest them? Do you generate a newsletter? Whatever it is, make it compelling and let them know what's in it for them.

 Check out chapter 5, "Making Proper Word Choices."

Listen to your speech patterns.

After you write your talk, record it and listen carefully. (A tape recorder works well.) Here are some things to listen for:

- Speech patterns that may distract the audience from what you're saying. For example, do you start with a low registration, work up to the emphasized words, then trail off? If so, this pattern will generate major yawns.

- Words that read well on paper, but are hard to say. I was writing a script for a YouTube video on email etiquette. I wrote: "People are overwhelmed by the large volume of digital dross they receive each day," and found myself tripping over the words *digital dross.* So I changed the sentence to read: "People are overwhelmed by the large numbers of emails they receive each day."

- *Um, like,* or other speech patterns you interject.

- Rate of speech. Are you speaking too quickly or too slowly? A speech rate of 175 to 190 words per minute works well for both speaker and listener.

Make a list, check it twice.

Use the following checklist for presentations:

- ❑ Will my purpose be crystal clear to the audience?
- ❑ Did I learn everything I can about my audience?
- ❑ Did I distinguish between what to say and what to project?
- ❑ Are my visuals informative and pleasing to view?
- ❑ Can my visuals be seen from the worst seat in the room?
- ❑ Have I organized my presentation into logical topics and subtopics?
- ❑ Have I anticipated questions?
- ❑ Am I prepared to answer them?
- ❑ Have I confirmed the date, time, and place of the presentation?

Should you use a ghost writer?

If you don't have the time or inclination to write your talk yourself, consider hiring a ghost writer. If you go that route, find someone . . .

- Who's worked with other speakers you know and trust.
- You like and can work closely with. You must be able to share your feelings, thoughts, and personal stories.
- Whose prices are affordable.

Some people download off-the-shelf speeches from the Internet. If you do, you may lose credibility and find yourself embarrassed if people in the audience have heard the same speech from someone else.

Delivering Your Talk

Okay, you've written your talk and now it's the big day! It may help to remember that celebrated personalities such as Elvis Presley and Barbra Streisand admitted to suffering from stage fright. Stage fright is actually healthy. The sudden rush of adrenaline is a form of positive energy that makes you appear excited about your talk.

Remember . . . people aren't attending your talk to judge you; they're attending to hear what you have to say and learn from you. There will be people in the room who admire you, respect you, and are cheering you on.

Please consider the following:

- If you're one of several presenters, and the order in which you speak hasn't been determined, try to go first. Not only will you get it over with, but you'll set the baseline for all other presenters and be able to enjoy listening to everyone else.

- If you're suffering from a cold or allergies, cough or sneeze into your elbow, sleeve, or handkerchief. After your talk you want members of your audience to come up and talk with you without being afraid of shaking a germy hand.

Fielding Questions

Anticipate that people will have questions, and let the audience know up front how you'll handle them. How you do so depends on your comfort level and the nature of your talk.

For questions throughout the talk or at designated times
- I'll be delighted to take any questions and comments as we go along.
- After each section, I'll be happy to answer questions about what was just discussed.

Down side . . . You must manage this well. Don't let the questions bog down the presentation, and don't let one questioner monopolize the floor. One solution may be to say, I'll give you the short answer now; we'll be discussing this later this morning.

For questions at the conclusion
- At the end, I'll be happy to take your questions.
- If you have any questions, I'll be available afterward for about a half-hour. I welcome you to stop by.
- Please jot your questions down, and at the end [person] will come around to collect them. I'll try to answer as many as I can.

Down side . . . Some people leave immediately and may not submit questions. Also, when people get up to leave, it's disruptive to those who want questions answered.

Beforehand

Practice your talk using your notes.

If you don't have the confidence to speak from memory, prepare notes to read from rather than a script. Use the notes as a skeleton of your talk and include key words you want to remember in the order in which you want to say them. Practice in front of your partner, parents, friends, canary, and/ or anyone who'll listen. Practice out loud rather than in your head, so you "hear" your words. Also, practice in front of a mirror to see what you look like. It's important not to overpractice! You want to appear natural and conversational.

Time yourself.

Time yourself with your visuals to make sure you're near your target time. The actual presentation will go faster than the practice, so allow for slightly more time than you actually need.

Envision success.

You care about what you're saying, and you've invested the time and effort. Now imagine a standing ovation. Hold this thought and use it again before you start speaking.

Visit the location where you will give your speech, and practice there if you can.

This will allow you to get a realistic picture as to where you'll be, where the audience will be, etc. If you can't visit the location, try to visualize it as best you can.

Get a good night's sleep the night before, and don't overeat.

Try to get a good night's sleep the night before, so you'll be refreshed when it comes time to present. Have a good meal that will give you energy and keep your stomach from growling, but don't overeat. Also, drink plenty of water so you're well hydrated, but not so much that you'll want to run from the stage for a "bio" break.

Dress to impress!

The first thing your audience will notice is what you're wearing. Wear something comfortable that's appropriate for the occasion and the topic. Avoid loud colors and flashy jewelry.

The time has come

Do the hokey pokey.

If you have a private area before you speak, do the hokey pokey, jump around, or do anything that will help you release energy. If you don't have a private area, flex your calves, make fists and release them, and do anything else to get rid of the adrenaline going through your body. Remember, some degree of the jitters is good; it will help you to present excitedly and passionately.

Start by taking a deep breath.

Before beginning to speak, glance at your notes, look at the audience, take a deep breath from your diaphragm, and begin. Imagine yourself being fabulous.

Stand tall.

Spread your weight evenly by placing your feet slightly apart, a little less than shoulder width. This will keep you from swaying from side to side and allow you to stand confidently.

Face your audience and look them in the eyes.

If you think that's too painful, imagine your audience sitting in their underwear, or look at their foreheads instead of directly into their eyes. When you look directly at people, they'll trust you. (Don't look at the floor; there's nothing to see there.)

Speak loudly enough and at an appropriate pace.

Your voice should be clear, even to those in the back of the room. Find out the size of the room beforehand so you can determine whether you need a microphone. Speak at a good pace that reveals your excitement and passion about your topic, but don't speak too fast.

Create a comfortable silence.

Silence (or pauses) can be powerful. Use pauses to emphasize key points or to give yourself time to think, change your pitch, or let your audience digest the impact of something you have said. Pauses make the message before and after much more important.

 Don't use fillers such as *um, ah, like uh, you know,* or *okay.* They are distracting, and no one is rushing you.

Use your style to your advantage!

Be yourself, and don't try to copy speakers you've seen or heard, no matter how good they were. If you're reading from a script or notes, be sure to look up at the audience, and don't lapse into a monotonous recitation.

 More to think about:
- If you start to shake while presenting, take a couple of steps to get rid of some of that energy and regain control of those muscles.
- It's okay to hold your index cards, but don't hold a sheet of paper. The paper will flutter with every tiny movement and exaggerate all your shakes.

Let your personality shine.

Don't think you have to be ultra serious; lighten up. Let your personality show. No matter how serious your talk is, be yourself, use appropriate humor, share stories from your experience, and laugh at yourself. Laugh at your mistakes. If you drop the microphone or bump into a chair, forgive yourself and make light of it.

Turn the floor over to the next speaker.

If you're one of two or more speakers, graciously turn the floor over to the next speaker. (The audience should know from the outset if there's to be more than one speaker.) Before you end your talk, make sure to turn off your projector. You can say,

- *Before I conclude, I'll be happy to take two or three questions.*
- *Before I turn the floor over to [name], are there any questions?*
- *It's now my pleasure to introduce [name], who will be speaking about [topic].* You can continue with a brief intro, if appropriate.
- *At the end of [name's] presentation, she and I will be happy to answer any questions. Thank you.*

 Plan to stick around after your talk. If people liked your talk and identified with you, they'll come up to you afterward with comments and questions. When that happens, you know you did a great job.

Even the most eloquent speakers misspeak.

It was a mulligan for Barack Obama. During his inauguration in January 2009, both President Obama and Supreme Court Chief Justice John Roberts "flubbed" the oath of office. Here's the text:

ROBERTS: Are you prepared to take the oath, Senator?
OBAMA: I am.
ROBERTS: I, Barack Hussein Obama . . .
OBAMA: I, Barack . . .
ROBERTS: . . . do solemnly swear . . .
OBAMA: I, Barack Hussein Obama, do solemnly swear . . .
ROBERTS: . . . that I will execute the office of president of the United States faithfully . . .
OBAMA: . . . that I will execute . . .
ROBERTS: . . . faithfully the office of president of the United States . . .
OBAMA: . . . the office of president of the United States faithfully . . .
ROBERTS: . . . and will to the best of my ability . . .
OBAMA: . . . and will to the best of my ability . . .
ROBERTS: . . . preserve, protect and defend the Constitution of the United States.

OBAMA: . . . preserve, protect and defend the Constitution of the United States.
ROBERTS: So help you God?
OBAMA: So help me God.
ROBERTS: Congratulations, Mr. President.

Just to be on the safe side, Obama took the oath of office again the following evening at the White House. So if you ever watch *Jeopardy* and hear the answer, "The U.S. president who took the oath of office twice within two days," you'll know the question: "Who is Barack Obama?"

Resources

If you don't want to go it alone, here are a few resources to check out:

Professional Coach

Abraham Lincoln once said, "If I had eight hours to chop down a tree, I would spend six hours sharpening my axe." Sharpen your axe and prepare to boost your career by delivering great speeches. You can find speaking coaches through your personal or virtual network. Or Google words such as "professional coach," "public speaking coach," or "professional speaking coach" together with your region. You're bound to find a few you feel comfortable with.

National Speakers Association (NSA)

NSA is a professional organization that has regional chapters to provide education, publications, and resources.

    1500 S. Priest Drive, Tempe, AZ 85281
    480.968.2552
    www.nsaspeaker.org

Toastmasters International

Toastmasters is a nonprofit organization of groups that meet to practice speaking. Speeches are critiqued by members in a positive and constructive manner.

    Box 9052, Mission Viejo, CA 92690
    949.858.8255
    www.toastmasters.org

SpeakerNet News (SNN)

Get a free e-subscription to SpeakerNet News for technology tips, travel tips, miscellaneous tips, webinars, and other topics of interest to speakers. Send an email to editor@speakernetnews.com to sign up.

Looking for the perfect gift?

If you're ever looking for the perfect gift for a speaker in your life, here are a few suggestions:

wireless presenter with laser pointer

I like the Targus Wireless Presenter with Laser Pointer. It has a button to darken the screen when not projecting; most others don't. (Darkening the screen is important, because it moves the focus away from the screen and onto you and the audience.)

extendable pointer

Consider a laser pointer necklace or pocket laser pointer so the presenter doesn't have to keep looking for the pointer.

aluminum easel

If you work with documents in a range of size and weights, the Quartet Heavy Duty Telescoping Aluminum Easel is an excellent choice because it's relatively lightweight and portable.

self-sticking easel pad

The 3M Post-it Self-Stick Easel Pad has specially coated paper so markers don't bleed through. The tabletop version can be set up anywhere. Self-stick sheets adhere to walls without damage, so there's no need for tacks or tape.

attention-getting gavel

When you need to restore order, the Valley Forge Gavel in solid walnut gets the point across with style and elegance. Approximately 10 1/2 inches long, it comes with a sound block. Buyers receive up to three lines of custom engraving.

And, of course, there's an endless supply of books about speaking in public.

Teach children the life-long skill of speaking in front of people.

Many adults fear public speaking because they never overcame the fear as children. Encourage "public speaking" with the children in your life and open the doorway to opportunities in their lives. It's a skill that gives children confidence in school, a boost in social situations, and an edge in the job market.

Here are some suggestions for starting children along this path at an early age:

- *Set a good example by speaking well, encouraging your children to speak well, and praising them when they do. This will have the added benefit of helping you to know the children better and get into their emotional worlds.*

- *Encourage them to stand up in front of family to recite poems or anything else they have learned in school. Follow with applause, of course.*
- *Ask children to cut pictures from magazines, then stand up and create a story about the picture. Make it interactive and participate with them.*
- *Encourage show-and-tell at home as well as in school.*
- *Sign children up for drama classes and encourage them to participate in school plays.*
- *Acknowledge the* what-if *fear (What if* I *forget my lines . . . What if people laugh . . .), and let children know it's perfectly natural.*

With each experience, children's confidence levels increase. Whether the talk is a simple presentation of a snippet of information or something more lengthy, well-spoken experiences foster feelings of self-worth, build confidence, and prepare children for the future.

10

Everybody can look good on paper.

— John Y. Brown, Jr., former governor
of Kentucky

Interviewing and Being Interviewed

In this chapter

- Get Ready, Get Dressed, Go!
- Typical Interviewer Questions
- Typical Candidate Questions
- Dealing with Difficult Issues
- Checking References
- Interviewing Gen Xers and Gen Yers
- Types of Interviews

Okay. You look good on paper. Your resume enticed a company to call you in for an interview. Now you're ready to "meet the Fockers."

One way to reduce interview jitters is to go on a series of practice interviews. This may involve asking someone you know in a professional position to put you through the paces of a mock interview or setting up interviews for jobs you don't really care about just to get the practice. Either will give you an idea of what questions interviewers ask, how you answer them, and how well you do.

Get Ready, Get Dressed, Go!

Your first impression will be a lasting one. It's always better to overdress than to underdress.

Men
- Blue, gray, or navy suit (Pinstripes are fine if they're muted.)
- Long-sleeve shirt (Choose white or a light color to coordinate with your suit.)
- Leather belt and leather shoes to match your suit
- Conservative silk or polyester tie

- Socks to match your suit (They should be high enough that you don't show your hairy legs when you sit down.)
- No jewelry other than a watch and standard rings (Leave any excess piercings at home.)
- Hair clean-cut and neatly combed
- No aftershave lotion
- Neatly trimmed nails
- Leather (or leatherlike) portfolio or briefcase

Women
- Dark-colored suit or conservative skirt and blazer (The skirt should be long enough that you can sit down comfortably and loose enough that you don't look like a streetwalker.)
- Conservative leather shoes (No spike heels.)
- Blouse to coordinate with your suit (Nothing see-through or showing cleavage.)
- Very limited jewelry, such as earrings, simple necklace, and watch (Don't draw attention to excess piercings.)
- Neatly combed hairstyle that won't keep falling in your face (You don't want to constantly be putting your hair back behind your ears.)
- No perfume or scented lotion
- Neatly trimmed nails
- Neutral pantyhouse
- Conservative purse
- Leather (or leatherlike) portfolio or briefcase

 Eat lightly before the interview so you don't arrive with a rumbling stomach. A heavy meal with lots of carbs can make you feel and appear sluggish.

Typical Interviewer Questions

Federal, state, and local laws limit the questions an interviewer may ask you during personal interviews, phone interviews, or testing. The questions must be related to the position for which you're applying.

 Check out chapter 6, "Using Politically Neutral Terms," for guidelines on interviewing candidates with disabilities.

 When you're scheduled for an interview, plan to arrive about 10 minutes early. If you arrive too early, you may sit and worry. If you arrive too late, you may be huffing and puffing. Don't put yourself under any undue stress. And turn off your cell phone.

Prepare for questions you may be asked.

Always learn as much as you can about the company, its products and services, and the industry. (The Internet and social networks are great resources.) The following are more questions than you'll ever be asked, but they'll help you to do your homework before going for the interview. The higher the position, the more questions you can expect.

- Before answering a question, make sure you understand it. If not, ask: *Would you please be more specific?* or *Would you mind repeating that?*
- If you don't know the answer to a question, don't lie. It's okay not to know. Often the interviewer is more interested in how you find answers than in your having the answer.
- Keep your answers simple and succinct.
- When a question requires a lengthy answer, after you answer, ask, *Did I give you enough detail?*
- Let your motto be: *Confidence implies competence.*

General Questions

- How would you describe yourself?
- What do you really want to do in life?
- Why did you choose this career?
- What motivates you to go the extra mile on a project or job?
- How do you determine or evaluate success?
- Do you have any hobbies? What do you do in your spare time?
- What qualities should a successful manager possess?
- What two or three things are most important to you in your job?
- Are you seeking employment in a company of a certain size? Why?
- What are your expectations regarding promotions and salary increases?
- What criteria are you using to evaluate the company for which you hope to work?
- What's the most recent book you've read?
- What two or three accomplishments have given you the most satisfaction? Why?
- In what kind of work environment are you most comfortable?
- How well do you adapt to new situations?

 If the interviewer says, *Tell me about yourself,* you may answer, *Where would you like me to start?*

Interest in the Company/Position

- What do you know about our company?

- What interests you about our products/services?
- What do you know about our competitors?
- Why do you want to work for [company]?
- Why should we hire you?
- What can you contribute to [company]?
- What interests you about this job?
- What challenges are you looking for in a position?
- What attributes/experience do you have?
- Are you overqualified for this job?
- Why are you the best person for the job?
- Why should I hire you?
- What makes you qualified for this position?
- What qualifications do you have that will make you successful in this position?
- What do you think it takes to be successful in a company like ours?
- Is there anything I haven't told you about the job or the company that you would like to know?
- What would it take for you to accept this position? (That's a wonderful question to be asked, because it means they want you.)

Objectives and Goals
- What are your long-range and short-term goals and objectives?
- What specific goals other than those related to your occupation have you established for yourself for the next ten years?
- How do you plan to achieve your career goals?
- What do you see yourself doing five years from now? Ten years from now?
- What do you expect to be earning in five years?
- Do you have plans for continued study? An advanced degree?

Prior Employment
- Why did you leave your last job?
- How well do you work with people?
- Do you prefer working alone or in teams?
- Describe the best supervisor you've ever had.
- What would your last boss say about your work performance?
- How would you evaluate your ability to deal with conflict?
- Have you ever had difficulty with a supervisor? How did you resolve the conflict?
- What's more important to you, the work itself or how much you're paid for doing it?

- What do you consider to be your greatest strengths (weaknesses)?
- What's the most rewarding experience of your career thus far?
- Can you explain this gap in your employment history?
- Describe the workload in your current (or most recent) job.
- How do you work under pressure?
- Are you good at delegating tasks?
- What's one of the hardest decisions you've ever had to make?
- Have you ever been fired or forced to resign?
- Describe the best job you've ever had. What made it the best?

Leadership Abilities
- Do you consider yourself a leader?
- What are the attributes of a good leader?
- Are you good at delegating?
- What's your management style?

Travel and Relocation
- Do you have a geographic preference? Why?
- Are you willing to relocate?
- Are you willing to travel for the job?
- Why do you think you might like to live in the community in which our company is located?

If you're asked about weaknesses, turn your weaknesses into strengths. *I realize I may not have direct experience in [area], but I have [specific] experience in [something comparable].* Or express confidence that you can get the job done and share a story about how you handled a similar challenge. (Once I was asked to name a weakness. I thought for a moment and said, *Chocolate.* The interviewer appreciated my sense of humor and laughed. I got the job.)

Here's how I have turned my biggest weakness into a strength: I try to avoid having to work under pressure, so I put myself under a lot of pressure to get assignments done well in advance of deadlines.

Consider social networking to be your public relations tool.

Remember that www can stand for "wild, wild West"—and there are dangers out there. Employers don't like surprises, so many are combing social networking sites of potential candidates. You'd be surprised how many candidates have been disqualified because of embarrassing statements or photographs. And it doesn't have to be you who posted. It can be someone you considered to be a friend. Here are a few things you can do to protect yourself:

- *Google your name regularly to see what pops up.*

- *Switch your MySpace or Facebook profile to "private."*
- *Edit what people write on your wall.*

Typical Interviewee Questions

Remember that an interview works two ways. The interviewer is trying to determine if you'd be a good fit for the company, and you're trying to determine if the company would be a good fit for you. Too many people take jobs only to find out within the first few months that the company and its people aren't a good fit for them.

Before the interview, get the name(s) of the person or people you'll meet with. Learn all you can about them. (The Internet and social networks are good places to start.) Below are some questions you may ask.

 Mention the name of the company throughout the interview, rather than saying *the company* or *your company*.

Ask about the company.
- What are the core values of [company]?
- Do you perceive that [company's] actions are consistent with these values?
- What are some of the challenges [company] faces? (This gives you an opening to share how you may have solved similar problems in another environment.)
- How do you plan to meet those challenges?
- What are [company's] goals for the next year?
- What gives [company] the edge over the competition?

Ask about the interviewer.
- What is your approach to solving problems?
- Have people who work for you ever told you that you're wrong? (If you ask that, do it lightly and with a smile.)
- Have you been able to balance your life outside the company while still growing your career?
- What is your management style?

Ask about your position.
- What are the keys to being successful in this position?
- Is this a newly created position? If not, what did the former person go on to do?
- How much travel may I expect?

- What are the prospects for advancement and professional growth?
- Can you tell me about the people I'd be working with?
- Will you or someone else in the company mentor me?

Ask in closing . . .
- When may I expect to hear from you?
- If I do get the offer, when would you like me to start?
- Would you like a list of references? (Have about three references you can hand the interviewer, just in case.)

 At the end of the interview, the interviewer may ask, *Do you have any questions?* An appropriate answer may be, *What about my background would make me a strong candidate for this position?* This forces the interviewer to recap your strengths. Then, before you get up, hesitate for a moment and ask, *Is there anything else I could have told you to help you make the decision to hire me?* If at the end of the interview the interviewer doesn't ask if you have any questions, turn around briefly before you leave the interviewer's office and ask the two questions suggested above.

All candidates need stories.

What do political candidates and job candidates have in common? Everything. If you listen closely to any political campaign, the candidates go to great lengths to tell stories of challenges they overcame, problems they solved, passion for their commitments, and strategies for the future. They want people to vote for them because of their determination, enthusiasm, proven success, and can-do attitude. They try to prove they can get the job done and get it done right.

As a job candidate, tell stories of challenges you overcame, problems you solved, passion for your career, and strategies for helping the company in the future. You want a vote of confidence based on your determination, enthusiasm, proven success, and can-do attitude. Convince the interviewer you're the best person to get the job done and to get it done right.

Dealing with Difficult Issues

Following are a few "sticky wicket" issues you should prepare for.

Be attuned to illegal questions.

Occasionally an interviewer may pose a question that's illegal to ask. Often it's a misstep taken out of ignorance or innocence. If you want the job, don't be confrontational or hostile. Here are a few suggestions:

- Answer the question briefly if you're comfortable doing that.
- Politely say you're not comfortable answering the question.
- Skirt the question and go to another topic.
- Answer the intent of the question, which may be your best option. For example, if the interviewer asks if you're a legal US citizen (which is illegal to ask), you may say, *If you're asking if I'm legally authorized to work in the United States, the answer is "yes."*

Legal and illegal questions

Illegal	Legal
Age related	
• How old are you?	• Are you over 18?
• When is your birthday?	• Can you, after being hired, provide proof of age?
• In what year were you born?	
• In what year did you graduate from college/high school?	
Family status	
• Are you married?	• Travel is an important part of the job. Do you have any restrictions on your ability to travel?
• Do you have a permanent partner?	
• With whom do you live?	• Would you be willing to relocate, if necessary?
• Are you pregnant?	
• Do you expect to have a family? When?	• Do you have responsibilities or commitments that will prevent you from meeting specified work schedules?
• How many children will you have?	
• How many children do you have?	• Do you anticipate any absences from work on a regular basis? If so, please explain the circumstances.
• Do you have child-care arrangements?	
Nationality	
• Where were you born?	• Do you have any language abilities that would be helpful in doing this job?
• Are you a US citizen?	
• What's your native language?	• Are you legally authorized to work in the United States?
• What language did you speak when you were growing up?	
• Are you [any specific nationality or ethnicity]?	• What other languages do you speak? (if job related)

Illegal	Legal

Health

- Have you had any recent illnesses or operations?
- Do you have any preexisting health conditions?
- When was your last physical exam?
- How is your family's health?
- When did you lose your eyesight/leg/hearing, etc.?
- Do you have a drug or alcohol problem?
- Are you taking any prescription drugs?

- Could you lift a 50-lb weight and carry it more than 100 yards for this job?
- Are you able to perform the essential functions of this job with or without reasonable accommodations?
- Will you be able to carry out all job assignments necessary for this position in a safe manner?

Personal

- How tall are you?
- How much do you weigh?
- Have you ever filed for bankruptcy?
- What's your religious affiliation?
- Do you go to church?
- Are you in the National Guard?
- Have you ever been convicted of a [specific] crime? *(Unless it's related to the job. For example, a bank could object to hiring someone who had been convicted of embezzling.)*

Deal with salary issues strategically.

You may hear questions such as *What are your salary requirements? What are your salary requirements for the long and short term? What's the range of salary you would accept? What were you making at your last position?*

It's best if you can let the interviewer make an offer without locking yourself into a salary suggestion that may be too high or too low. If you're pressed for an answer, however, here are a few statements to consider:

- My requirements would be based on the position and the overall compensation package.
- I'd like to learn more about the position before discussing a specific salary.
- I'd be more comfortable not giving a specific dollar amount right now.
- I'd be interested in the range of [dollar amounts].

- Please make me the best offer you comfortably can.
- In my prior position I was making [dollars]. (Don't inflate the amount you earned.)
- While salary is important, I don't want it to stand in the way of a career with [company].
- Well, that depends on the scope and responsibilities of the position, and I need more time to get my arms around that.
- The quality of the company and the people I work with are more important than salary. (Say this only if you truly mean it.)

 If you're offered a salary that's less than what you'd hoped for but you want the job, be prepared to negotiate. Discuss a sign-on bonus, the ability to telecommute, more vacation time, and the like.

Handle questions about why you were furloughed from a position.

This is always tricky. If you handle this well, you'll come across as mature and responsible. It's important not to lie—although a former employer can't give out information that would prevent you from finding another job, word may get out. Here are some suggestions:

Before the Interview
- Mend fences with your former employer or company if possible.
- Talk to the former HR department or to an executive recruiting firm about how best to address the question.
- Line up former colleagues who can speak positively about you in case your former employer is a loose cannon.

During the Interview
- Never badmouth a former employer (or company), no matter how much of an ogre he may have been.
- Avoid blaming the situation on office politics or on incompatibility. A potential new employer could conclude that you're not easy to get along with and can't handle conflict.
- Discuss what you did while you were unemployed. For example, did you do volunteer work?
- Be ready with answers that may include any of the following:
    - My position was outsourced.
    - I highly respect my former boss, but we didn't work well together. I'm not sure why.
    - A new manager came in and replaced many of us with members of his old team.

- My skills weren't quite right for [company], but I believe they're a good fit for yours.
- I made it through several downsizings, but not the current one.
- On reflection, I realize I might have handled things differently. I learned a lot from that experience and am ready to move on.

Come to each interview armed with a few one- or two-minute stories about how you made or saved a company money, a major contribution you made to a team effort, a failure that occurred and how you overcame it. Also, collect business cards from everyone you speak with so you can send them thank-you notes.

Explain lapses in employment.

There are many reasons for lapses in employment—becoming a stay-at-home parent, taking care of ill family members, returning to school, and more. The key is to be honest and not make excuses. Even though you weren't employed, that doesn't mean you became a couch potato. Capitalize on the activities you were involved in that enhanced your skills.

- Did you volunteer?
- Were you involved in community activities?
- Did you have consulting engagements?
- Did you earn a degree or certificate?
- Did you stay involved in professional associations?

Discuss how you kept current with changes in your industry. Draw the interviewer's attention to the strengths you gained during this period, and downplay the lapse.

 Don't attempt to explain these lapses in your resume. If you're asked at the interview, that's the time to discuss them.

Focus on positives if you job-hopped.

Consider preparing a functional resume to focus on what you've done, and downplay lapses in your employment history. In some fields (information technology, project management, consulting, and the like), short periods of employment are commonplace because people look for new challenges. Anticipate questions in advance and be prepared with answers, so you don't appear hesitant or fidgety.

- Prepare a strong list of accomplishments.
- Bring written recommendations from previous employers.

- Discuss your long-term commitment to volunteer work for specific organizations.
- Omit from your resume some of the short-term experiences you've had. (Remember that a resume is a marketing piece, as opposed to a job application, which is a legal document.)

Provide a list of references.

The people on your reference list are members of your team. Select them carefully and include those who can say positive things about you and your work. Ask your references what they'd say if called, and coach them if necessary. Remind them of times you worked late to finish certain projects, times you went beyond the call of duty, things you excelled at, your accomplishments, and more. Make sure to give each one a copy of your resume, so they're in sync.

Bring to the interview a list of five references and include phone numbers, email addresses, and the persons' relationship to you. (Many people ask for three, but not everyone is easy to reach.) Never give people's names without first asking their permission. If anyone has any reservations about recommending you, cross him off the list.

As much as you want to manage your reference list, savvy interviewers may ask people on your list for secondary references. For example, if you list your past supervisor, the interviewer may ask the supervisor for the name of one or two peers. So give the names of references who will speak highly of you and can refer other colleagues who will do the same.

Other things to consider:

- If the interviewer asks if he may contact your present employer, the answer should be *No*, unless your employer knows you're in the job market.
- Don't list references on your resume, because no company will check references until they've met you and determined you're a strong candidate.

Checking References

Hires that don't work out cost businesses hundreds of thousands of dollars every year. Checking references is one more way to satisfy yourself that the candidate you select is the right one.

As the potential employer

Ask basic questions.

Here are some basic questions to consider:

- Would you please verify dates of employment?
- What was [name's] starting and ending salary?
- Did that include bonuses/overtime?
- What was [name's] job title?
- What responsibilities went along with that job?
- Was [name] promoted while working at your company?
- What was [name's] reason for leaving?
- Where did [name] work prior to joining your company?
- Is there anything I haven't asked that you think will help me make my decision?

Ask probing questions.

Probing questions go deeper into understanding how the candidate fits into your environment.

- How does [name] compare with his replacement?
- On average, how often was [name] absent from (or late for) work?
- When there were urgent assignments, what steps did [name] take to step up to the plate?
- What was [name's] biggest accomplishment?
- Can you describe [name's] experience as a team member?
- How does [name] perform under stress?
- Since no one is perfect, how would you describe [name's] shortcomings?
- Please describe [name's] oral and written communication skills.
- Did [name] get along with management, peers, and subordinates?
- Would you rehire [name] if the opportunity presented itself?
- If I describe the position we're looking to fill, would you describe how good a fit [name] would be?
- Tell me of a time [name] worked with staff from multiple generations.

And there's more.

- Be alert for red flags. If a referral is evasive or doesn't return your call (after you've left several messages), that may be a clue that he's trying to hide something.
- Will this candidate go into people's homes? Will he have contact with children? Will he be trusted with large sums of money? Other sensitive issues? If so, consider engaging a credit-checking agency that can give you the lowdown on the candidate.
- Go on the social networking sites. If you see the candidate dancing on the table with a lampshade on his head, is that someone you'd want to hire?
- If you're hiring a high-level employee, check the references yourself

rather than delegating the task to a reference-checking company, human resources, or someone else. It's in your best interest to get the information directly from the horse's mouth, as the cliché goes.

Get secondary references.

Of course, candidates will give references who have positive things to say. A savvy interviewer will ask for secondary references. Ask, *Would you please give me the name(s) of (managers, peers, subordinates) I may speak with?* Or, if the candidate is applying for a high-level position, ask to speak with your counterpart at that organization. One company president is likely to speak candidly to another company president. Then ask that secondary reference many of the same questions you asked the primary reference.

More to think about:

- Conduct the questioning over the phone, rather than through email. You get inflections, hesitations, and other key indicators from the voice. You also avoid any "traceable" details the person may be reluctant to put in writing.
- Check the social networking sites to learn of people you may know who worked at the candidate's past companies.

As the candidate

Name only people you are sure will speak well of you. (If in doubt, leave them out.) Coach your references. You can't control what someone will say about you, but you can review some basic questions to ensure that the answers match your expectations about their opinions of your abilities, history, and ethics.

Older Workers Interviewing Gen Xers and Gen Yers

Job search strategies have changed. While many traditionalists and baby boomers once relied on word of mouth, search firms, or the newspaper as the main vehicles for job searches, Generations X and Y rely on online social networks, online job sites, members-only postings for trade associations, and sites such as craigslist.org. Companies need to adapt their recruitment strategies and their interview questions accordingly. Following are some commonly asked questions from both sides of the desk.

Questions interviewers may ask:

- What qualities do you think are necessary for this position?
- Where do you see yourself five years from now?
- When you have a dilemma, how do you approach it?

- How do you spend your free time?
- Describe what an outstanding job would be.
- Describe your ideal work/life balance.
- After I hire you, what steps will you take to advance from this position?
- Do you believe the concept of "paying your dues" is archaic?

Questions interviewees may ask:

- May I work from home?
- How high-tech are you?
- Will I advance within the next six months?
- What benefits do you offer?
- Will I be able to travel outside the country for this position?
- How diverse is your company?
- May I bring my dog to work?
- May I wear flip-flops?
- Why? Why? Why?

 Questions interviewees ask change with economic conditions. For example, during difficult employment periods, candidates won't be very interested in whether they can wear flip-flops or bring their dog to work. They'll be happy to get a job offer. And that goes for candidates of all generations.

Types of Interviews

Prepare for the following types of interviews as you would for the first interview. Dress properly, anticipate what questions you'll be asked, know what questions you will ask, and think about how to respond to difficult situations. The specific types of interviews you may encounter are discussed below.

Plan for a second interview.

The phone rings; it's great news. You wowed them at the first interview, now you're being invited back. This interview may last longer, as the prospective employer wants to make sure you work and play well with others. You may meet with your potential manager, coworkers, and other staff members. Here are some things to remember:

Dos
- Relax. It went well the first time.
- The guidelines that applied to the first interview apply to this one as well.

- Be alert for clues that get to the heart of what the company's looking for and the problems you'd be expected to handle.
- Observe the work environment to determine whether this is for you. Is it frantic, boring, calm, or stimulating?
- Before you leave, ask about the next step in the process and/or when they plan to make a decision.
- Ask for the job.

Taboos
- If you get an offer, don't answer immediately. Ask for time to consider the offer. (If they want you, they'll wait.) Find out when they need an answer.
- Don't hesitate to talk with people in addition to those you're interviewing with.

Get ready for a phone interview.

Prepare for a phone interview as you would a face-to-face interview. Employers often conduct an initial phone interview as a way of screening candidates. Leading candidates are called in once the pool is narrowed. If you're called without prior warning, ask if you can schedule the call. This will give you time to mentally prepare. You may say, *I'm very anxious to speak to you, but I was just walking out the door. I'd like to schedule a time that would work for us both. What would you suggest?*

Following are a few suggestions to make your phone interview successful:

Before
- Make sure you have a strong phone connection. Don't use a cell phone that can fade in and out.
- Turn off call waiting.
- Conduct the interview in a quiet space, away from kids, pets, and other noises or distractions.
- Have a glass of water nearby to keep your throat from drying.
- Put on professional attire. Even though the interviewer can't see you, the more professional you feel, the more professional you'll sound.

During
- Stand up during the interview, because you'll have more power in your voice.
- Smile, because the interviewer will be able to "hear" a smile in your voice.
- Don't smoke, chew gum, or munch on anything.
- Keep a pen and paper handy for taking notes.

- Speak slowly and enunciate clearly.
- Give verbal feedback such as *I see, I understand.*
- Ask for clarification when needed.
- Inquire about the next step. (Remember, the main purpose of this call is to get a face-to-face interview.)

After
- Keep a log of the issues covered and those you feel went well.
- Send a typewritten or handwritten thank-you note.

Set up a cheat sheet

In addition to having your resume handy, set up a cheat sheet with information you can see at a glance. Here's an example:

Experiences relevant to position

1.

2.

3.

Education: Training, courses, apprenticeships, or internships

1.

2.

3.

Core competencies

1.

2.

3.

Questions you want to ask the interviewer

1.

2.

3.

End by thanking the interviewer.

Prepare for an interview over a meal.

If you're invited to a meal, perhaps the potential employer wants to check your demeanor or see how you function under pressure. Unless you have abominable table manners, this type of interview can be more relaxing, because you're not sitting in the employer's office. However, it's just as important. So, brush up on your dining etiquette.

Dos

- Turn off your cell phone.
- Consider having a snack before the meal, so you won't be ravenously hungry. You don't want to have your mouth constantly full of food.
- Be familiar with the basic table set-up. Beverage glasses will be on your right, and food that's not part of your main plate (such as your bread plate) will be on your left.
- Order sensibly.
  - Ask the host what he's ordering to get a sense of the price range to consider.
  - If you like what the interviewer is ordering, say, *That sounds good. I'll have the same thing.*
  - Order food you can cut into bite-size pieces.
  - Be decisive when ordering, otherwise you give the impression that you can't make decisions.
- As soon as everyone is seated, put your napkin in your lap.
- Chew and swallow before you speak so you don't spew airborne particles.
- If the interviewer orders coffee, tea, and/or dessert, do the same. Otherwise, don't.
- Say *Thank you for the meal.*
- Expect the interviewer to pay.
- Send a typewritten or handwritten thank-you note.

 Remember what you learned growing up . . . keep your elbows off the table, sit up straight, and don't talk with your mouth full!

Taboos

- Messy foods such as spaghetti, lobster, ribs, saucy items, hamburgers, and the like.
- Crunchy foods such as potato chips or celery.
- Food that can get stuck in your teeth.(Just in case, carry dental floss and excuse yourself to go to the restroom if you think you have something stuck in your teeth, such as spinach from your salad.)

- Alcohol, even if the interviewer orders some.
- Garlic and onions.
- The most expensive item on the menu.
- Criticizing the meal or the restaurant.
- Asking for a doggy bag.

Be organized and focused for a panel interview.

A panel interview is where two or more people take turns asking you questions. This lets them assess how you interact with different people under pressure. (Some people refer to this as a committee interview, tag-team interview, or firing squad.) Consider the pros and cons of a panel interview. For you, it may be more stressful because there are several people asking questions. On the other hand, this type of interview gives you a chance to evaluate the group dynamics. With a bit of preparation, this can be a positive experience for you.

Before

- Find out in advance the names and job titles of each person who will be in attendance.
- Study the description of the job for which you are applying, and know how your skills match.

During

- Engage with each interviewer by making eye contact, shaking hands firmly, and mentioning their names. (Don't rush through this process, or you give the impression of being nervous.)
- Ask each person for a business card.
- Take out a piece of paper and ask if they mind if you take notes. The first thing to do is write down each person's name in the order in which they're seated.
- Size up each person's agenda. For example, the needs of operations and of marketing will be different, so try to prepare answers that will resonate with each.
- Cross-reference a question that's been asked by a different panel member. For example: *I'd like to expand on my answer to Jim. My experience in operations includes. . . .* This reinforces the positive answers you've already given.
- Respond to the person asking the question, but acknowledge the others with a comfortable level of eye contact.
- Use interviewers' names throughout. *[Name], my strong background in [area] will enable me to. . . .*
- When you finish your answer, focus your attention on the person who

asked the question.

- At the end of the interview, shake each person's hand and mention each one's name.

After

Send separate typewritten or handwritten thank-you notes to each member of the panel.

Prepare well for a behavioral interview.

While you're sitting in the waiting room, you won't know what type of interview to expect. If you're applying for a high-level position, a behavioral interview may be a possibility. In this type of interview, the interviewer hopes to learn how you acted and reacted in specific situations during past employment. The premise is that past performance will determine future performance.

Be prepared to discuss one or two difficult situations, the tasks that you needed to do (or supervise), the actions you (and your team) took, and the results. You'll be asked probing, straightforward questions that may include the following:

- What major problems or challenges did you face at [prior company]? How did you handle them? How successful were you?
- Have you ever had to motivate teams to work on projects they weren't thrilled about? How did you do it? How successful were you?
- What was a typical work week like?
- How do you deal with difficult subordinates, peers, or superiors?
- Describe an unpopular decision you made and how you implemented it.
- Tell me about how you worked effectively under pressure.

Do some research for an informational interview.

You can gain knowledge of a company or industry by talking to people employed in that field. This is a low-stress interview that allows you to make contacts in the field. Here are some benefits: You . . .

- Are asking for information, so you're in control of the interview.
- Gain confidence in talking with people while acquiring some valuable industry information.
- May become a job candidate.
- Build a network of people who can help you down the line.
- Gain valuable insights into your strengths and weaknesses during the interview.

Sending a letter requesting an informational interview

Gather a list of companies and people you want to meet. Then write a letter requesting a 20- to 30-minute informational interview.

- Make it clear your purpose is to gather information, not ask for a job.
- If you were referred by someone, mention that person's name.
- Don't enclose your resume, but mention your background in one or two sentences.
- Mention in the letter that you'll follow up with a phone call. (And don't forget to make that call.)

Here's a sample letter:

Dear [name]:

I'll be graduating from [college or university] in June with a major in [major]. My passion is to become a [profession] such as you are. You and your company have an excellent reputation, and I'd welcome the chance to meet with you to learn how to become successful in this field.

Would you be willing to meet with me for 20 to 30 minutes for an informational interview? I'll call you the week of [date] to see when would be a mutually convenient time to meet. Thank you for considering my request, and I look forward to meeting you.

Sincerely,

Doing your homework

Get names and companies from friends, relatives, college placement offices, and colleagues. Learn all you can about the company and the person you want to interview. Check the Internet and social networking sites. The more you learn, the more confidence you'll have, and the more valuable the interview will be.

Compiling a list of questions

The following are just a few questions that serve as guidelines. Your questions should reflect your interest in the person you're interviewing, the company, and the industry.

- How did you get started in [industry]?
- What are the key characteristics to being successful in [industry]?
- How does this job influence your lifestyle?
- What skills, degrees, or certifications would be of value?
- What are important buzz words to include in my resume and cover letter?
- Can you suggest some related occupations?

- What types of technologies are you using?
- Can you predict the future need for employees in [industry]?
- Can you suggest reading materials or professional associations that can give me further insights into [industry]?
- Is there anyone else you could suggest I might meet with at your company or another?

Evaluating the interview

What did you learn? What do you still need to know? How does [industry] fit your interests and lifestyle? What plan of action will you formulate?

Sending a thank-you note

After the interview, send a handwritten note to the person you met with, thanking him for his time. Mention that you'll keep him informed of your progress. If you were referred by someone, send that person a thank-you note as well.

Need additional help?
- For help preparing your resume, go to www.pongaresume.com.
- For interview savvy, go to www.interviewmastery.com.

If Michelangelo wasted as much time in meetings as most business executives today, he would have never found time to take on the Sistine Chapel job. They would have given it to that da Vinci fellow.

—John Cleese

Conducting and Participating in Business Meetings

In this chapter

- The Proof Is in the Planning
- Put on Your Meeting Strategist's Hat
- Selecting an Ideal Speaker
- Virtual Meetings
- Multilingual meetings
- Multigenerational considerations

Americans suffer from a rare condition called *meetingitis*. Do you have any idea how many meetings are held in the United States each day? Exclusive of seminars and educational conferences, I've heard numbers ranging from 750,000 to over 12 million. Meetings are either very productive or are marathon sessions that leave you with an empty head and a full bladder.

When one is necessary, though, a well-planned and well-conducted meeting can be magic. It can bring out the best in us—the best ideas and the best decisions. With the following guidelines, you can conduct action-oriented meetings that are so meaningful that participants will be energized rather than checking their email or mentally packing for a vacation to Hawaii.

The Proof Is in the Planning

We've all attended chaotic meetings that may have been planned by the Mad Hatter from *Alice in Wonderland*. He's the character who spoke utter nonsense and had no clear purpose. The March Hare was ill-mannered, and the Dormouse was so bored he snoozed. Many of us have seen characters just like this in modern-day business meetings.

Meet only when necessary.

Never call a meeting merely because you haven't called one in a while or because you feel compelled to assemble people each week. It's a waste of everyone's time and costs the company money. Just think of the salaries of the participants and how much work isn't getting done because they're at your meeting.

Before you call a meeting, ask yourself these questions: Is the meeting really necessary? If so, do you need to meet face to face? Can the information be communicated via email, phone, memo, virtual meeting, video-conference, or phone conference? People typically hold meetings for any or all of the following reasons:

- Analyze or solve a problem
- Brainstorm
- Communicate essential information
- Demonstrate something
- Ensure that everyone has the same understanding of a situation
- Gain support or acceptance of an idea, program, or decision
- Reach a decision in which group judgment is required
- Foster team spirit
- Reconcile clashing viewpoints or ideas

Treat the agenda as your blueprint for success.

George J. Lumsden, former manager of sales and training at Chrysler Corporation, said, *We don't prepare food without recipes or build houses without blueprints. Why should we expect meetings to be successful without plans?* Your agenda is the blueprint of the meeting. Without it, the meeting lacks order and may never accomplish its purpose. Give attendees clear objectives before the meeting time and at the start of the meeting itself.

Put on Your Meeting Strategist's Hat

Business meetings (whether formal or informal, inside or outside the office, live or virtual) are one area where proper etiquette can enhance your career. Comfort, trust, attentiveness, and clear communication are just a few ways to demonstrate good etiquette. The linchpins of all successful meetings are good manners, courtesy, and consideration.

Manage the before, during, and after of a meeting.

Before the meeting

- **Schedule your meetings at appropriate times.** You know what's appropriate for your group, your organization, your clients, and the like. For example, if your group has flextime, arrange an important meeting during the hours everyone is in the office.

- **Pick a suitable place.** Don't try to squeeze 15 people into a room the size of a closet.

- **Prepare a realistic agenda and distribute it in advance of the meeting.** List the date, time, place, purpose, participants, roles, pending decisions, how people can prepare, and whatever else is relevant.

- **Take multigenerational differences into consideration.** Learn more about this later in the chapter.

During the meeting

- **Make sure your meetings start on time.** Even the laggers will be there on time when you have a reputation for starting on the dot.

- **If the meeting is small or informal, make sure people know each other.** Start with a roll call, or ask participants to introduce themselves.

- **Create an inclusive environment.** Set ground rules at the outset of the meeting to make sure everyone will feel comfortable speaking up without fear of mockery, condemnation, or reprisals.

- **Minimize distractions.** Shuffling papers, side conversations, text messaging, ringing cell phones, and the like are distracting.

- **Stick to the agenda.** No matter how interesting a diversion may be, stick to the agenda. If the group veers too much, bring it back to focus. If issues arise that aren't on the agenda, "park" them. If time allows, you can address them at the end of the meeting. If time doesn't allow, discuss how best to handle those items.

- **Follow parliamentary procedure.** If this is a formal meeting, parliamentary procedure should dictate the process for making motions, seconding motions, voting, and more.

- **Involve people in the group.** Even if you're doing a presentation, make it interactive.

- **Create a plan of action.** What are the outcomes? Who has to do what as a result of the meeting?

- **End on time.** It's important for people to be able to leave on time so they can keep to their schedules for the rest of their day.

Here are a few things to keep in mind:

- According to Toastmasters, at a formal meeting you should not clap until the speaker being introduced has shaken the hand of the person making the introduction.
- As a participant, never interrupt anyone, even if you disagree strongly. Make a note of what's been said and return to it later. When you speak, make sure you're brief and make a relevant contribution.
- End the meeting once you complete all the items on the agenda. There's no reason to "fill time" if the one-hour meeting you had planned takes only 45 minutes.

Manage Conflict

When a conflict arises, it's up to the meeting leader to promote positive conflict while avoiding personal attacks.

Tips for Promoting Positive Conflict
- *Create a safe, open environment.*
- *Encourage all participants to speak up.*
- *Use decision devices such as pros and cons, evaluation sheets, and grids.*
- *Set the ground rules and enforce them.*

Tips for Defusing Negative Conflict
- *Listen to views.*
- *Identify common goals.*
- *Build on agreements.*
- *Avoid placing blame.*
- *Depersonalize through your own words.*
- *Look for a win-win outcome.*
- *Communicate respect.*
- *Use a positive tone.*
- *If conflict persists, take the issue off-line.*
- *Maintain zero tolerance for personal attacks.*

Permission from Suzanne Bates, President and CEO of Bates Communications, and author of Speak Like a CEO *and* Motivate Like a CEO. *Learn more at www.bates-communications.com.*

After the meeting
- Distribute the meeting notes as quickly as possible.
- If there's a speaker, always extend a warm thank-you.

I agreed to give a lunchtime talk to a group of HR professionals. When I arrived, I was told my 30-minute talk would be cut to 15 minutes due to a schedule change. Okay. Then the woman in charge (I'll call her Paula, to protect the guilty) introduced me as follows: *I'd like to introduce today's speaker, Sheryl Lindsell-Roberts.* As she was about to sit down, someone from the audience called out, *I didn't know we were having a speaker.* Paula casually said, *Oh, I forgot to put that in the invitation. . . . Okay, Sheryl, you can start now.* When I finished, Paula got up and was on to the next item without a thank-you or any acknowledgement that I had just made a presentation. What was wrong with that picture? Here's what:

- When you send out invitations, include a brief write-up about the speaker and the topic.
- When you introduce a speaker, always include some brief tidbits about the person's background/business.
- At the conclusion, always thank the speaker and end with some closing words such as *Thanks, [name]. We were delighted to have you share [topic], and I'm sure we'll all go back to our offices with tips we can implement immediately.*
- Additionally, send a handwritten thank-you note.

Facilitate good conversation.

It's important for everyone to be involved and not to have one or more people filibustering. It's okay to interrupt someone who's monopolizing the conversation. You may say, *In order to finish on time, we'll need to stick to the agenda* or *Perhaps we can discuss this offline.* It's not okay, however, to interrupt someone in order to redirect the conversation to yourself. It's just as important to be a good listener as it is to be a good talker.

Stay on track, but be willing to be derailed slightly. That's called flexibility. Some of the best ideas come from all-over-the-place conversations. If the conversation shifts to a topic not on the agenda, politely ask the group if they've completed discussing the prior issue. If they have, continue along the path.

Deal tactfully with disrupters.

Some people bring their own agendas to meetings. Sometimes they pose questions to undermine, stump, or embarrass the speaker or other attendees. To maintain the confidence of others in the room, maintain your composure, be courteous, don't argue, be honest, and deflect the question. Merely say, *I believe that question takes us off track, but I'd be happy to discuss it with you offline,* or *That's straying from today's agenda. Perhaps we could cover it at the next meeting.* This maintains your credibility and shows others you're in control of the meeting.

We all know who these disrupters are. They hog the floor, interrupt others, discuss off-topic issues, and respond sarcastically to other people's thoughts or ideas. Here are some ways to calm the savage beast:

- Prior to the meeting, line them up as allies and give them roles to play at the meeting. They can write on flip charts, take notes, or whatever. The key is to make them feel important; that's what they're looking for.
- During the meeting, agree on what is and isn't acceptable. If someone makes a comment that's inappropriate, merely say, *[Name], please don't get personal. Confine your comments to the issue at hand.*

Think on your feet.

Always be ready for the unexpected. You never know whether you'll lose electricity, there will be a fire drill, your equipment will fail to work, outside noises will drown you out, or whatever. Murphy's Law has a way of pouncing on us all. You must always think on your feet and make the most of any unexpected situation.

 I was doing a two-hour workshop at a large military base when we had an impromptu evacuation drill. There was no time to gather any materials, and thousands of people were ushered to a large building. I gathered my group, found a corner, and used that time for questions and answers.

Dress appropriately.

Before you dive into your closet looking for just the right thing to wear, ask yourself a few questions:

Who will be at the meeting?
- When you meet with people from your own company, you know the culture.
- When you meet with people from outside your company, understand the culture and dress in their style. For example, young high-tech executives rarely show up in pinstriped suits.
- If you don't know the culture, err on the side of dressing up.

What is the meeting about? or **Why** are you meeting?
- Are you trying to get someone's business? Dress up.
- Are you being pursued? Dress as the pursuer.
- Are you out to impress, or to put someone at ease?

When is the meeting?
- If it's a breakfast meeting, you'll probably go straight to work and should dress accordingly.

- If it's an after-hours meeting, you can either wear your business attire or bring a change. It may mean changing only a blouse or shirt.

Where is the meeting?

- Are you going to a ball game or a fancy restaurant? There's a big difference in how you dress.
- Are you meeting at a client's office? If so, dress appropriately for the culture of the client. If you don't know it, dress up.

How can you prepare?

- Is there anything you need to prepare for the meeting? For example, if you need to set up, perhaps you'll need to change your clothes.
- Are there arrangements you need to make for transportation? If you're flying, do you want to fly in your business suit, or should you change when you arrive?

Plan for last-minute meetings.

No, that statement isn't an oxymoron. If you've ever found yourself scrambling to organize a last-minute meeting, you know how overwhelming this can be. Here are some tips to help you be prepared on short notice.

- **Have a list of basic questions ready to go.** Purpose? Date? Time? Place? Agenda? Attendees? Equipment? Budget?
- **Develop lists of resources with names, emails, and phone numbers.** This is the dream team you can call in a hurry.
- **Consider Plan B.** If something goes awry at the last minute, what's your backup plan?
- **Laugh and keep your sense of humor.** You'll have a much saner perspective on life, because laughter is a great survival technique. Studies show that laughter reduces stress and lowers blood pressure.

Meal Meetings

Conducting business over breakfast, lunch, or dinner is an effective way to build relationships, hold interviews, make a sale, or seal a deal. Even though meeting in a restaurant may appear more casual than meeting in someone's office, it's still a business meeting. Here are a few basic guidelines:

- *Find a restaurant that lends itself to conversation, one that's not too noisy.*
- *Give your guest the most desirable seat—the one with the good view.*
- *Keep the initial conversation pleasant and free of controversy.*
- *Don't talk with food in your mouth.*
- *Chew with your mouth closed.*

- *Never smoke, and limit your alcohol intake.*
- *Avoid finger foods or messy food (such as spaghetti).*
- *If you don't know the other person(s) well, engage in small talk before talking business. (It's the host's responsibility to start the business part of the meeting.)*
- *The host should give her credit card to the maitre d' or waitperson.*

Selecting the Ideal Speaker

Are you overwhelmed by the plethora of speakers out there and want to make sure you don't hire a dud? You want a speaker with entertainment quality, knowledge of the topic, a good education, and motivation. Check chambers of commerce, convention and visitors' bureaus, the Internet, industry colleagues, speakers' bureaus, and friends.

- **Know what your audience needs.** Today's workforce is younger and more diverse. They want content, they want to learn, they want to have fun, and they want take-away value.

- **Check for reputation.** Avoid speakers who claim to be all things to all people. Many have glitzy marketing materials, but are desperate for work. What experience does the speaker have? How familiar is the speaker with the industry? Who can the speaker provide as references?

- **Look for certifications.** Although association membership is no assurance of great platform skills, look for certifications such as Certified Speaking Professional (CSP), Council of Peers Award for Excellence (CPAE), or National Speakers Association (NSA) to offer some level of professionalism.

- **Test drive.** You wouldn't buy a car before taking a test drive, so don't hire a speaker without doing so. Either attend an event where you can see the speaker live, or ask for a video or audiotape of a previous presentation recorded before a live audience. Notice the rapport the speaker builds with the audience.

- **Trust your instincts.** You'll have an initial reaction—I like / don't like this person, or I feel comfortable / uncomfortable working with this person.

 Check out chapter 1, "Making Introductions," for tips on introducing a guest speaker.

Virtual Meetings

Virtual meetings are a great way to assemble groups from around the corner or around the world. They're less expensive than face-to-face meetings, take less time, and allow people to communicate less formally. There are some rules of etiquette, whether you're teleconferencing, videoconferencing, or web conferencing.

- **Make introductions.** Make sure everyone is introduced to each other. If it's a phone conference and people can't see you, state your name before you speak. *This is Bob. I'd like to mention....* (Don't interrupt someone; wait until the speaker has finished.)

- **Keep meetings focused by sticking to the agenda.** Start the conference on time, regardless of who's present. It's just as inconsiderate to arrive late for a teleconference call as it is to walk in late to a meeting. Honor the time of those who are on time.

- **Listen carefully.** Although you are not all gathered in the same room, you should still pay attention. People can hear you rustling papers over the phone, and they can see you in a videoconference or web conference.

Teleconferences

A successful teleconference (conference call) starts by treating everyone as if this were a face-to-face meeting. Be on time, be prepared, pay attention, and participate. However, you must be comfortable knowing that you'll be talking with a group that gives you no visual cues or feedback. Here are some guidelines to help you:

Apply these tips when you're the moderator.

Send out advance invitations that include the purpose of the call, dial-in number, PIN, name of the moderator, start and end times, participants, agenda topics. Try to limit the number of participants to 10; more than that is unmanageable on the phone.

- Test the teleconferencing equipment several days before the actual meeting.
- Conduct a few trial runs with the other locations to ensure that everything is working well and audibility is good.
- Arrive a few minutes early so you can greet each participant. Note when everyone is "present" so you can start the meeting.
- Ask people to introduce themselves so others can hear their voices.

- Discuss agenda items that you sent prior to the meeting.
- Make sure people stick to the agenda. Keep people on course by being polite but firm.
- Close the meeting by thanking participants for their time.
- If a follow-up call is needed, get a consensus on date and time.
- Conduct a roll call at the end to allow for latecomers.
- State very clearly when the call has ended by summarizing highlights, action items, and follow-up items.

Apply these tips when you're a participant.

- Use a phone in a quiet room where there will be no background noise. You don't want people to hear your barking dog or crying child. This gives the impression that you're sitting there in your pajamas waiting for the call to end.
- Read the agenda beforehand and be prepared to participate actively.
- Say your name before you speak, even if you think everyone will recognize your voice. Begin with, *This is Marty,* and then speak. When you pick up the conversation again, repeat, *This is Marty again.*
- Come to the call with all relevant documents you need.
- Listen carefully to what others are saying.
- Participate without interrupting.
- Stay on topic, and stick to the agenda and anticipated timeframe.
- Use the mute button when you're not speaking and when you're taking notes on the computer, coughing, sneezing, and the like.

Other things to consider:
- Don't sit in a leather chair. (When you move around, an embarrassing sound may be heard.)
- Don't shuffle papers, tap your pencil, chew gum, munch on chips, or anything else along those lines. The sound will be magnified and indicate that you're not fully engaged in the conversation.
- If you have call waiting, disconnect it.
- Don't breathe heavily into the mouthpiece.
- Avoid using speakerphones and cell phones when possible.
- Stay focused. It's easy to drift away or multitask. All too often we hear, *Can you please repeat the question; I wasn't paying attention.* It's unprofessional.

Videoconferencing

Videoconferencing is a great way to have "face time" and reduce travel budgets. Participating in a videoconference engages the same rules of meeting etiquette as an actual face-to-face meeting, so it's only common sense that you should treat participants as if they're in the same room.

Prepare the space to avoid facing the camera toward bright windows or bright lights. Remove unnecessary equipment such as computers, televisions, or anything that would draw attention from the people at the meeting. Also, have a contingency plan in case there are technical difficulties.

- Introduce all participants. If you don't know everyone, ask people to introduce themselves.
- Review items on the agenda (which the participants should already have) and remind everyone how important it is to stick to the agenda.
- Give participants instructions on what to do in the event of technical problems or disconnection.
- Urge participants to address each other by name when responding to questions or comments. This will avoid confusion during interactions.
- Build in time for participants to interact to create the feeling of a more traditional meeting.
- Plan a short break if the conference lasts more than 1½ hours.
- Be attuned to body language on both sides of the camera.
- At the end of the meeting, summarize the key points, reiterate any decisions, and review action items.
- Agree on the date and time for a follow-up conference if one is needed.

 Be sure that someone at each site is in control of the camera so the speaker will always be in view.

Apply these tips when you're participating in a meeting.

- Allow the current speaker to finish speaking before you start.
- When you start, begin by saying your name. *This is [name].* For multipoint conferences, this gives time for the camera to switch to the speaker.
- Speak in a normal tone, without yelling or whispering.
- If using a PowerPoint presentation or other visuals, don't focus on them for longer than necessary.
- Use a flipchart or whiteboard to capture information.
- Be aware of your body language. Tapping your pencil, swiveling your chair, drumming your fingers, and the like may convey anxiety or boredom. Also remember that people may be able to read your lips.
- Consider muting your audio when you are not speaking.

More to think about:

- Always assume the equipment is on and that you can be seen and/or heard. Many important people (including presidents of countries) have gotten into serious trouble when they made damaging comments thinking they were muted.

- Expect time delays. A weak video signal could cause a delay or echo, so expect lag time between when you speak and when your message reaches the other site. Wait for a response before you resume making new remarks.

- Don't wear very bright colors, stripes, plaids, or flashy jewelry.

- Use small gestures. Actions are amplified on videoconferences. Wild, sweeping movements can result in distorted, fuzzy images.

Web conferencing

Web conferencing is similar to videoconferencing, but it's easier and consumes less bandwidth. Participants sit at their own computers and are connected to other participants via the Internet. Web conferencing is a popular option for communication with employees, customers, prospects, etc. It's also great for seminars, training, presentations, press conferences, and the like. Web conferencing yields the effectiveness of a live meeting without the travel expense. Most of the tips for videoconferencing apply to web conferencing. Here are a few more:

- **Make the most of your time with your audience.** Know what you want to convey. Would the best method be slides, streaming video, whiteboarding, application sharing, or something else? Keep the visuals simple so they load quickly.

- **Keep the conference to less than an hour.** If you need more time, segment the conference. Otherwise you run the risk of your conference becoming tedious.

- **Set up more than one computer.** The person initiating the conference should be able to see everyone. This will let you see the formatting and presentation from the perspective of the participants.

There are many free conferencing services. A couple are: www.confreecall.com and www.freeconferencecall.com.

Multilingual Meetings

Business today is conducted globally, and although English is becoming the language of business, there may be times when you need to conduct a meeting for bilingual people or for people who don't speak English. Following are a few things to keep in mind.

Keep the language simple.

Address the lowest common denominator. Technical language generally isn't a problem, because people quickly learn the terms associated with their fields. The problem comes with idioms and common expressions people outside your realm may not recognize. Explain immediately any terms you think participants may not understand.

Engage a language services company.

A good language services company may be essential. The company can supply an interpreter and translate your written materials. Here's how to work with an interpreter:

- Prepare a script.
- Give the script to the interpreter well in advance of the talk.
- Follow the script to the letter.
- Remove your headphone and speak directly into the microphone.
- When speaking, address the audience, not the interpreter.
- Keep the talk unified for the audience by speaking in small chunks of information, giving the interpreter a better chance to be accurate.
- Remember that when you have an interpreter, this doubles the time the meeting takes.

Multigenerational Considerations

 The following is from an article I wrote with Nancy Settle-Murphy, principal of Guided Insights. Learn more at www.guidedinsights.com.

For the first time in the history of the workplace, organizations need to accommodate the contrasting communication styles of four distinct generations. Although they go by a variety of names, let's call them traditionalists (born between 1927 and 1945), boomers (born between 1946 and 1964), Gen Xers (born between 1965 and 1980), and Gen Yers (born in 1981 or later).

Most work teams consist of people representing at least two generations. Yet, when deciding how best to communicate across teams, we often employ a one-size-fits-all approach that may not work well for *anyone*, let alone *everyone*. And because so many managers are from the boomer generation, these channels typically mean "conventional" communication styles such as face-to-face meetings, phone conferences, email, and the like.

Regardless of their ages, many managers fail to take generational preferences and styles into account when mobilizing and motivating their teams. Instead, they develop team norms and operating principles that may run counter to what individual members might need or value. For example, a boomer manager may insist that all people work from a central office during typical working hours. However, many Gen Yers are most productive at 10 p.m., working from the comfort of home. Some Gen Xers, on the other hand, may need an afternoon off for family obligations, coming back online later in the evening. Instituting a rigid policy about work hours or locations may leave some team members feeling alienated, excluded, and ultimately not very productive.

There are many generalizations in these guidelines, and while each person must be treated as an individual, making some "best guesses" about communication styles and preferences is a great first step toward creating a team communications plan that works for most people on the team.

Rethink "normal" work hours.

Apart from some government offices and banks, the 9-to-5 business day has given way to more flexible work times and locations, with people working at all hours from multiple locations. For a team that works virtually, it's much harder to find an agreed-upon window for group meetings, whether face to face, phone, web conference, or videoconference.

A boomer manager may feel more comfortable when all team members meet face to face for the weekly 8 a.m. status meeting. But consider a Gen Xer who's caring for a family and needs to battle traffic for 90 minutes to get there. Or the Gen Yer who insists he or she is most productive from 11 a.m. to 11 p.m. Many traditionalists easing their way into retirement are also demanding more flexible work arrangements. Managers must consider the comfort level and preferences of all participants when deciding which team meetings really need to take place face to face and which can be done via telephone or over the web.

Share vital information.

When time is of the essence and you need to get critical information to team members, what's the best meeting option? It depends on a host of factors, including the likely preferences and habits of members representing different generations. Older generations tend to rely on email, phone, or face to face as the default, while many younger members may look to instant messaging, blogs, wikis, or phone texting as their primary means of giving and getting important information.

Consider multiple channels for information sharing, especially if you have people with strong preferences for different communication methods. At the same time, make sure you have an agreed-upon method for sharing urgent information, such as news likely to affect the work of the team or missed deliverables that will trip up others. Keep in mind that younger generations tend to be natural and eager collaborators, and often do so from a distance as a matter of routine.

Remember that there's no place like "home."

Create a team portal that's easy, quick, and intuitive for members of all generations to use. Younger generations expect and demand highly efficient websites where needed information takes just one or two clicks to find. Otherwise they may tune out quickly. Older generations may require a bit of prodding to regard the team portal as the place to go to share and view the latest and greatest information.

If people are slow to gravitate to your team portal, try pushing out emails that contain a sentence or two about what content can be found on the team site, and refrain from including the actual information in emails so they have more incentive to visit the portal. Constantly seek feedback from team members representing all generations as to how the team space can be made even more useful.

Understand generational differences in regard to instant gratification and patience.

Younger workers typically expect responses and information right *now*, as evidenced by the popularity of social networking sites (such as Twitter, Facebook, LinkedIn, and others) and the proliferation of text messaging and IM. Waiting a day or two to receive a return email or voice mail is a nonstarter. Older workers tend to expect a reply to take a little more time, and likewise may be slower to respond themselves, especially if they have to wade through a jammed inbox to reply.

Create agreed-upon norms for responsiveness to certain types of inquiries or issues, and then determine how best to use specific tools to get the job done. If one person insists on an IM or a blog update and another prefers an email, work together to agree on the best ways to meet as many needs as possible without extraordinary effort on anyone's part.

Be mindful of differences in expectations.

Older workers tend to prize consistency, predictability, accuracy, good grammar, and thoroughness in communications. Even the most creative ideas may be dismissed if such ideas crop up randomly, without context, and without a way to prioritize them. After all, if the ideas don't lead to something tangible, you've just lost a lot of time! Younger workers, on the other hand, are adept at brainstorming and collaborating with people who have shared interests, including total strangers—for the sheer joy of creating something new and fresh.

Social networks enable the type of spontaneous collaboration that may lead to great new ideas that may do nothing more than satisfy intellectual curiosity. Openness and creativity are especially valued by younger generations, while playing by prescribed rules of engagement is something their parents may be more comfortable with.

Ramp up and ramp down.

People from different generations have a lot to teach each other, if we create the right opportunities for knowledge transfer. Many younger people coming on board bring rich new perspectives, a keen appreciation of how best to apply the right technological tools, and a passion to learn. They embrace challenges with gusto and are devoid of the "this-is-the-way-we've-always-done-it" mindset. Older people, many of whom might be nearing retirement, have accumulated wisdom about the business, industry, and organization, and know what it takes to operate successfully within the enterprise.

Two-way mentoring programs, pairing a younger employee with a more senior counterpart, afford the opportunity for both to learn from each other. Agreeing on objectives, schedules, and viable processes for knowledge transfer will help ensure a mutually rewarding mentoring experience. The result: New people position themselves for success more quickly, and older workers can leave behind valuable knowledge as they take new skills and knowledge with them.

Develop high-performance multigenerational teams.

The bottom line is that organizations need to examine the most significant generational differences and determine how best to anticipate and address them within each work team. This will result in high-performing teams that consciously take advantage of generational differences instead of ignoring or dismissing them.

12

If you speak three languages, you're trilingual. If you speak two languages, you're bilingual. If you speak one language, you're American.

— Anonymous

Communicating Cross-Culturally

In this chapter

- Creating an Inclusive Business Environment
- Traveling Abroad

People once thought that if you just studied a foreign language, you could work, deal, entertain, and negotiate with colleagues from different cultures. It's not that easy. Cross-cultural communication can be a minefield if you're not prepared. Here are just a few examples:

- General Motors ran an ad with the slogan "Body by Fisher." In Flemish, it translated into "Corpse by Fisher."
- Chevrolet introduced the Nova, but in Spanish *No va* means "Doesn't go."
- Parker Pen wasn't able to advertise its famous "Jotter" pen because in some languages the translated word sounded like "jockstrap."
- Pepsi-Cola ran a "Come alive with Pepsi" campaign. The Taiwanese heard "Pepsi brings your ancestors back from the grave."

To prepare yourself for meaningful and clear cross-cultural communication, read books, take formal training, attend events where people of other cultures congregate, be patient with yourself, accept uncertainty, and read this chapter.

 When you're first beginning to interact with people from other cultures, notice the similarities, not just the differences. We all belong to the same species and are far more alike than we are different.

Creating an Inclusive Business Environment

The world continues to shrink and the world market continues to grow. This is rapidly changing the face of business. Businesses are very diverse in races, ethnicities, cultures, and generations. In the early 2000's, the majority of people in the United States were white. Many studies show that by approximately 2050, most people will be of Hispanic, Middle Eastern, Asian, and African descent. Successful cross-cultural communication is about making everyone feeling comfortable, welcome, and valued.

Focus your cultural eye.

You've successfully communicated across cultures when you minimize misunderstandings and maximize clarity. Poor cross-cultural communication often results in a loss of clients/customers, high staff turnover, internal conflicts, stress, poor working relations, misunderstandings, low productivity, and a lack of cooperation.

Check stereotypes at the door.

We all have preconceived ideas about people of different body types, ethnicities, genders, backgrounds, and more. Many of these were passed on by our families, and others were established based on people we've met along the way. *Always remember, you're meeting a person, not a stereotype.*

- Fill in the following blanks to help you understand some of the stereotypes you may be holding onto: "I've heard it said that _____ people are typically _____." Do you believe that? If so, on what do you base that belief? Whom have you met who isn't stereotypical?

- Ask yourself if anyone has ever said anything that wasn't true about your race, religion, body type, or anything else about you. If so, where do you think those people got their biases?

A nice attribute of the younger generations is that they tend not to stereotype. They don't notice or care as much about the differences between cultures or demographics. They're used to living in a global world and creating their own communities of interest—many through social networks and global travel that spans countries and cultures.

Establish one spoken language in the company.

A company today will probably employ people from a variety of countries. It's important to determine the primary language (in which all employees are conversant) that everyone will use. It's impolite for a few people to have a conversation that others don't understand. The language should be determined by the background of your employees and the nature of your business. For example, if you're a Chinese-owned company, your employees are all Chinese, and you deal exclusively with Chinese businesspeople, your dominant language would probably be Chinese.

Allow for cultural differences.

People from different cultures often have challenges in terms of language, values, business ethics, etiquette, business practices, and behavior. While these differences must be respected, the company has an obligation to manage communication so that everyone can work together productively and cohesively. Following are some ways to make people feel comfortable:

- **Enunciate clearly and slow your pace.** Even when English is the common language, enunciate clearly and slow your pace to ensure that everyone understands you. It's harder for people whose primary language isn't English, but it may still be difficult for native English speakers from other regions of the country.
  Example: I'm from New York City, and I developed a fast rate of speech. I was facilitating a workshop in the South (where people have a slower rate of speech). During the first break, I heard two participants say they thought I was very good, but I talked so fast they were having difficulty understanding me. I learned to slow down so people outside the New York City area can understand me. (No emails, please, from those who still can't.)

- **Avoid slang.** Although you should avoid slang in any business situation, foreigners will have an especially difficult time understanding slang, idioms, and the like. Of course, if you're in a group of peers, industry lingo would probably be inclusive.

- **Be careful with humor and jokes.** People in the Western part of the world often build rapport through humor, but this may not be universally appropriate. Many cultures don't appreciate humor and jokes, and see laughter in business as a sign of disrespect. Ethnic humor may be perceived as evidence of racial prejudice, even if you're a member of the subject group.
  Example: A colleague of mine who's Jewish told a joke about Jews while he was facilitating a seminar. Many people (Jews and non-Jews alike) took offense. It didn't matter that he told everyone he's Jewish; his joke was inappropriate and out of place.

- **Be clear with questions.** Don't end a meeting by asking, *Is this a good place to stop, or should we continue?* These two questions mentioned together may be difficult to understand.

- **Avoid words, images, qualifiers, and stereotypes that suggest that all or most members of a particular group are the same.** For example, don't make generalizations about someone's religion or ancestry.

- **Be mindful of politically neutral language.** Check out chapter 5, "Making Proper Word Choices," and chapter 6, "Using Politically Neutral Terms."

- **Be aware of body language.** You can always tell when people are comfortable by their body language. (Check out chapter 3, "Interpreting Body Language.")

- **Be aware that cultural differences exist within a race or nationality.** A variety of cultures can exist within a single race, language group, religion, or nationality. They can differ by age, gender, socioeconomic status, education, and exposure to other cultures. Think of cultures in the United States, for example. The South has a distinct culture, as does the Midwest, the Northeast, the West Coast, and any region I may have left out.

 If you have difficulty understanding someone with an accent, ask him to repeat what he has said, because what he's saying is important to you. That holds true for making sure you hear names correctly as well.

Traveling Abroad

Habla esperanto, monsieur? Wouldn't it be convenient if there was one language and you could use it anywhere in the world? In 1887, a Polish ophthalmologist and scholar named Ludwig Zamenhof invented Esperanto, a so-called "artificial language" because it was constructed by an individual for a specific purpose instead of evolving on its own. Esperanto was designed to facilitate communication among people of different cultures. Although more than two million people speak, read, and write Esperanto, it has never caught on as an international language.

Vive la différence.

Don't consider standards in the United States a guidepost by which you measure life elsewhere. And don't judge. Things are different elsewhere.

Different doesn't make them better or worse; they're just different. Enjoy the differences and think of them as a way to learn about a new and exciting culture. When you see Tibetan tribesmen greeting each other by sticking their tongues out or Latin Americans greeting each other with a firm hug (known as an *abrazo*), that's part of the culture and perfectly normal.

Much of the following will serve as guidelines. Customs differ from country to country, and people within those countries differ. For example, some people who have a lot of dealings with the United States may have adopted some U.S. customs; others may not have. Always do your homework before traveling abroad or hosting someone from abroad so you have an idea of what to expect.

 My husband had a group of people working for him in Japan. During a trip to Japan he was invited to the home of the project manager. The man's wife greeted my husband in a kimono, bowed at the door, and extended all the traditional Japanese customs. When the gentleman came to the United States, my husband reciprocated and invited him to our home for dinner. The gentleman spoke very little English, so there were lots of smiles, but little conversation. The evening went along well, and he seemed to enjoy the meal I had made. After the entrée, I went to the kitchen to get dessert. When I returned to the dining room, the man wasn't there and neither was my husband. Here's what happened: The man had abruptly gone to his car. My husband went out after him, but he drove away. We found out later, through an interpreter, that the man didn't know how to gracefully say goodbye, so he just left. True story.

Going to Europe

Some of these suggestions apply to traveling in any part of the world.

Serve as an ambassador.

When you travel outside the United States—whether you realize it or not— you're an ambassador. The image you create will affect how those you meet will view all Americans. Take the time to learn all you can about your host country. If you know nothing about the customs or language, you insult your hosts. The subtle message you communicate is that they aren't worth your taking the time to learn about them. To get information about a host country, speak with people who've been there, contact the country's embassy or consulate, get a travel guide, or tap into the Internet.

Learn some basic words.

When you learn a few key words in the language of the host country, you transform yourself from a stuttering, gesticulating gringo to a savvy traveler. Here are some common words and expressions to learn in the native tongue that will be helpful in social and business situations:

Please	Thank you
Good morning	Good day
Good evening	Excuse me
I'm sorry	Yes, I understand
No, I don't understand	Just a moment
Chairman	President
Vice President	Director

 I was at a lovely restaurant in Italy and a woman at the next table ordered fettuccine verde. When her order arrived, she complained bitterly to the waitperson because her fettuccine was green. (*Verde* means "green" in Italian.)

Lost in the translation

When you say something in a foreign language, be sure it translates properly. Following are some signs that were translated into English to accommodate Americans:

Bangkok dry cleaners: Please drop your trousers here for best results.
Acapulco hotel: The manager has personally passed all the water served here.
Budapest zoo: Please do not feed the animals. If you have any suitable food, give it to the guard on duty.
Paris elevator: Please leave your values at the front desk.
Paris boutique: Dresses for street walking.
Czech tourist agency: Take one of our horse-driven carriage tours. We guarantee no miscarriages.

Respect silence.

In Western cultures, 20 seconds of silence makes people feel uncomfortable, and people feel the need to say something. In other cultures, silence is to be expected before a response. It's a sign of thoughtfulness and deference to the original speaker.

Know the general dos.

The following tips may keep you from standing out like a tarantula on a piece of angel food cake.

- **Compliment your host.** Think about the beauty or accomplishments of the host country or city.

- **Become familiar with the dress code.** This applies to business and after-hours attire (formal, casual, or in-between).
- **Know the religious taboos,** if there are any.
- **Inform yourself about local customs.** Know the proper way to greet your hosts and make introductions.
- **Understand what gifts are considered appropriate.** If you're unsure, ask someone who's been to the country or someone from that country living in the United States.
- **Be aware of current events that surround the country or area, and be sympathetic to any problems.** But know what topics of conversation are appropriate.
- **Do some advance research.** Find out as much as you can about artistic, cultural, and sports figures.
- **Learn about the metric system if you need to.** The United States is among only three countries in the world that have not officially adopted the metric system.
- **Bring plenty of business cards.** Write your name, company, and address on the reverse side in the language of the host country. Offer the card with the native-language side showing.
- **Be cognizant of a person's personal space.** Some cultures foster physical closeness; others shun it. (Learn more in chapter 3, "Interpreting Body Language.")
- **Respect a country's monetary unit.** Their money is real money. On overseas trips, I've heard comments such as *What does this cost in real money? This is just like Monopoly money.* Not only are those comments rude, they make the people saying them sound like idiots.

Know the general taboos.

We've all heard of the Ugly American, and we have met many examples of the species. They're offensive, ill-mannered, and insensitive.

During a trip to Mexico, I was having dinner at a fine restaurant. I was enjoying the ambience, the strolling guitar players, and the wonderful food. Then, lo and behold, Ugly Americans reared their ugly heads at the next table. One was complaining about the slow service. Another loudly announced to the waiter that Mexican food tastes better in the United States. Perhaps these people should have stayed home and eaten at Taco Bell.

During another trip I took, this time to Russia (when it was the USSR), some Americans were making a scene because the street signs weren't bilingual (Russian and English). Where did these people think they were?

Following are blunders to avoid:

- **Gestures.** Know what gestures to avoid. For example, in many parts of the world, giving someone a thumbs-up or pointing your index finger is rude or obscene. (Learn more about gestures in chapter 3, "Interpreting Body Language.")
- **Conversation.** Avoid remarks that might be misinterpreted as social blunders. For example, if you're in Greece, you shouldn't tell your host that, in America, all the diners are owned by Greeks.
- **Profanity and racy stories.** Just don't.
- **Correcting language.** Unless you're asked to do so, don't correct a foreigner's English.
- **Photos.** Don't take people's pictures without their permission. (That holds true in the United States as well.)

Shake hands as you would in the United States.

Greetings in most European countries are similar to greetings in the United States—a handshake for greetings and departures. If you're unsure of protocol, observe those around you. Europeans tend to shake hands frequently, so be prepared to shake often.

 Don't call people by their first names unless you're invited to or you know them well.

Know what topics of conversation are appropriate.

Be sensitive about the topics you discuss. It's appropriate to talk about art, sports, the weather, and other topics that don't have historical or political implications. Although most Europeans are happy to talk among themselves about events that have blurred their borders, *you* must be careful. (It's like talking about your loved ones. *You* can say negative things about them, but no one else can dare!) Here are some additional tips:

- Don't ask business acquaintances about their families unless you know them well. Europeans tend to be private.
- Don't discuss money or the cost of living.
- When talking to someone (even casually), don't keep your hands in your pockets. Europeans may interpret this as a sign of disinterest.

Dress appropriately.

Most of the guidelines that apply in the United States hold true in Europe. However, some exceptions do exist. For example, in Europe, pantsuits aren't popular with women.

- If in doubt, dress conservatively.
- When dining at an elegant restaurant or attending the theater, women should wear skirts or dresses and men should wear business suits.
- At theaters, you might be expected to check your coat in the cloakroom rather than take it with you to your seat.
- For business meetings, men should wear suits and women should wear dresses.
- If you're at a beach resort on a business trip, wear conservative clothing. Women should avoid bikinis, and men should avoid Speedos.

Mind your table manners.

It's critical to display good table manners. In the United States, *you* are judged by your manners; abroad, *all Americans* are judged by your manners. Following are some things to keep in mind.

- Europeans hold their forks with the tines down and don't switch their knives and forks after cutting. If you want to eat like a European, hold your fork in your left hand and your knife in your right to cut your food. (Lefties do the opposite.) And don't switch to eat.
- Use your knife to push your food to the back of your fork, and hold your knife in your right hand, even when you're not using it. (Lefties do the opposite.)
- Keep your wrists on the table and don't put your hands in your lap.

Give gifts that are appropriate.

When it's appropriate to bring a gift, be sure it's appropriate. If you're unsure as to what to give, ask someone who's been to the country or someone from that country living in the United States. No matter what you select, wrap the gift nicely, because presentation is important. Also, buy something that isn't too costly, so it's not mistaken for a bribe. Following are some gift suggestions:

- Classical, jazz, or folk music (Stay away from rap.)
- Coffee-table book from the United States, your state, or your region
- Crystal, china, or porcelain
- Box of fine stationery
- Liquor (except in Muslim countries)

- Local handicraft or nonperishable food that typifies the United States or your area
- Pen and pencil set, with refills for the pen
- Something that reflects your colleague's special interest or hobby

Handle "nature" calls with class.

Leave at home any preconceived ideas about plumbing facilities. If you visit a major city and stay in a first-rate hotel, you probably will find business as usual. When you venture out, however, be prepared to either exercise camel-like staying power or set aside all cultural biases. Following are some of the experiences you may encounter:

- You won't necessarily find the words *restroom* or *bathroom*. Europeans do recognize *toilet*, *WC* (for water closet), or some equivalent in their native language. Also, you'll generally see iconic symbols of men and women.
- Be prepared to use unisex toilets. Men are often less intimidated by this than women.
- Always bring a roll of toilet paper. In some facilities outside major cities you won't find any paper; in others, you may find an attendant willing to sell you small sheets for pocket change.

Traveling in Asia

For many people, Asia conjures up images of *Madame Butterfly* or kung fu movies. Those images couldn't be further from reality. Asia is a distinct and remarkable part of the world, and each country is unique, with different customs, lifestyles, religious beliefs. Learn all you can about the country or countries you'll be visiting, and your trip will be more enjoyable.

Extend a proper greeting.

Unlike in Western cultures, where you normally greet the host and hostess first, in most Asian countries you first greet the oldest person in the room. Here are some things to remember in some of the popularly visited countries:

China and Hong Kong: Shake hands. (Older people may clasp their hands, shake them, and bow.)

India: Hold palms together at chin level and nod.

Japan: Bow and hold your head down. (Japanese businesspeople who are used to doing business with people from the United States shake hands.)

Korea: Bow slightly.

Malaysia: Shake hands.

Philippines: Shake hands.

Singapore: Shake hands.

Adapt to Japanese protocol.

Japanese businesspeople take protocol and customs very seriously. Following are tips from Henry M. Seals, author of *Making It In Japan: An Insider's Journey to Success.*

- **Distributing business cards:** Give and accept business cards with both hands. When you accept a business card, look at it, touch it, and keep it in an obvious spot. Never stuff the card in your pocket or write on it in front of the person who gave it to you.

- **Making a deal:** Japanese rarely make business decisions right away. When you're invited to an initial meeting, the people you meet with are probably there to evaluate you and your business, not to make the deal. They'll take the information back to their superiors, and you'll be invited back if negotiations are to continue.

- **Taking a bow:** Japanese businesspeople bow to show deference and respect; they don't typically shake hands. Japanese businesspeople bow 60 degrees; the chief executive bows 45 degrees. Americans should bow deeply.

Seals states, "To the Japanese, manners and etiquette are very important. . . . If you can perform correctly, if you know the rules of etiquette, then the feeling is that you can be trusted to act prudently in another environment, the business environment."

Prepare for "squatters' rights."

In some parts of Asia, toilets are level with the floor. For flushing, you may find anything from a pull chain to a bucket of water. Some toilets don't flush, but have a wastebasket in which to deposit the toilet paper. Take nose clips or a mask, because some facilities are quite odorous.

 When I was in China recently, I bought a small jar of Tiger Balm, used for relieving various aches and pains. It has a strong but not unpleasant smell that helped to reduce the odor.

Dress appropriately.

Unless you're Asian, you can't blend in. People's attitudes toward you, however, won't depend on the color of your skin or hair. Their attitudes will depend on other initial impressions, such as your manners and the way you dress. To avoid stares—other than those of mere curiosity—be conscious of what you wear.

- Err on the side of being too conservative.
- Avoid sleeveless garments, miniskirts, halters, and other items of clothing that might be too revealing.
- Dress up for an evening on the town, such as theater and dining.

Develop a yen for conversation.

The following tips can be useful in casual conversation:

- In some Asian cultures, expect to be asked personal questions, even by people who don't know you well. Don't be surprised if you're asked your salary or your age.
- Asian people tend to deny compliments paid to them, so if you're paid a compliment, deny it graciously. *Thank you, but. . . .*
- Avoid any topics about politics or World War II.

Enjoy the cuisine.

Dining in many of the Asian countries can delight the senses. Of course, you can head for the nearest Kentucky Fried Chicken or McDonald's—and they're all over—but why would you? Be an intrepid diner and experience local culinary delights. Religious dietary laws influence the foods people eat. For example, many Muslims don't eat pork; Hindus don't eat beef; and Buddhists tend to be vegetarians.

Asian Cuisine

Rice is a staple in Asian countries, and it's served at every meal, even breakfast. Tea is the standard beverage. The Asian food you eat in the United States may be quite different from what you'll eat in the native country. For example, in China, fried rice is white.

Here are some things to enjoy while you're out and about:

China: There are four major regional styles of Chinese food: *Cantonese* dishes are stir-fried or steamed in light oil to keep the natural flavors. Favorites are sweet-and-sour. *Peking-style* is often deep fried, and is hot and spicy. *Shanghai cooking* is sweeter and more oily than the first two, and often contains fish. *Hunan-Szechuan* can be hot and fiery.

India: Indian food is often flavored with spices such as coriander, cumin, tumeric, ginger, and chili. *Tandoori* dishes are cooked in a clay oven. They are often chicken based and not too spicy.

Indonesia: Indonesian food is famous for its *rijsttafel* (rice table), a legacy of the Dutch colonials. Expect chicken, meat, seafood, vegetables, coconut, tropical fruits, and assorted relishes.

Japan: Japan is well known for *sukiyaki* (thin pieces of beef, noodles, mushrooms, and bamboo shoots), *tempura* (deep-fried fish or shrimp and vegetables), and *sushi* (raw fish).

Korea: While in Korea, try *kimchi*, which is a vegetable (generally cabbage) that has been pickled with garlic, red peppers, and onions.

Malaysia: *Satay* is marinated chicken, beef, or mutton on a bamboo stick that's roasted over a charcoal grill and dipped in peanut sauce.

Philippines: A favorite in the Philippines is *adobo*, which is chicken, pork, or squid simmered in a marinade.

 Although you can request a fork and spoon in most restaurants, many Asians will appreciate your attempt to use chopsticks. You won't need a knife, because your food is generally served in small pieces.

 To learn more about eating with chopsticks, check out http://www.ehow.com/how_3261_chopsticks.html.

Understand the rules of business.

Asians have a great deal of respect for age, wisdom, and experience. Therefore, if you send a business delegation to one of the Asian countries, it might be wise to include some of your more mature staff members. Also, Asians tend to form personal relationships before establishing business relationships. So, your first meeting might be a getting-to-know-you session involving very little business.

 Use up-to-date terminology. The Asian people are *Asians*, not *Orientals* or *Far Easterners*. Better yet, refer to them in relation to their countries: *Japanese*, *Chinese*, and the like.

Trekking through Latin America

Latin American people tend to be very warm and open. Spanish is the primary language, except in Brazil, where they speak Portuguese. (If you speak Spanish, you may be able to understand some Portuguese; there are many similarities.)

Latin Americans aren't as casual about greetings as Americans. When people stop to say, *Hello, how are you?* they really want to know. They often shake your hand and wait for a reply. Friends and relatives often greet each other with a kiss and a hug, and it's not uncommon for men to embrace or throw their arms around each other's shoulders.

Confirm appointments in advance.

When you have a business appointment, always confirm it a day or two in advance. Meetings don't necessarily start on time, but you should arrive on time. Latin Americans tend to make small talk before actually getting down to business, and may sit and schmooze over a cup of coffee. Refusing a cup of coffee is considered rude, so sip it if you're not a coffee drinker.

Eat, drink, and be merry.

A typical breakfast may consist of coffee with hot milk, rolls with butter or jam, eggs with bacon and sausages. The midday meal—which is the main meal of the day—may consist of dishes with staple foods such as beans, corn, and rice. The evening meal is a scaled-down version of the midday meal. Always bring along a pocket menu guide so you know what you want to order.

If you're in a restaurant that's not fancy, don't be surprised to see locals clapping their hands or banging silverware to get the attention of the wait staff. In cosmopolitan cities, you find very elegant restaurants that may serve European-style food. If you don't like spicy food you can say, *No muy picante, por favor,* which means "Not too hot, please."

Mingling in the Middle East

Many Americans avoid the Middle East because parts have been in conflict or at war. However, these events are typically random and have little effect on daily life. By and large, the Middle East is a safe place to travel. Crowds enjoy freedom of movement at all hours. English is widely spoken, so language is rarely a problem.

Enjoy the food.

Many hotels and restaurants cater to tourists and offer international food; therefore, it's not uncommon to find Western and Asian food on menus. Here's what you may expect at mealtimes:

Breakfast: Coffee and tea are standard, accompanied by pita bread with white cheese, jam, and honey. You may also expect scrambled eggs or omelets.

Main meal: Middle Easterners prefer to eat their main meal at midday, although hotels serve main meals in the evening, also. Favorite appetizers are *hummus* (a dip made of ground chickpeas), *tahini* (a paste of sesame seeds with lemon juice and garlic), *tabbouleh* (a mixture of bulgur or cracked wheat with chopped tomatoes, onions, parsley, and mint leaves with olive oil and lemon juice dressing).

Popular main dishes: These include *shish kabob* (skewered and grilled cubes of meat or chicken and vegetables) and *kofta* (a popular Arab dish of minced meat, onion, and seasonings shaped into balls then grilled, baked, or fried). Fresh vegetables are abundant, especially eggplant, cabbage, onions, peppers, zucchini, and tomatoes.

Desserts: You must try *muhallabiya*, a rice pudding that's part of every Arab cook's repertoire. You may also expect dessert to be fresh fruits, including apricots, dates, figs, watermelon, and oranges. If you eat in an authentic Arab restaurant, you may see a communal wash sink in the entrance. You wash your hands as you enter the restaurant and when you leave. Watch what others do.

 Strictly observant Muslims don't drink alcohol. It's wise to refrain from drinking in their presence.

When in Israel . . .

Israel's population is predominantly Jewish. Many other citizens are Arabs (Christians and Muslims). Israelis are rather casual in dress and style. A traditional greeting is Shalom, *which means "hello," "good-bye," and also "peace."*

Religious Jews have customs such as not doing business on Sabbath (from sundown on Friday to sundown on Saturday) and eating only kosher food—food conforming to special dietary laws that govern what may be eaten and how it is prepared. For example, religious Jews eat only mammals with cloven hooves that chew their cud, and only fish with fins and scales. Animals must be properly slaughtered. Meat products must not be eaten together with dairy products.

When you're introduced to an Orthodox Jew or a conservative Muslim of the opposite sex, it's best not to offer your hand in greeting. Instead, bow your head slightly as a nonphysical way of saying hello. This will show respect and save the awkwardness of the other person not offering his or her hand in return.

13

Generational differences can be a source of creative strength and a source of opportunity, or a source of stifling stress and unrelenting conflict.

— *Generations at Work* by Ron Zemke, Claire Raines, and Bob Filipczak

Harnessing the Power of Today's Multigenerational Workforce

In this chapter

- Understanding What Makes Each Generation Tick
- Common to All Generations
- Younger Workers Reporting to Older Generations
- Older Workers Reporting to Younger Generations

In this chapter I attempt to bring cohesiveness to—yet make distinctions among—the generations in today's workforce. Each generation spans approximately a 20-year period. People on the cusp of two generations may have attributes related to both, but may be more aligned with one than the other. Regardless of when you were born and where you are on the continuum of these generations, remember four golden rules to create a positive and inclusive professional environment:

1. Don't attach labels.
2. Don't make assumptions.
3. Show understanding, respect, and dignity to everyone.
4. Focus on what you have in common, rather than on what's different.

Businesses have consistently relied on the influx of young talent to regenerate the workforce. Through the generations, people have always had different ideas, ways of approaching an issue, and ways of communicating. That there are differences between generations is nothing new. What's new is the magnitude of these differences, brought about by events of the time and new products, types of entertainment, and technology. In the table on page 202 you see a snapshot of what has shaped each generation.

Understanding What Makes Each Generation Tick

Peek back over the last 30 years. We've gone from status quo to constant change; from job security to risk taking; from paper-based research to the information superhighway; from completed educations to life-long learning; from private offices to cubicles; from hierarchical to participatory; from labor focus to knowledge focus; from one-company-per-career to frequent job changes; from national to global; from wired to wireless; and the list goes on.

Understand traditionalists (born 1927–1945).

This is a generation that lived through tough economic times and saw their parents out of work, many standing on bread lines. Those who went to college sought practical professions that would offer long-term or lifetime job security. They have high respect for authority, leadership, and the government.

During their peak employment years, the workforce was the realm of white males, while women and people of different races and ethnicities had supporting roles. Male managers were in command, and the subordinates did as they were told. Many became "organization men" because they stayed with one profession and in one job for a long time—often a lifetime. They were steeped in loyalty to a company, and that loyalty was returned. Many are remaining longer in the workforce, by choice or necessity.

Defining values: Patriotic, fiscally conservative, hard working, conformists, duty bound, rule bound, loyal, conscientious, and respectful of authority.

Characteristics:
- Call for respect for the wisdom they've acquired over the years.
- Enjoy mentoring younger, newer employees.
- Use good grammar and expect it from others.
- Avoid slang and profanity and expect others to do the same.
- Learn best from stand-up training, rather than electronic.
- Appreciate the personal touch, such as handwritten letters and notes.
- Value public recognition with plaques and traditional rewards.

What has shaped each generation*

Events of the time	Products introduced	Entertainment

Traditionalists (Born 1927 to 1945)

Atomic bomb	Aerosol can	Big Bands
Cold War	Bubble gum	Bing Crosby
GI Bill	Car radio	Charlie McCarthy
Golden Age of Radio	Commercial airlines	Duke Ellington
Great Depression	FM radio	Flash Gordon
Korean War	Frozen vegetables	Frank Sinatra
Lindbergh flight	Penicillin	The Lone Ranger
The New Deal	Scotch tape	Mickey Mouse
Pearl Harbor	Tape recorder	Swing
World War II		Tarzan

Boomers (Born 1946 to 1964)

Booming birthrate	Air conditioning	Beach Boys
Civil rights expanded in most countries	Barbie doll	The Beatles
	Bar codes	Bob Dylan
Economic prosperity	Credit cards	The Brady Bunch
Human rights movement	McDonald's	Bruce Springsteen
JFK shot	The Pill	Captain Kangaroo
Man landed on moon	Polio vaccine	Diana Ross and the Supremes
Oil embargo	Television	
The peace sign	Tupperware	Elvis
Space flight		Hula Hoops
Urban flight		Laugh-In
Vietnam		Rock 'n roll
Watergate		
Woodstock		

Generation X (Born 1965 to 1980)

AIDS epidemic	Personal computers	Bon Jovi
Challenger explosion	Microwave ovens	Cabbage Patch dolls
Death of Princess Di	Post-it™ notes	Disco dancing
Fall of the Berlin Wall	Rollerblades	ET
Hostages in Iran	VCR	MTV
Kuwait invaded	Walkman	Pet rocks
Lennon shot		Prince
Nixon resigns		Rap music
Oklahoma City bombing		Reggae
Y2K		Sesame Street
		The Simpsons

Generation Y (Born from 1981 to the present)

Attack on World Trade Center	CDs	Barney
Columbine shooting	Cell phones	Beanie Babies
Iraq war	DVDs	Puff Daddy
Personal computer age	The Internet	Remix
	Personal computers	Spice Girls

---

*Each generation is also influenced by the prior generation(s).

Note: It's interesting to note that this generation is considered to be the happiest. According to a Duke University study on the aging (as reported in *The Boston Globe* on April 19, 2008), "This is partly because older people have learned to lower their expectations and accept their achievements. An older person may realize that it was fine to be a schoolteacher and not a Nobel Prize winner." The article went on to say that the odds of being happy increased 5 percent with every 10 years of age. The survey did not include nursing home residents.

Know the boomers (born 1946–1964).

Boomers grew up in the post-Eisenhower era, with the *Leave It to Beaver* scenario of the working father and homemaker mother. They were brought up to believe they were wonderful, were the center of the universe, and could accomplish anything they set their minds to.

Leaders such as Richard Nixon and Lyndon Johnson caused boomers to become cynical and question authority. This group grew up during times of economic prosperity and worked relentlessly to pursue their goals. Many sought liberal arts degrees to get away from what they saw as the trappings of their fathers' narrow career paths. This is the first generation with a high divorce rate and with two-income households as the norm, and they learned to distinguish themselves as individuals.

Defining values: Workaholic, entrepreneurial, in need of personal gratification and personal growth, involved, materialistic, sandwiched, optimistic, and respectful of authority.

Characteristics:
- Value power, perks, prestige, and public recognition.
- Work long hours with salaries they expect to be commensurate with their experience.
- Participate in professional projects, associations, and affiliations with others in their fields.
- Appreciate long-term perks such as profit sharing, health care, long-term care.
- Tie concepts to the mission at hand.
- Work best with a team approach and consensus.

Meet Generation X (born 1965–1980).

Nearly 40 percent of the Xers experienced the divorce of their parents while they were young or had both parents working outside the home and became latchkey children (or they knew children who were). The impact of this can be seen in the fact that they have married later, hoping to make good choices in life partners.

They tend to seek professions (and companies) that allow them to establish a work/life balance, and they often like to work independently. They want to be more available to their families. They work to live, rather than live to work, and believe they must construct their own futures. Also, they don't work and play as well with others as do the boomers.

They have experienced the period in which American industry has become leaner and has outsourced large amounts of work to foreign countries. Therefore, they seek a mixture of skills and experiences to help them move from one company to another. They often work long hours because they view this as training for their next opportunity.

This is the first generation to have diminished expectations, be weaned on television, and have wide access to computers. Yet, Xers are less informed about world events than past generations.

Although many made small fortunes during the dot-com boom, the dot-com bust shattered many dreams. This is the first generation expected to earn less than their parents, and many boomeranged back home after college.

Defining values: Eclectic, resourceful, self-reliant, diversified, adaptable, pragmatic, independent, informal, in the moment, rule benders, global thinkers, distrustful of institutions and politics.

Characteristics:
- Need flexibility to control their own needs (not wants), such as children, aging parents, and outside interests.
- Work best with teamwork and collaborative efforts.
- Are straightforward and use language-based results.
- Enjoy lots of interesting projects with leading-edge technology.
- Need time to pursue outside interests.
- Make commitments to their work, not to employers.
- Will change jobs when a more interesting or exciting opportunity comes along.
- Want flexibility to work offsite.
- Focus on the present and the future.

Welcome Generation Y (born 1981–present).

During their early years, "baby-on-board" signs in car windows showed a resurgence of protective family values. Their parents married later, and nearly three-fourths of their fathers were present for their births. Although many Yers had two working parents, there was a large infrastructure (from daycare to after school programs) to keep their lives structured. Play dates were popular—when they weren't taking music lessons, dancing lessons, or playing team sports. This generation has grown up trusting older people, and they often relate well to traditionalists and older boomers.

During their formative years, technology drove much of their communications, and Googling, chatting, blogging, WiFi-ing, instant messaging, text messaging, podcasting, and more are practically coded in their DNA. This generation has yet to evolve, as many are just entering the workforce.

Defining values: Civic minded, globally concerned, media savvy, confident, sociable, street smart, realistic, critical of government, environmentally conscious, and social networkers.

Characteristics:
- Earn to spend and question the status quo.
- Require flexibility as to where and when work is done; they shun rigid workday schedules.
- Realize that coming in late isn't irresponsible. (They often work late hours, nights, and weekends.)
- Expect to use the latest technology, such as instant messaging, texting, and the like, in their jobs.
- Will change jobs when a more interesting or exciting opportunity comes along.
- May have a number of careers over their lifetime.
- Make commitments to their work, not to employers.
- Challenge in order to change. (Treat rebelliousness carefully.)
- Appreciate mentoring programs.
- Ask for and respect input.
- Focus on the present and the future.

Think Age Diversity Doesn't Affect You?

Check off the situations you've experienced personally.

❏ No sense of urgency among the youngest generation.

❏ Older people who are set in their ways.

❏ Baby boomers who insist on meeting just to have a meeting.

❏ Younger employees who use up sick days and earned days off as quickly as they accumulate them.

❏ No one under the age of 40 is in the office after hours.

❏ Workers in your office over the age of 40 are now in the minority.

- ❑ Inappropriate work attire being worn by younger workers.
- ❑ Gen Xers and Gen Yers who can't write a formal business letter.
- ❑ Seasoned employees who still don't use email.
- ❑ Baby boomers who treat younger people the way they treat their children.
- ❑ Three words—tattoos, piercings, tattoos.
- ❑ Younger workers who assume that if you don't have an iPod you are computer illiterate.
- ❑ Baby boomers who monopolize conversations.
- ❑ Traditionalists who constantly let everyone know how things were different in their day.

Used with permission from Roberta Chinsky Matuson, Generational Workforce Expert and President, Human Resource Solutions (www.yourhrexperts.com).

Common to All Generations

As mentioned in the introduction, the companies that thrive (not merely survive) are the ones harnessing the potential of today's rich and diverse multigenerational workforce. This increases the bottom line and serves customers better.

 I wrote the following in collaboration with Dave McKeon, Managing Partner, Game On! LLC (www.gameonllc.com). Although our attempt is to get away from specific labels, we do need to make distinctions. For lack of anything more appropriate, we've chosen to use the terms *older generation* and *younger generation*.

Pay attention to demographics and create a balance.

Pay attention to generational demographics in your environment and be ready to shift when the need shifts. For example, if you need someone who's willing to travel on a moment's notice, do you have the right people? If customers need people to work all weekend, do you have staff members willing to work weekends at the last minute? Rather than creating a conflict and asking people to do something they're uncomfortable with, put the right mix of people in place. People of the older generation are typically more willing to travel and put in the extra time. And if you have only one person of the older generation in the mix, you can't expect her to constantly travel or put in overtime.

Leverage appropriate communication methods.

Dave absolutely believes that Newt Gingrich was correct with the observation, "The biggest problem with communication is the belief that it has actually occurred." Effective communicators are masters in the technique of flexing their own style to mirror the preferred styles of others. A best practice in today's multigenerational workplace is to factor in generational communication preferences.

- Older workers respond well to phone calls, face-to-face meetings, letters, and memos.
- Younger workers prefer instant messaging and texting. Both use email, which is a common denominator.

Notice how presidential candidates have used technology to their advantage. Ronald Reagan was an older candidate and a wonderful speaker and debater. He leveraged the technology of the time—television—to swing voters into his corner. It was his final TV debate against Jimmy Carter that is credited with Reagan's winning the election. Barack Obama, a younger candidate and wonderful speaker and debater, was the first to leverage the new technologies of texting and blogging to reach people of younger generations. This played a dramatic role in his winning the election.

Remember the golden rules.

As we start to get into specifics, it's worth repeating the four golden rules for creating a positive and inclusive environment:

1. Don't attach labels.
2. Don't make assumptions.
3. Show understanding, respect, and dignity to everyone.
4. Focus on what you have in common, rather than on what's different.

The objective is to accomplish common goals in the best and most cost-effective way possible. *No generation has the best way, the right way, or the only way.*

Avoid age-related remarks.

In the workplace, we're all on equal footing, and no one should make age-related comments. It's not okay for an older person to say to a younger person . . .

- *You're too young to be a manager. I have kids your age.*
- *I don't know much about computers. Better get one of those younger guys.*

Conversely, it's not okay for a younger person to say to an older person . . .

- *How's it going, Pops?*

- *Can I have my mother sit in on my performance review?* (A manager told me about that one.)

 Check out chapter 10, "Interviewing and Being Interviewed," for tips on interviewing people from the younger generations.

Younger Generations Reporting to Older Generations

Leadership is as much about creating "followship" as it is about anything else. As Franklin D. Roosevelt once said, "It's a terrible thing to look over your shoulder when you are trying to lead—and find no one there."

Key for older generations leading younger generations is that they be seen as leaders that truly value what the younger generations bring to the table. Fail to achieve that, and your younger workers will leverage their preexisting networks for advice instead of coming to you for guidance on the projects you've assigned to them.

Arguably, many performance problems are directly related to breakdowns in communication between leaders and subordinates. These breakdowns go right to the bottom line as hidden costs in the form of missed opportunities, delayed results, and high turnover. Members of the older generations must leave their egos at the door and not expect the younger generations to feel compelled to conform to their styles and preferences.

The following dos and taboos will help you to create the followship you need to be an effective leader:

Dos
- Be respectful to everyone and expect respect in return.
- Provide constructive feedback constantly.
- Be open to change. Even though something has worked well in the past, welcome new ideas and let the younger generation be the contributors they see themselves to be.
- Take the time to explain the business logic behind requests that might be challenged when compliance isn't really a choice.
- Encourage collaboration. The younger generation takes teamwork seriously and works well in groups.
- Treat younger workers as peers and colleagues, not subordinates and interns. Involve them in decision-making processes.
- View questions as opportunities to revisit the appropriateness of how you're doing things. "My way or the highway" no longer works.
- Encourage younger workers to chat. Learn their motivations. Understand what they like about the workplace and what they'd like to change. Find out what matters to them.

- Make your language, tone, and body language reflect your intentions.
- Provide challenging work opportunities that really matter.
- When delegating, delegate both the assignments and the freedom to determine how to achieve the outcome.
- Allow for flexibility when planning and scheduling.
- Offer increasing responsibility as a reward for accomplishment.
- Acknowledge a job well done.
- Spend time getting to know the people you lead as individuals and learn of their capabilities.
- Provide ongoing training and learning opportunities.
- Maintain a focus on the work, but be personable.
- Mentor and collaborate on plans for career development.
- Have a sense of humor.
- Talk the talk and walk the walk!

Taboos
- Using words such as *Read my lips . . . Just do what I'm asking . . . Make it easy, just do it my way . . . I don't care how it's done somewhere else, this is how we do it here . . . I've been down this road before, this is the way we need to do it . . . Do what I'm telling you and stop questioning.* Words or expressions such as these marginalize the younger worker.
- Engaging in a monologue versus a dialogue.
- Talking down to or bullying people.
- Showing unethical, immoral, dishonest, or illegal behavior.

Understand a different perspective.

People from younger generations bring a different perspective. For example, if a younger person finishes her work at 3:00, she may want to leave early to attend her child's soccer game. If that creates a conflict, ask yourself:

- Whose values are showing up?
- Is there a need to have this person remain until 5:00?
- Are these repeated requests that deviate from the norm?
- What other types of allowances and concessions can be made?
- What's the impact of saying yes and saying no?
- If I do this for her, will others expect the same treatment?

The caveat, of course, is to have sufficient staff and a good generational mix that will allow you to be flexible and still satisfy any coverage requirements.

Benefit from a team-approach mindset.

The younger generation grew up with strong team bonds. They learned that when everyone does their best, everyone is rewarded. For example, in youth soccer leagues, everyone gets a trophy for participating, not just the winning team. In the big leagues, known as the business world, only the winners get the trophies. This is a major paradigm shift. It helps to understand it.

 Be current with the new lingo. For example, *onboarding* is the process used to introduce a new hire into a role within an organization. This can be either someone who's new to the organization or someone who's assuming a new role within it.

Keep an open mind.

I composed a questionnaire for an article I wrote on multigenerations from the perspective of the younger generation, and received this wonderful advice from Bobby DiMarino, Human Resource Assistant at Roche Brothers Supermarkets: "The best way to overcome any communication-based problem is to just keep an open mind. . . . I never want to come off to anyone that's asking me a question [about technology] that they're bothering me. So during these times, no matter how busy I might be at that moment, I listen carefully and explain thoroughly. There isn't a better feeling in the world than after you help someone with a problem, and they are absolutely satisfied and comfortable."

Older Generations Reporting to Younger Generations

Many older workers are electing to "power down," or step out of management or leadership roles, to spend their remaining working years as individual contributors. If you're one of them, you may report to a younger manager. Remember, it's what you've done in the past that allows you to make a valuable contribution.

If you feel your expertise is being challenged, what's your first emotion? What's your reaction? In your new role, you need to craft and define the framework of your responsibilities and how you choose to work going forward.

- Get clarity on the purpose of your role. Why does it exist?
- Create relationships with younger managers that will work for all of you.
- Get clarity on the boundaries of your role so you're all able to shift from the implicit to the explicit. Honor those boundaries and behave

accordingly so they don't collide with your ethical, moral, or legal constraints.

- Watch your body language. (Learn more in chapter 3, "Interpreting Body Language.")
- Anticipate that the majority of your communication won't be face to face.

Check your ego at the door.

If you're in a situation where your needs and values aren't aligned with the job's rewards and you opt not to adapt, you're a misfit (to put it bluntly.) If you can adapt, remember that you're selling your time for money. If you can't adapt, the situation will drain your energy and everyone's around you—both at home and at the office. Before this happens, leave before you're asked to leave. Don't worry about not being employable. You will find a more suitable setting.

Continue learning.

Every moment represents a choice of how you can act and behave. Don't become obsolete. If you want to be taken seriously, shift and adapt. Learn the latest technologies and methods. Although you may not figure things out as easily as younger people, you can learn by being shown. Ask your manager about taking courses, getting a technology mentor, and anything else that will help you continue to grow.

As a young manager, do you feel you'd rather put your training dollars into your younger workers? If so, remember this: Younger workers may move on as soon as the next opportunity presents itself. Older workers are more likely to remain loyal and stay. The dollars you spend on them will be returned to you in kind.

Older people are working for personal satisfaction, the need for insurance, or to be challenged. As a younger manager, you should . . .

- Recognize the wealth of experience older workers bring.
- Be humble about your own shortcomings.
- Consider options such as part-time, flextime, seasonal, or contractual work.
- Pick their brains. When they do retire, they take their knowledge with them.
- Appreciate their loyalty. While younger people change jobs frequently, older ones remain loyal.
- Keep the lines of communication open. Discuss differences and the best way to deal with them. So, if an older worker asks to schedule a meeting, don't dismiss him by saying, *Shoot me an email.*

Remember Dave McKeon's best practices.

- Leverage the communication differences that are common to each group.
- Realize that one approach doesn't fit all, so flex your generational communication style to other generational style preferences.
- Use employee satisfaction surveys to get feedback and address challenges head on.
- Create a dialogue, not a monologue. It's only through dialogue that communication works.
- Talk openly about your environment and cultural values so that the boundaries and norms are clear.
- Be clear about performance goals and expectations, and give feedback on a regular basis.
- Communicate with and treat people as the individuals they are, not as stereotyped members of a generation.
- Get in the habit of catching people doing things right and acknowledging them.
- Listen with the intention of being influenced.
- Shift from past and present; focus on the future. That's the behavior that can be influenced and controlled.

Survey Results: Multigenerational Differences from the Point of View of the Younger Generations

Much has been written about multigenerational differences from the point of view of the older generations. Nancy Settle-Murphy and I have written several articles on the multigenerational workforce, and we decided to take a look at these generational differences from the point of view of the younger worker. Although this is a limited sampling, many of the issues relate to differences in communication styles and technical abilities. Following are responses to questionnaires we sent to Gen Xers and Gen Yers:

What are some of the communication challenges you face when working with members from older generations?

- Many people from the older generation aren't very savvy when it comes to technology.
- I made a chart this past week for [an older generation team member], showing the differences in training for new hires held in our stores. It took maybe two hours. It was simple to me, but when I gave it to [name], his eyes opened so wide, it was like seeing a four-year-old opening a Christmas gift.
- Older workers tend to put people into categories. My boss often makes generalizations about the communication styles of New Yorkers, Midwesterners, and so forth. He categorizes them as either direct, nice, or passive-aggres-

sive. I find people from the younger generations interact individually and don't apply generalizations about communication styles to demographics.

- The older generation is more formal with their writing. They use formal language and proper grammar. Younger people are used to adapting their style, depending on the medium.
- Multitasking is a driving force behind quicker, faster messages.

How do you overcome some of the communication challenges with members of older generations?

- I try to keep an open mind and be willing to help, especially when it comes to technology. When someone comes to me for help, I help them with whatever they need by taking it step by step.
- I try to keep it simple. My company is loaded with politics and agendas, and navigating the environment is very difficult. Rather than try to understand the angles and intentions, I just go about my work. When confronting an older coworker (or one higher on the food chain), I try to be direct but respectful.
- With an older person who's my superior, I adapt to his or her style. If I'm communicating peer to peer and there's a generational difference, it makes sense to use my own preferences.
- The bottom line is to always be respectful.

What aspects of your generation would you like other generations to honor (or understand and value)?

- Everyone treats me like I have been working here for 20 + years. I know my knowledge will only grow in this field as I see more and more situations, but I always offer a younger point of view, or ideas that might reach out to associates at a younger age, because I can relate to them.
- The older generation tends to look past us when dealing with situations. For instance, they don't ask for that younger point of view, or accept the views we have. I think the best mission any company can have is to work as a team and listen to all points of view. One point of view from a 20-year-old might not be the perfect fit, but it might spark another view from across the table, and then you can piece it all together for a solution.
- Respect that tone and style can be variable.
- Recognize that being familiar doesn't imply disrespect.
- Emoticons and acronyms like IMHO and BTW are okay to use.
- Build a culture of trust that's not about age, but about what you can contribute.

What aspects of older generations do you most admire?

- I am really happy you asked this question. I could honestly write pages on how much I admire the view of the older generation. The one thing I admire most is their stories, and their way of dealing with situations. One thing I do as a new associate working in an office atmosphere is to watch how others of older generations conduct themselves. I watch how they interact with people, how they treat business situations that arise, and also how they interact with associates of all generations.

- Their reservedness and modesty.

How would you advise teams that include both older and younger members to create communication plans that work well for everyone? What process can be used, and what aspects are most important to agree upon?

- My department excels at teamwork. I would advise any company working with older and younger generations to work as a team. It's the best process you can have, and it's the only way that will lead to solid team-based solutions. As I mentioned before, if a younger [person's] view can spark up another view of an older associate, that idea could be the best idea that is presented. I see it all the time working in my department, and I know it's the reason I am always involved with meetings.

- Be open and direct.

- Use a neutral tone—not overly polite or familiar or otherwise alienating.

- Avoid jargon that isn't relevant or understood by all, such as catchphrases.

No problem can be solved from the same level of consciousness that created it. We must see the world anew.
—Albert Einstein

Employing Appreciative Inquiry

Appreciative Inquiry (AI), as described by Wikipedia, is "a particular way of asking questions and envisioning the future that fosters positive relationships and builds on the basic goodness in a person, a situation, or an organization." AI seeks to tap into opportunities, values, high-point moments, wisdom, stories, traditions, competencies, innovations, and achievements. In a nutshell, AI is a paradigm that allows people to master their successes, learn from positive experiences, and focus on what works. Here's a real-life example most everyone can relate to:

Typical Approach

Your manager calls a meeting with your team to discuss a problem. He puts the problem statement on a PowerPoint slide or whiteboard and people discuss ways to solve the problem. Morale is low. The mood is negative. People are edgy. Everyone plays the blame game.

AI Approach

Given the same scenario, the manager focuses on what the team is doing well and incorporates those positive aspects into the area that needs to be strengthened. Morale is high. The mood is positive. People are at ease. There is no blame.

Who Uses AI and Why

If you're thinking AI is too touchy-feely, think again. Here are some words from high-level people from two major corporations who have successfully used AI:

> *Appreciative Inquiry gets much better results than seeking out and solving problems. We concentrate enormous resources on correcting problems . . . [but] when used continually over a long time, this approach leads to a negative culture, a descent into a paralyzing sense of hopelessness. Don't get me wrong. I'm not advocating mindless happy talk. Appreciative Inquiry is a complex science designed to make things better. We can't ignore problems—we just need to approach them from the other side. (Thomas White, President, Telephone Operations, GTE Wireless)*

> *When you focus on what works and you dream of the possibilities, it's very inspiring to people. (Bob Stiller, CEO, Green Mountain Coffee Roasters)*

AI is an organizational development process developed by David Cooperrider and his associates at Case Western Reserve University School of Management in the mid-1980s. It's been successfully used by Green Mountain Coffee Roasters, the U.S. Navy, GTE Wireless, Yellow Roadway (formerly Roadway Express), Hunter Douglas Windows, Save the Children, Habitat for Humanity, British Airways, United Religions Initiative, McDonald's, and many others. It has become a valuable and successful methodology for

- team building
- product development
- core business design
- mergers and acquisitions
- focus groups
- process improvement

- strategic planning
- labor-management relations
- jump-start innovation
- joint ventures
- customer relations
- and more.

 AI is also used outside of the business world. It's becoming one of the most popular change methodologies in religious communities, municipalities, and many organizations.

Four Stages of AI

The four stages are discover, dream, design, and destiny.

Learn the four stages of AI.

AI involves a four-stage methodology built around the positive core competencies of your group. Those competencies can be innovation, strong financial assets, religious beliefs, commitment to the community, best business practices, personal strengths, world-famous CEO, or whatever.

Discover

People talk to one another through structured interviews to discover when they were at their best. We all like to tell stories and listen to stories. We all like to pass on our values. We all like to be heard in a positive way. That's what past and present discovery is about.

It's done through a series of positive, open-ended, and thought-provoking questions that use experiential words. Ask questions that encourage storytelling. And ask questions to which you don't know the answer. The answers will broaden personal and collective visions. Questions may include . . .

- What's right about where we are now?
- You've done that before. What was your experience with . . . ?
- When did you achieve your goals?
- What's your most cherished memory of . . . ?
- What makes this . . . particularly appealing?
- What do you like most about the . . . ?
- Why was . . . important to you?
- If you had three wishes for . . ., what would they be?
- Please tell me more about. . . .
- What do you think really made . . . possible?
- Would you briefly describe . . . experience?
- What made that possible?

Once you focus on the successes in your life, they become magnified and make current challenges appear more controllable.

 It's a good strategy to create diversity with groups or pairs of "unlike" people, such as people from diverse ethnic backgrounds, multigenerational backgrounds, or different departments.

Dream

This stage is about envisioning the process as it would work in the future.

- Describe what it may be like a year from now when we get it right.
- What would this look like if . . . ?
- If . . . didn't exist, what would . . . look like?

Design

During this phase, groups analyze the input from the discovery and dream phases. They use the findings to design a roadmap of actions and resources from inside and outside the group. This is more an activity than a process of questioning.

Destiny (or Deliver)

This involves a strong top-down commitment and is where the rubber meets the road. Groups of committed people make a commitment to follow the roadmap. Questions may include . . .

- What should we set as our priorities?
- What should our focus be over the next . . . ?
- Who from outside the group would be interested in working on . . . ?
- How will we measure success along the way?
- How will we know when . . . has changed (improved)?

 AI is a continuous process. The destiny step leads to new discoveries that start the process anew.

Why AI works well with children.

Some of the most inspiring AI interviews were with children. Why? They have the natural ability to be honest, open, curious, and amazed. Somewhere early in life, we all lose that innocence. Perhaps it's because we hear expressions such as these all too often:

- *Why? Because I said so.*
- *If I've told you no once, I've told you no a thousand times. You can't (or don't) . . .*
- *No means no.*
- *What don't you understand about the word no?*

As adults, we continue to receive negative reinforcement.

- *We've tried that before and it doesn't work.*
- *Yes, but . . .*
- *The problem with that idea is . . .*
- *That won't work because . . .*
- *That's just not a good idea.*

Turning Negatives into Positives

Think in terms of negative and positive things around you. For example, your company probably offers the mandatory sexual harassment training. The title itself is negative and misleading—the focus isn't about training people to sexually harass. Even if you called the program *sexual harassment prevention training*, it's still negative. Why not call the program *positive gender interactions training*?

Try this at your next session when you hope to solve a problem.

Divide people into groups and present a scenario. Perhaps it has nothing to do with the issue at hand. Here's one possible scenario: You're going to start your own business (you determine what it is), and you have all the resources you need.

1. The first person makes a suggestion.
2. The next responds by saying, *Yes, but* . . .
3. Then the next person adds to that another *Yes, but* . . .
4. Keep that going until everyone on the team has had a turn, or until you've had six or seven *Yes, but* . . . contributions.

Then switch the scenario with one slight change: *Yes, and* . . .

1. The first person makes a suggestion.
2. The next responds by saying, *Yes, and* . . .
3. Then the next person adds to that another *Yes, and* . . .
4. Keep that going until everyone on the team has had a turn, or until you've had six or seven *Yes, and* . . . contributions.

Notice the difference when you switch to a more positive *Yes, and* . . . conversation. People get excited and want to contribute. They create a positive energy.

Use positive words and phrases.

Presenting yourself as an optimist is always a winning strategy. Sometimes it's as simple as letting people know what you can and will do, rather than what you can't and won't do.

Positive: With the proper equipment, we can do our jobs.
Negative: Without the proper equipment, we won't be able to do our jobs.

Positive: The meeting should last until 10:30.
Negative: Don't plan to get out of the meeting until 10:30.

Be mindful of the phrases you use. For example, *Please remember to . . .* is positive; *Please don't forget to . . .* is negative.

Applying this to words in a resume

When writing a resume, use specific positive and powerful words such as consolidated, directed, improved, launched, led, pioneered, reorganized, saved, strengthened, supervised, wrote, *and others. They're stronger than wishy-washy terms such as* assisted with, exposed to, involved in, helped, knowledge of, participated in, *and the like.*

15

The real art of conversation is not only to say the right thing at the right place but to leave unsaid the wrong thing at the tempting moment.

—Lady Dorothy Nevill, English writer

Speaking in General

This chapter is a depository for speaking situations that didn't have enough information for separate chapters.

Asking for a Raise

Perhaps your loved ones are always telling you you're priceless. But what value does your employer place on you? Do you feel you deserve a higher salary but are afraid to ask? Asking for a raise can be intimidating. However, armed with substance, you can proceed with confidence.

Know your value in the marketplace.

Although you may be envious of friends who are earning more than you, make comparisons only if they're working in similar positions, have similar experience, and are in your geographic region. Talk to others in your field, attend trade and professional association meetings, read professional publications, and look at salary surveys to get an idea of salary ranges. A few good websites are www.salary.com, www.payscale.com, and www. monster.com.

 Don't ask colleagues you work with about their salaries. People are sensitive about those questions.

Determine the financial health of your employer.

As an employee, you probably know your employer's fiscal health. Don't ask for a raise during down times. Check out the company's financial reports and follow business news. Up and down industry trends are always spotlighted.

Time it right.

There are a few factors that go into the timing, and you know the expression, "strike while the iron is hot."

Ask for a raise . . .

- when you're at peak performance, have finished a major project, have just received special recognition, or have just been handed a new or major responsibility.
- on a Friday. Managers are typically in their best moods on Fridays because they're anticipating the weekend.

Don't ask for a raise . . .

- on a Monday. That's the day people catch up from the weekend and plan the upcoming workweek.
- if your company just lost a major contract or client—even if the company's bottom line is healthy.

Treat this as a business meeting.

To show your manager you're serious, ask for an appointment for a face-to-face meeting. (Of course, wait until your manager is in a good mood.) Don't approach this topic on the phone, by email, or at the copy machine.

Plan your argument.

Think of how you sold yourself to get this job, and use similar tactics. Make sure you deserve a raise and are ready to prove it. Write down the following so you present your case in terms of the value you provide the company.

- Start with your contribution to the company's bottom line and quantify it in terms of dollars and percentages, if you can.
- Mention how your performance makes a contribution to the company's goals.
- Start with your most recent accomplishments.
- List other key accomplishments since your last raise.
- Incorporate mention of additional skills you've gotten or additional tasks you've undertaken.
- Talk about the salary you deserve.
- Be concise and direct.
- Ask for a little more than you'll accept so there's room to negotiate. (Everyone likes to save face.)

 Don't use higher living expenses as a reason for a raise. You must base your case on merit (rather than having three kids in college).

Let negotiations begin.

Play out several scenarios before you set the appointment. Of course, if your manager says *yes*, you walk away delighted. But there are other scenarios that may play out.

- **You're offered less than you want.** Compromising is okay provided each side is satisfied. The key is to know how much you're willing to compromise and what you'll do if you won't get what you want.

- **You get turned down.** Will you quit your job or ask again at a later date? Of course, only you can answer that question. If your manager denies your raise and offers criticism of your work, are the criticisms valid? If so, take corrective action and plan to revisit the issue when you've made the improvements.

 Prepare other bargaining chips. If your manager doesn't give you a raise or the raise you're asking for, have a few options in your back pocket. Perhaps you can negotiate additional vacation time, flextime, time off, or something your company can write off such as a laptop, cell phone, and the like.

If you don't get what you feel you deserve, you can always look for another job. Don't show agitation and don't walk out angry. Leave on a high note and say something like, *I appreciate your time and candidness. I hope we can revisit this issue [next month, next year, or whenever].* Then, get your resume and your network in gear.

Exit Interview

Employees leave jobs for many different reasons, including poor management practices, lack of advancement opportunities, low salary, harassment, conflict with coworkers, lack of appreciation, and more. Companies conduct interviews with exiting employees to discuss their reasons for leaving. Exit interviews help employers diagnose and improve performance and benchmark employee expectations. Savvy companies use this information to retain valuable employees and change the climate of the organization.

- Don't treat this interview casually; it must be structured.
- Have someone who is not closely connected with the employee conduct the interview. (This is often the responsibility of HR.)
- Have a series of questions ready to be asked. (Some appropriate questions follow.)
- Provide an opportunity for the employee to speak freely.
- Make sure the interview isn't confrontational.
- Guarantee confidentiality.
- Inform the employee of anything that's due, such as salary, benefits, and the like.
- Keep a written record for the employee's file.

 Some companies use online exit interviews. This allows exiting employees to be more honest than they might be during a face-to-face interview. If you're preparing one, ask five to seven multiple-choice questions and a few open-ended questions so employees can include anecdotal experiences.

Tread carefully with terminated employees.

Employees who are terminated may be angry and disgruntled. Some may not participate in an exit interview; others may value the opportunity to express their side. Perhaps they still have friends at the company and would like to improve the workplace for them. Exit interviews with angry employees may help employers avoid costly litigation.

Build your repertoire of questions.

Compose open-ended questions, rather than ones requiring a simple *yes* or *no*. Following are some basic questions for employers to ask during a short exit interview:

Basic questions
- What made you want to join this company originally?
- What were your best experiences here?

- What were your worst experiences?
- If you could change anything here, what would it be?
- What message would you give to management upon your departure?
- What is your reason for leaving?
- If a friend or colleague asked you, would you recommend that they take a job here?

Additional questions
- Did the training you received help you to perform your job properly?
- If not, what additional training would have been helpful?
- Did you receive adequate support from your superiors and peers?
- Did you receive your performance appraisals on time?
- Did this company help you fulfill your career goals?
- Based on your experiences here, what do you think it takes to succeed at this company?
- What is your new company offering you that ours doesn't?
- Would you be available to train your successor?
- What suggestions do you have to improve this workplace?

Press Interview

Congratulations! Your company is ready for its first product launch and you're going to be interviewed by the press. Proper preparation can mean the difference between a good and bad interview. Whatever the nature of your interview, you want to be well prepared and control the story.

If the phone rings out of the blue and an interviewer wants to speak with you, don't hesitate to say you'd like to call back. Ask what the deadline is and schedule something in that time frame. This gives you the opportunity to formulate your thoughts.

 If your interview contains time-sensitive information, ask the interviewer to sign a non-disclosure agreement (NDA) before the interview starts. The NDA can detail the timing for the release.

Prepare for the interview.
The interviewer may ask for something in writing from you to become better versed in the topic. Have something that's well written ready to go.

- **Determine the format.** Will this be live or over the phone?
- **Find out how long the interview will take.** It may take anywhere from a few minutes to an hour or longer.

- **Ask for questions in advance so you can prepare.** But even though you have seen the questions, your answers may prompt other questions, so be prepared.
- **Generate a list of talking points.** This will help you steer the interview in the direction of the points you want to cover.
- **Learn as much as you can about the interviewer.** Listen to or read other interviews by the person you'll be speaking with, if that's possible.
- **Know your message.** Before your interview, review your message points. Identify two or three essential points that you must get across during the interview.

Interview with enthusiasm.

You've prepared properly and now you're ready. Right?

- **Think before you speak.** Take the time you need to gather your thoughts, and don't hesitate to use your notes. Those few extra seconds will help you sound thoughtful and deliberate.

- **Articulate and talk slowly.** If the interviewer is taking notes, you want to be sure she understands you. If the interview is on the air, you may have an audience of people who speak different languages.

- **Be descriptive.** Use concrete examples that convey your points and provide images the interviewer can picture.

- **Be mindful of jargon and acronyms.** Keep explanations simple. It may be fine to use industry-specific jargon or acronyms if you're being interviewed for a technical publication and your readers will understand your language. Know the audience.

- **Be positive and upbeat, but not like a cheerleader.** If you're discussing a controversial topic, remain positive, upbeat, and natural. But don't overdo it.

- **Flag key points.** Use phrases such as *The bottom line is . . ., The most important thing is . . .,* or *Let me be clear about. . . .*

- **Don't bluff.** If the interviewer asks you a question you can't answer, simply say *I don't know the answer to that. I'll find out and get back to you within. . . .*

- **Stress your key points.** Notice how politicians answer questions. They always bring the conversation back to the points they want to make.

You can do that as well. One way is to avoid yes and no answers.

- **Ask for clarification when necessary.** If you don't understand the question, ask for clarification. Otherwise you run the risk of giving the wrong answer or an inappropriate one. This also gives you time to formulate your answer.

- **Avoid speculation or agreeing to unfamiliar facts or figures.** Keep your answers factual to avoid being misquoted or misinterpreted. If the interviewer quotes something he wants you to agree with, simply say *I'm not familiar with that, but let me tell you what I do know. . . .*

 Don't speak "off the record" and say something you wouldn't want to have go live. Anything you say is fair game, even if the interviewer agrees to hold the information in confidence. And don't answer questions that seem unsuitable.

Think about the next step.

- **Thank the interviewer.** Thank the reporter at the conclusion of the interview and follow up with an email. The follow-up builds rapport for future interviews and gives you a chance to add or change something.

- **Ask to see a printed copy before release.** Most interviewers will be happy to provide one.

Office Gossip

As a child, you may remember playing a game called "telephone." You'd whisper something into someone's ear, that person would repeat the message in the next person's ear, and the process would continue down the line. By the time the message reached the last person, and that last person said the message out loud, it often bore little resemblance to the original message. The same holds true for office gossip. Gossip is often a cesspool of misleading, damaging, and false information. But not always.

Use gossip beneficially.

For many baby boomers, the words "I heard it through the grapevine" conjure up a song popularized by Marvin Gaye in 1967. Office gossip (also known as *the grapevine* or *rumor mill*) is the conduit for people complaining about the latest benefits package, the spat between the VP of marketing and the VP of sales, and more. Gossip is part of corporate culture. But it is good or bad? It all depends.

Used correctly, gossip can be beneficial. Let's say you just finished a major project that didn't get you a lot of recognition, and you want to toot your own horn. You talk it up because it may trickle down to people you want it to reach. Sharing a story about someone's humanity; alerting senior-level people to a problem; discussing someone's pregnancy, marriage, promotion; and things of that sort can bring people closer together.

What's your gossip barometer? Ask yourself what your motives are for participating in gossipy conversations and be honest about them. More often than not, when you talk about someone who's not present, you're gossiping.

Recognize the difference between sharing information and gossiping.

The major difference is intent. Telling stories you know to be untrue, stories you heard through the grapevine, stories to destroy someone's career is gossiping and is malicious. Telling stories about office culture and politics with a new hire is sharing information. If people are complaining about the performance of a coworker and you mention that the person has a terminally ill family member, sharing that information may help coworkers to be more understanding.

 Savvy managers should be tuned in to the grapevine to clarify or dispel rumors.

Don't ignore the elephant in the room.

Some people start rumors because they feel they're shoring up their social networks, building status, and boosting their importance. These people may propagate rumors about an impending downsizing, year-end bonuses, and anything else that makes them "sources of knowledge" (in their own minds).

For people who are victims of the rumor mill, consider how politicians squelch rumors. During the 2008 presidential campaign, Barack Obama rejected controversial statements by launching a Fight the Smear website. He placed his rebuttals alongside the rumors. Sarah Palin squelched rumors that her youngest child was actually the child of her daughter by releasing a strong statement to the contrary. If you're the victim of a vicious rumor, don't hide from it. If you come out immediately and lay the facts on the table, you may be able to steal the thunder and set the record straight.

Beware of the office gossiper.

Every office has at least one or two, and you typically know who they are. They gain your confidence to gather information, then they sneak around behind your back filling up the cesspool. Sometimes they even share personal information about themselves to gain your trust. Here are some red flags. Office gossipers . . .

- Need to get a life. They don't have much of a life outside the office, so gossiping becomes an attention-seeking device.
- Try to make points with the boss by running with "information."
- Thrive on discord and arguing.
- Talk about others behind their backs, so you can be assured they're talking about you too.

Pull in the reins.

When you find yourself in an uncomfortable position with a gossiper, don't participate. That means not defending the person who's being attacked, because the gossiper may twist your remarks around. Here are a few lines you may try:

- *I don't think it's professional to talk about [name] that way.*
- *I'm not comfortable talking about [name] when he's not here. Why not ask him to join us?*
- *I didn't hear you. Would you mind speaking a little louder?*
- *Would you say that if [name] were standing here now?*
- *Why would you say something like that? I'm sure you're not trying to be hurtful.*
- *When I hear you say things like that, I wonder if you say those same things about me when I'm not listening.*

Getting Along with Coworkers

Difficult people are everywhere—from the pushy salesperson in the department store to the abrupt customer service representative. You can always go somewhere else to find another pedicurist or barber, but there's one person you can't get away from—the noxious coworker.

Meet the challenge head-on.

The workplace, unlike any other environment, brings together diverse groups of people—varieties of personality types, abilities, speed, temperaments, goals, and agendas. Add those to dissimilar cultures and several generations, and you're bound to have some challenges. Here are some common-sense tips to help everyone get along better and be more productive.

- **Listen more and talk less.** In chapter 4, "Developing Listening Skills," we talked about having two ears and one mouth. Use them in equal proportion.

- **Be friendly to everyone.** You don't have to stop to converse with someone every time you visit the water cooler, but a smile goes a long way.

- **Avoid controversial topics.** Topics such as politics, religion, values, and sex, to name a few, should be off-limits in the workplace. Keeping conversations light and focused on business can go a long way towards peaceful coexistence. Even things said in jest can be misinterpreted and hurtful.

- **Agree to disagree.** You won't get along with everyone and you won't share the same opinions or ways of approaching things. It's okay for people to disagree and still work in harmony.

- **Be a team player.** Many companies list this as one of the top three qualities in a valued employee. Volunteer to help a coworker who's overwhelmed, get a stressed coworker a cup of coffee, and do other things you'd like people to do for you. If you're leading a team that consists of disparate styles (which is very common), arrange the workflow so people can contribute productively. For example, if someone works better alone, give that person individual projects that add to the total effort.

- **Involve a third party.** When you can't defuse problems on your own, enlist a neutral third party to help navigate the choppy waters. This person can be a sounding board for both parties. Come with an open mind and be willing to compromise.

- **Watch your own back.** Do your job and avoid involvement in explosive situations.

- **Shun toxic types.** You know these people . . . Charlie the *complainer*, who whines incessantly and gets on your nerves . . . Diana the *delegator*, who pushes work off on others . . . Carol the *credit monger,* who takes all the credit and never gives credit to others . . . Bob the *blabbermouth*, who talks too much and interrupts everyone . . . George the *gossiper*, who constantly feeds the gossip mill . . . and the *bully*, you know, the kind you dealt with on the school playground. (You probably can name a few types I missed.)

 Bullies are often fragile on the inside and are trying to protect their vulnerabilities. Break down the barriers and you may find a loyal friend and coworker.

Be a desirable coworker.

We all think we're desirable (and most of us are), but there may be little things we do that annoy others. Do you break any of these rules?

- Moderate your voice when on the phone or having meetings in your office, especially in an open environment.
- Clean up after yourself in the kitchen area. (It's too bad that many offices have to put up signs asking people to do this.)
- Be on time for meetings.
- Remember to say *please* and *thank you.*
- Return anything you borrow.
- Avoid eating odorous food in your office; some people find food aromas offensive.
- Don't sell your daughter's Girl Scout cookies in the office. (Leave your pet projects at home.)
- Choose your battles wisely.
- Honor your commitments.

Apologize with sincerity.

When you owe someone an apology, apologize sincerely. Don't ever send an apology via email. Say you're sorry in person, send a handwritten note, or make a phone call if the injured party isn't nearby. Simply say . . .

- I was wrong and I apologize.
- I embarrassed you in front of your coworker and I had no call to do that. I sincerely apologize.
- That was unkind of me. I apologize.

If you made the remark in front of others, be sure they know you have apologized. You may send them an email stating your regrets and letting them know you apologized personally to the person you offended.

Communicate with people in their own styles.

People with good social skills can get along with almost everyone. Understand what matters to others, what makes them tick, and communicate with them in their own style. The following is a slide I use in my business-writing workshop that shows how to communicate with dominant, influential, steady, and compliant people. The same methods apply when speaking.

Communicating with People in Their Own Styles		
Style	Trait	Best method of communication
Dominant	Need to direct Results oriented Motivated by challenge and power	Direct, to the point, stick to business Provide win-win situations Focus on bottom line and results without overemphasizing data
Influential	Need to interact People oriented Motivated by recognition and involvement	Use positive introduction to break the ice Highlight benefits and generate excitement Show samples, if appropriate
Steady	Need to serve Cooperation oriented Motivated by stability and appreciation	Use a step-by-step process Leave time for recapping and review Attach supporting materials
Compliant	Need to comply to high standards Quality oriented Motivated by standards and desired expectations	Avoid new ideas, stick to proven facts Be detailed and provide statistics Use lots of graphs and charts Examine arguments from all sides

Dealing with a Toxic Boss

A recent Gallup Poll surveying one million workers found that having a toxic boss is the most common reason people look for other jobs. Jack Welch quit his first job because of a toxic boss. At the time he had a wife, a baby, and no money. He went on to become chairman and CEO of General Electric, gaining a solid reputation for his uncanny business acumen and superior leadership strategies.

There are many kinds of toxic bosses that make people go home at night with blood boiling—bullies, yellers, micromanagers, know-it-alls, insecure jerks, and more. Although it won't make your job any easier, know that toxic bosses generally have low self-esteem; they push others around to bloat their egos.

 Before you implement any of the following strategies, look yourself in the mirror and ask if you may be part of the problem. Can any of your actions and behaviors be causing or contributing to the problem?

Discuss the issue with your boss.

Sometimes bosses don't realize they're treating people unkindly or unfairly; others just don't care. Your boss may be having personal problems, may be unclear when giving directions, may suffer from an inferiority complex, may have antisocial behavior. Whatever the reason, don't get stepped on like a doormat! Tell her what you need. Do you need feedback, support, or independence? Use diplomatic, nonthreatening language such as:

- *Have you noticed that . . .*
- *Do you think we should take another approach?*
- *I'd appreciate your helping me to reach my goals. Can we outline what that will . . .*
- *I've noticed a change in our relationship in the last [time frame] and am wondering what's gone wrong.*
- *I am not being critical, because I respect your judgment, but . . .*
- *I'm having a difficult time because . . .*
- *I know you've been under a lot of pressure lately and I'm not sure you realize . . .*
- *If the situation were reversed, I know you would want me to tell you . . .*

 Plan ahead what you want to say and schedule an appointment for a private face-to-face meeting. Don't accuse and don't make it personal. Just state your feelings.

Put things in writing.

Notate your achievements and bring them to your boss's attention. This will show your worth and the status of your key projects. Even if you do weekly or monthly reports, a short conversation about a success you or your team had may help your cause. Remember that the better you look to your boss, the better she looks to her superiors.

Try to get things in writing when you can. You may send your boss an email that reiterates a conversation. For example, *I just want to confirm that you asked me to. . . .* If your boss makes threats, make sure you keep careful notes of the conversation, including where and when the conversation took place. As a last resort, you can approach HR and your notes can be evidence.

Here are a few things to consider:

- Don't do something rash that you'll regret just because it may relieve momentary stress and feel good at the moment. It takes a very mature person to put long-term career goals ahead of the thrill of telling the bully where to get off.
- If the situation is impossible and you think your rights are being violated, approach HR. If the situation doesn't improve, you may think about consulting an attorney.

Manage the stress.

- ***Eat lunch away from the office to decompress.*** *If your boss can't find you, perhaps she'll unleash her hostilities on some other unfortunate soul.*
- ***Don't be on call.*** *If your boss calls during nonoffice hours, monitor your calls and don't answer the call.*
- ***Exercise.*** *Exercise reduces stress. Join a gym, run, walk, or do something energetic.*

Develop a support system.

Build relationships with coworkers, clients, customers, vendors, former employees, and managers who can attest to your good ethics and good work. Find a mentor you can go to for advice and support. These relationships can be an important source of support if you need to approach HR or need a recommendation for another job.

Know when it's time to fire your boss.

While your goal may be to outlast your boss, if the situation becomes unbearable, your only option may be to jump ship. Don't do this prematurely; look for other opportunities while you're still employed. Get your resume in order, network, and start interviewing. Having an exit strategy will put you in charge.

Try these top 10 employee motivators.

According to a survey by the American Society for Training and Development (ASTD), there are many ways to motivate employees—and they don't cost a dime. Here they are:

1. Say thank-you when it's appropriate.
2. Allot time.

3. Give feedback.
4. Provide a positive work environment.
5. Engage in ongoing communication.
6. Provide opportunities to grow.
7. Engender a sense of ownership.
8. Celebrate success.
9. Trust individuals.
10. Show respect.

Saying No to Your Boss

No is one of the smallest words in the English language and the toughest word to say, especially to your boss. Yet, there are times when you have to deny a request. You must do it without saying the word *no*, without creating ill will, and without losing your job. Remember that your boss doesn't always know all that is on your plate and may appreciate your candor.

Say no without saying "no."

Rather than saying *no*, propose an alternative, agree to the request if you can get some assistance, ask if anyone else may be available, and the like. If you're asked to do the following, consider the bulleted responses:

Take on a project you know you couldn't finish on time.
- That sounds very interesting. I'm really on a tight deadline with the [assignment] right now. Do you want me to reprioritize?
- I'll be happy to undertake that. Can you provide me with a team?
- I'm working [xx] hours a week to meet the deadline on [project]. Is there anyone else who can help out?

Attend a meeting that just won't fit into your schedule.
- I'd love to go to that meeting. Perhaps [name] would be more appropriate; he'll be working on [project] [when].
- I was planning to be in [destination] that week. Is there anyone else who would benefit or contribute?

Mentor a new employee.
- I'd enjoy doing that, but I'll be traveling most of the month of [month] and it wouldn't be fair to [person]. May I suggest [another name]?
- I'll fully tied up on [project] and wouldn't want to shortchange [new employee]. Let's see who else may be appropriate.

Take on new assignments on an ongoing basis and you're already up to your eyeballs.

- I enjoy working on the projects you often ask me to do, but they make it hard to do my primary job. Would you like me to drop [task]?
- Would you like to review my job description so it includes this type of work? (Consider if added salary should be part of this review.)

Other retorts may include . . .

- *I'm already working on several important assignments with tight deadlines; that doesn't give me any time for new projects right now.*
- *If I take on this assignment, I'm afraid it may jeopardize other projects I'm working on now.*
- *I'm not sure I have the skill set.* (Suggest someone who may.)
- *Is there anyone else who can pitch in? I'm working at 110 percent capacity.*
- *Can you delegate some of my other work?*
- *Can I put some other assignments on the back burner for a while?*

 If you're pressured to do something contrary to your moral ethics, say so. If the request continues, get assistance from your human resources department or your state's department of labor.

Decline calmly and tactfully.

Be calm and tactful, and speak in a normal voice. Here are some things to consider:

- Find the right location and time to have this discussion.
- Don't have this conversation in front of anyone else.
- Explain why you can't perform the task.
- Tell your boss what's on your plate that would make it difficult to accept this new assignment.
- Suggest one or two alternatives.

Remain positive during tough times.

Gregory Berns, a neuroscientist at Emory University, wrote in The New York Times *that people should disconnect from things that breed "negative emotional contagion." When we're fearful, our brains shut down and stifle creativity, risk taking, and innovation. When times are tough, therefore, limit media exposure and resist the urge to engage in negative conversations with others.*

Dealing with Outsourced Service Providers

Very few companies have all the resources to handle every project in-house. Therefore, outsourcing can help to save money, access new technologies, gain an outside perspective, and add industry experience. Preserve a good relationship with your consultants, contractors, and vendors. (These terms are often used interchangeably.) It's crucial to your business, as they may be the "face" of business to customers in various situations. The goodwill you establish will translate into business growth and may see you through difficult times.

Make sure you need a consultant.

Examine your current staff, their skill sets, your requirements, and the costs. Even though outsourcing may cost more than your employees, you typically pay only for services performed and delivered. You save on payroll taxes, medical benefits, pensions, profit sharing, 401k contributions, and any other benefits you offer.

Get recommendations or go out for competitive bidding.

There's nothing like a good, solid recommendation from someone you trust. It's not always about the price, but about the quality of the service. If you go out for bid, let everyone bid on the exact same information so you compare apples with apples. It's a good idea to discard the lowest and the highest bids. The lowest price may mean the lowest quality; they'll cut corners. The highest may be overcharging.

Interview extensively.

Interviewing is key to finding a person or group you feel comfortable with. If the candidate is trying to snow you with fancy lingo and buzzwords, that may be a warning sign. If the consultant can't express herself clearly, this indicates a major communications problem that spells trouble.

- **Make sure the candidate is a good listener.** The candidate should listen to your needs and objectives. If she doesn't, she isn't the right person.

- **Ask about membership in professional associations.** Candidates who are members of professional organizations are generally serious about their businesses and are on the cutting edge of their industries. There are too many people who lose jobs and hang out a "consulting" shingle just to tide them over until something else comes along.

- **Learn what is and isn't billable.** What is and isn't included in the fee? Is there a charge for travel time? Is there a charge for telephone or online support? What does the candidate bill clients for and what does she absorb internally? Are there any gray areas?

- **Inquire about backups.** Depending on the nature of your project, question who the consultant's backup will be if the consultant can't finish the assignment.

- **Request a list of references and check them carefully.** It's not critical that the candidate has done the exact work for someone else; it is critical that she learns quickly and has delighted clients.

Put everything in writing.

Even with the best relationship, put everything in writing. Include expected outcomes, fees, responsibilities, method of payment, time frame, and anything that may possibly create a misunderstanding later on. If this is a long-term relationship or a complicated assignment, you may ask your attorney to prepare a formal agreement. Also, many professional organizations have standard contracts you can use.

Treat consultants as partners, not vendors.

Building a solid collaborative relationship with your consultants will be a win-win situation. When the going gets rough, whom would you rather have on your team—a partner or a consultant? Here are some ways to accomplish that:

- **Display your loyalty.** If you do a lot of business with a particular consultant, she may reward your loyalty by offering you discounts, putting you at the top of the priority list for emergency projects, and other things that will help your business to thrive.

- **Provide adequate training.** When consultants are part of your business model, make sure they have adequate training. This will help them to market your goods and services better.

- **Share your business goals.** A consultant who understands your business goals will be able to make strategic decisions that align with those goals.

- **Get ongoing status reports.** You undoubtedly get these reports from your employees; get them from your consultants as well. This can avert glitches and problems.

- **Don't play the blame game.** Just as employees sometimes make bad decisions, consultants will as well. The key to a lasting relationship is trust, so always get the facts and don't jump to conclusions.

Effective Feedback

Giving positive feedback is easy! We all need feedback (positive and negative) in order to grow. When you give negative feedback, your purpose is to improve future behavior, not focus on past behavior. Put yourself in the other person's shoes and be mindful of her feelings.

Giving Feedback

- **Give negative feedback in private.** Praise in public; criticize privately.

- **Limit feedback to important issues.** Too much feedback at a single time can dilute your key message. Stick to the point.

- **Focus on the behavior, not the person.** One strategy behaviorists recommend is to mention the behavior, how you feel about it, and what you want to change.
  Say, *I haven't seen you at most of the team meetings. I'm concerned about your missing important information. Let's set up a time to discuss this* . . .
  instead of saying, *You obviously don't care much for the project we're working on or the people in the group.*

- **Be specific and offer tangible steps the person can take.** The person you're speaking with should leave the meeting with specific action items to correct the behavior.

- **Use the sandwich approach.** Mention something positive, state the concern, and close on a positive note.
  Say, *Great presentation. I can see you were well prepared and had good information. The next time you may want to make more eye contact with your audience. Other than that, keep up the good work* . . .
  instead of saying, *You didn't make eye contact with your audience. Otherwise, your presentation was good.*

- **Be realistic and timely.** Avoid using words expressing extremes, such as *never* or *always*, and give feedback promptly. Feedback becomes stale if you wait too long.

- **Offer ongoing support.** Feedback should be a continuous process, not a one-time deal. Let the receiver know you're available for help and questions.

- **Schedule a follow-up.** After a reasonable period (and you'll know what reasonable is), set up another face-to-face meeting to discuss progress.

Giving Feedback to Sensitive People

This takes a very special mindfulness, so plan carefully.

- **Put your comments in writing.** In addition to meeting with the person, put everything in writing. This will avoid misinterpretations and the twisting of your words.

- **Ask for clarification.** Ask the person to clarify what she heard. She may have "heard" something very different from what you said.

- **Meet more frequently.** When someone is overly sensitive, short sessions held more frequently may work better than a long session.

- **Be prepared for an emotional rollercoaster.** If someone begins to cry, stop and wait for her to calm down. If someone becomes emotionally charged, take a short break and reconvene later on. If you know someone is prone to losing her temper, ask for a third party to be present.

Receiving Feedback

- **Listen carefully.** Don't interrupt and don't get defensive. Listen to what the person is saying rather than focusing on your rebuttal.

- **Be open.** There's often more than one way to do something, and we often learn by listening to the comments of others. Don't take them personally.

- **Ask for clarification, if necessary.** If you don't understand something or disagree, ask for clarification. *Can you please tell me when you noticed that* or *Can you please give me an example so I can learn from it?*

- **Decide what to do.** Assess the value of the feedback. Not all feedback is valid. If you disagree, what's the downside of ignoring it?

Performance Appraisals

Second to axing an employee (where the manager is the executioner), giving the performance appraisal (where the manager is the judge) is the task managers dread most. Why? The appraisals are time consuming, managers are concerned that the employee's emotions may be unleashed, and they fear not being able to defend the rating if put on the spot. Also, if the manager gives high ratings and can't give a raise commensurate with the evaluation, the employee may be demotivated. If the manager gives low ratings, the employee may be demotivated as well. Employees also dread performance appraisals. They don't want to be criticized, they're reluctant to speak up, and they worry about becoming defensive.

 Keep communication constant. A good manager gives ongoing feedback and doesn't wait until it's time for the annual appraisal. This includes praising people for a job well done. Some managers don't praise because they feel people are paid to do their jobs well. While this is true, we all need to hear we're appreciated.

When you give a performance appraisal, follow the same guidelines you would for delivering effective feedback. While feedback can be given for a wide variety of situations, a performance appraisal has specific objectives: evaluating past performance, improving future performance, reviewing the job description, planning upcoming goals and objectives, and creating an individual development plan that includes training/coaching needs. Following are ways managers can make the dreaded performance appraisal into a meaningful and productive exchange:

- **Set a positive tone.** Be clear that the discussion is to help the employee excel, not to punish or berate.

- **Describe the facts.** Do this without exaggerating or accusing.

- **Invite dialogue.** After you've explained the issues as you see them, give the employee a chance to rebut.

- **Empathize and clarify.** Use empathy when necessary and be prepared to give clarification if asked.

- **Prepare joint action items.** Rather than dictate what should be done, prepare a joint action plan so you get the employee's buy-in. This makes the manager more of a mentor in the employee's success, rather than a judge.

- **Get a commitment and schedule a follow-up.** Summarize the meeting, reiterate the action items, and select a time for a follow-up meeting. Don't wait too long—perhaps one month or one quarter.

Giving and Accepting Compliments

People are often reluctant to tell others they're great, special, or did something well. Why? As explained in *Find Something Nice to Say,* by Debby Hoffman and Kathy Chamberlin, "Many of us were brought up in homes and schools where compliments were rare and seldom given, where it was thought that bestowing praise would give a child a swelled head and cause them to be conceited." Others are just shy, don't know what to say, or don't think of it. We all need praise and shouldn't neglect giving it meaningfully and accepting it graciously.

Give a compliment sincerely.

When you pay someone a compliment, make sure it's sincere, otherwise it will sound as if you're "kissing up." Whenever you do give a compliment, focus on the other person by starting with the word *you. You* . . .

- *have a great way with words.*
- *always know the right thing to say.*
- *inspire me.*
- *really did a good job.*
- *gave a great talk. I learned a lot.*
- *are such a good listener. Thank you.*

Accept a compliment graciously.

Some people have trouble accepting compliments; they get nervous, defensive, or feel undeserving. Graciously accept someone's compliment or you risk downgrading it. Consider expressions such as . . .

- *Thank you.*
- *I'm glad you liked [what you're being complimented for].*
- *Thanks. Coming from you, that's a real compliment.*
- *Thanks. I worked very hard on that.*
- *As that comes from someone I respect so much, I appreciate it.*
- *That's the nicest thing I've heard today.*
- *Thanks. I got a lot of help from [person].*
- *I'm delighted you noticed the extra effort, and I will share your compliment with others on the team who helped me to achieve this.*
- *You made my day. Thanks so much.*

Avoid responses such as these that sound as if you disagree . . .

- *I was just lucky.*
- *It was nothing.*

- *You shouldn't have.*
- *I don't deserve it.*
- *There were more deserving people.*
- *Thanks, it cost me a lot of money.*
- *Thanks, but it didn't turn out as well as I expected.*

Lots of ways to say "You're welcome"

We all learned on our mother's knee to say please *and* thank you. *Those are words that go a long way. The response to* thank you *has typically been* You're welcome. *I was listening to a conversation between coworkers that went like this:*

> Person A: Thanks for staying late yesterday to help me meet that tight deadline.
>
> Person B: No problem.
>
> Person A: If I thought there would have been a problem, I wouldn't have asked you.
>
> Person B: I'm only saying it was no problem. Why are you making a big deal?

(The conversation continued to degenerate.)

There are many way to express "You're welcome," and "No problem" is just one. Rather than bicker over the words, accept the gesture. Here's how this nicety is handled in other countries:

> *Australia and New Zealand: No worries.*
>
> *England: No verbal response; just a nod. (The service was rendered, the person was thanked, and that's the end.)*
>
> *France and Spanish-speaking countries: It's nothing.*
>
> *China: No thanks are necessary.*

Giving and Accepting Gifts

Gift giving can be a daunting experience. When you select a gift, it speaks to your taste and expresses your feelings towards the recipient. We've all received white elephants we hide in the closet and try to remember to pull out when the giver visits.

Accept white elephants graciously.

A gift is supposed to be a pleasure, so keeping something you don't want or can't use is foolish—unless you know the giver would be upset. If you think the giver . . .

- would be upset, haul it out when she visits.
- wouldn't be upset and you don't know where the gift was purchased, politely ask. *I love the [item] but would enjoy having it in another color. Would you mind exchanging it or would you mind if I do?*
- wouldn't be upset and you know where the gift was purchased, exchange it for something you'll enjoy and tell the giver you've done that.

 Many years ago the people I worked with gave me a bridal shower. One of my colleagues gave me a gift in a Lord & Taylor box. The gift was a duplicate of something I already had (and I knew I wouldn't be seeing that person because I was moving away), so I went to Lord & Taylor to exchange it. Imagine my embarrassment when the clerk told me Lord & Taylor didn't stock that item. I found out through the grapevine that my colleague had bought the item at a discount store. The moral of this story is never to give a gift in a box that doesn't indicate where you purchased the item.

Know whether to send a thank-you note for a gift.

If you don't open the gift in front of the giver, you should send a note. If you open the gift in front of the giver, a face-to-face thank-you will often suffice. However, if the gift is something very special, you may want to send a note as well. After all, you write a note because you want to, not because you have to.

Save price tags and receipts.

When you give a gift, save the price tag and receipt until you're certain the recipient is satisfied. When you give a gift, you may say . . .

- *If you'd like to exchange this, I bought it at . . .*
- *I'd be glad to exchange this for something you'd rather have.*
- *The moment you opened this, I realized the chartreuse and pink ceramic monkey doesn't match your décor. Why don't you let me return it for something more to your taste?*

Refuse a gift tactfully.

It may be awkward to refuse a gift, but occasionally you have to. For example, certain companies and branches of the government deem it inappropriate for their employees to accept gifts because the sentiment may be viewed as an impropriety. In such a situation, if a gift is handed to you, simply say with a warm smile, *I can't tell you how much I appreciate your thoughtfulness, but it's against company policy to accept gifts.*

Giving gifts to foreigners

If you're not sure about the appropriateness of a gift, ask a business colleague who's been to the country, a person from the country, or an official at the consulate. Also check the Internet. Buy something that isn't too costly so it isn't misconstrued as a bribe. No matter what you select, wrap the gift nicely, because presentation is important. Gift ideas may include:

- *classical music*
- *coffee-table book*
- *china or porcelain*
- *local handicraft*
- *pen and pencil set*
- *specialty item from your region (such as maple syrup from Vermont)*

Here are just a few gift-giving taboos:

Argentina: Knives (They suggest you wish to "cut off" the business relationship.)
China: No personal gifts (If you have a relationship with someone, however, privately give something mentioned above.)
France: Bottle of wine to dinner (The host has already made the selection.)
India: Item of cowhide (The cow is sacred.)
Mulsim countries: Liquor or wine
Spain: Dahlias or chrysanthemums (They're for funerals.)

Wining and Dining

When you host a business dinner or luncheon, pick a restaurant that sets the tone for the meeting and be sensitive to the person or people you host. For example, if you're trying to win the business of a start-up company that has limited capital, opt for a conservative restaurant. On the other hand, if you have a long-standing relationship with a client whose business is prospering, opt for a more lavish restaurant.

Call ahead.

Call ahead and let the restaurant know your needs. For example, you may say, *Hello, this is [name] from [company]. I'd like to reserve a table for [number of people] in the Colonial Room for [date] at [time].* With that simple statement, you accomplish more than reserving a table. You identify yourself as a person with authority, establish a table that will be yours, and inform the restaurant you're planning a special meal.

Leave coats and other paraphernalia in the coatroom.

When you enter a fine restaurant, leave your coat, umbrella, and other paraphernalia with the coatroom attendant. If you'll be conducting business, you may need your briefcase. (Place your briefcase next to you, not on the table.)

Introduce guests.

When you host a dinner or luncheon for a large number of people, wait in the lobby for the first of your guests to arrive and escort them to the table. Let the maitre d' or server escort the stragglers. If your guests don't know each other, be sure to make the introductions. If the host neglects to introduce you, introduce yourself.

 Check out chapter 1, "Making Introductions."

Place your order with care.

The server generally takes the women's orders first. Here are a few ordering tips:

- **Be sensitive to pricing.** Ask the host what he's having and let that price be your guide. In an expensive restaurant, guests may get menus without prices, so order what you like.
- **Order food that isn't messy.** Avoid foods such as spaghetti, anything with lots of sauce, and finger food.
- **Order the special.** Chefs take great pride in preparing special meals, so they're generally a good choice.
- **Ask for explanations.** If there's something on the menu you'd like explained, ask the server.
- **Mention food allergies.** If you have any food allergies, make sure the server knows. You may say, Please check with the chef to make sure there's no gluten in [choice]. I'm allergic.

Be inconspicuous when a serving error occurs.

You may have heard the story of the man dining in a fine restaurant who noticed a fly in his soup. He called over the server and asked, "What's a fly doing in my soup?" The server answered, "The backstroke." On rare occasions alien life forms appear in food, and sometimes you get the wrong order. When this occurs, deal with it inconspicuously. Call the server over and quietly report the problem. Smile and say, *There's something in this soup I don't recognize. Would you mind getting another bowl?* or *I believe I ordered my steak rare, and this is well done.*

Conversely, when you order a meal that's very good, be sure to tell the server, *Please give my compliments to the chef.*

Remember the name of your server.

I once heard a server say, "I can remember the orders for a party of 12, but a party of 12 can't remember my name." Your server will always introduce herself; remember her name. If you need to get her attention, call her by name.

Refuse alcohol if you don't drink.

People refrain from drinking for a variety of reasons. If you don't want the server to pour you a glass of wine, touch the rim of your glass with your fingertips as an indication you don't want any. If the server isn't savvy enough to get the message, simply say, *None for me, thanks.*

Know when to start the conversation.

At breakfast, start the conversation as soon as the coffee is poured. At lunch, make small talk until the server has taken all the orders; then talk business. At dinner, wait for the host to introduce business into the conversation.

Find different ways to say the same thing.

Here are a few ways to say the same thing	
Giving people a choice	•It's up to you. •It's your decision. •Make up your own mind. •It would be fine if you want to. . . . •The choice is yours.
Asking someone's opinion	•What do you think about . . .? •What's your opinion of . . . ? •What would you say to . . . ? •Are you aware of . . . ?
Disagreeing with someone	•Actually, I think you'll find that . . . •Where did you hear that? •You may want to check those facts. •Did you get that firsthand?
Postponing giving an answer	•Now, let me think. •How can I put that? •It's on the tip of my tongue. •Now, that's an interesting question.

Apologizing	• I'm so sorry. It was my fault.
	• Please excuse my ignorance.
	• Please don't be angry.
	• That was very thoughtless of me. I'm sorry.
Seeking approval	• Do you think it would be okay for me to . . . ?
	• What's your opinion on the idea of . . . ?
	• Would you mind if . . . ?
	• Do you think anyone would mind if . . . ?

Pay the check if you're the host.

When you're the host, arrange with the server or maitre d' upon arrival that the check be presented to you. Put the meal on your credit card so guests don't see money exchanged. If you notice an error and the problem can't be straightened out easily, pay the bill and discuss the matter immediately afterward. Escort your guests to the lobby, and say, *Please excuse me for just a moment.*

Other things to consider:

- As a host . . . If you're at a restaurant you typically frequent and your company doesn't have a credit arrangement, you may present your credit card when you enter so you avoid the hassle of getting the check.

- As a guest . . . Turn your head away or converse with other guests when the check is presented.

Tidbits

Whether you're the host or the guest, never ask for a doggie bag. Make a clear distinction between social meals and business meals. At a business meal, the focus is on strengthening the relationship, not on the food.

If you're asked a question and have food in your mouth, politely hold one finger up with your palm outward and continue chewing. That indicates you can't talk at the moment.

Index

meetings, business
agendas, 169, 170
conflict, managing, 171, 172–173
conversation and, 172
declining, 235
dress codes for, 173–174
generational differences, 180–183
last-minute, 174
multilingual, 180
networking at, 104
planning for, 168–169
speakers, selecting, 175
strategies for, 169–175
virtual, 176–179
Melanson, Steve, 92, 105
memory lapses, introductions and, 6
men. *see* gender differences
mentoring, 183, 235
messages, accurate, 82, 83, 85–86,
89–92
Middle East, business travel and,
197–199
mirroring technique, body language
and, 29, 38
misunderstandings, preventing, 34, 67
motivation, employee, 234–235
multigenerational differences. *see*
generational differences
multilingual meetings, 180

N
name badges, 8, 110–111
names. *see also* nicknames
cold calling and, 94
conversations and, 14
introductions and, 6
networking and, 114
pronunciations, 9
telephone use and, 83
National Do Not Call Registry, 88, 89
National Speakers Association (NSA),
143
negatives, double, 59
negativity, body language and, 25–26

networking. *see also* social networking
websites
business cards and, 108–110
defined, 101–102
"elevator pitches," 102–105
follow up, 115–116, 120
groups, 118
introducing yourself, 8
name badges and, 110–111
referrals, 116–119
selling, compared to, 111
tag lines and, 105
trade shows/conventions, 119–121
verbal branding, 105–108
"working the room," 111–116
niches, identifying, 103
nicknames, 6–7, 13, 68
Non-Disclosure Agreement (NDA),
225
nonverbal communication. *see* body
language
note taking
introductions and, 8–9
networking and, 115
public speaking and, 136, 139

O
Obama, President Barack, 142–143,
207, 228
onboarding, defined, 210
openings, proper. *see* phrases, opening
outbound telephone calls, 85–87, 91
outsourced service providers, 237–239

P
pairs, word. *see* word pairs
Palin, Sarah, 228
panel interviews, 164–165
paralysis, coworkers with, 74–75. *see
also* disabilities, people with
paraphrasing, listening skills and, 38
parentheses, use of, 56
parents, 41–43. *see also* children
participles, dangling, 58

About the Author

 When Sheryl Lindsell-Roberts emailed her sons the good news about getting a contract for this book, her son Marc sent her a message saying, "If *anyone* can honestly write a book about speaking your way to success, it's you, Mom." She scratched her head, wrinkled her brow, and assumed he meant that as a compliment. At least she wanted to think so.

Since Sheryl was a small child, she's had the gift of gab. (Her granddaughter Brooke inherited it, much to the dismay of Sheryl's daughter-in-law.) Sheryl's father once told her that she should talk less because each person is given only so many words, and she wouldn't want to run out of words so early in her life. Asking her to talk less was, and still is, like sitting on an ocean beach and asking the tide not to come in.

Her words continue to flow in her professional life. She's a successful business and technical writing workshop facilitator, public speaker, and coach. She attributes her success to her passion for speaking, sharing knowledge, and helping people to achieve their potential—and to having a good sense of humor and thoroughly enjoying what she does. She thinks that passion shows whenever she's in front of clients, because they keep asking her back.

She spends her leisure time reading, sailing, kayaking, cross-country skiing, gardening, painting (pictures, not walls), making pottery, traveling, going to the gym, and enjoying her grandchildren. She tries to live each day to the fullest because she believes each one is precious.

To learn more about Sheryl's business writing, workshop facilitation, and coaching, please visit www.sherylwrites.com.

More Praise for *Speaking Your Way to Success*

Sheryl Lindsell-Roberts has presented in a clear, very readable, and extremely interesting manner a guide to prepare us—as professionals, employees, or executives—for purposeful, confident, and powerful communication and presentation techniques in all aspects of our business life.

—Warren M. Bergstein, CPA, AEP, Partner, Adelman Katz & Mond, LLP

Sheryl Lindsell-Roberts writes the way she teaches, in a very organized and engaging way. This is one of those books I'll keep as a desktop reference for a long time to come. It is packed with helpful tips for all kinds of everyday business challenges.

—Marianne Brush, Executive Vice President, Massachusetts Society of CPAs, Inc.

An amazing book, covering difficult business situations that are ignored by many authors.

—Joe Curtin, Director of Recruiting, Training and Development, Roche Bros. Supermarkets

Succinctly stated (you'll soon see why this is important), *Speaking Your Way to Success* is comprehensive, engrossing, invaluable, and necessary.

—Helen Graves, Founding Editor, *Women's Business*

Speaking Your Way to Success is a "must have" for everybody's personal or business library. This excellent resource addresses hundreds of situations in which the way a person communicates determines their success or failure, and Sheryl ensures success with each recommendation. . . . I will be recommending *Speaking Your Way to Success* as a tool to all of our employees.

—Linda J. Jackson, Assistant Vice President, Training Manager, Workers' Credit Union

This book offers practical speaking tips for every age and walk of life. It's like a vast medicine chest for anyone anticipating a speaking challenge: you open the cover, scan the contents, and pluck out the perfect remedy for your situation.

—Sue LaChance, Director, Organizational and Leadership Development, Constant Contact

Sheryl Lindsell-Roberts is one of my favorite facilitators. The passion and energy that she brings to the classroom also radiate throughout this book. *Speaking Your Way to Success* is the perfect toolkit for presenters, facilitators, and public speakers—whether they are new to the field or polished veterans. I've been in the learning and development field for ten years, and this book will become a key resource for both me and my participants.

—Paul Papierski, Learning and Development Specialist & Coach, American Cancer Society

This book is an invaluable tool in helping you to build confidence and share your own expertise. Sheryl uses a quick wit and deep experience to tease you toward successful speaking in any situation.

—Bard Williams, Ed.D., Director of Marketing, TiVo Inc.